MONSTERS IN LOVE

Praise for *Monsters in Love*

"*Monsters in Love* delivers one truth bomb after another. Busting the myth that surface harmony is the sign of a good relationship and that fiery conflict is the mark of one on the brink, this book makes the case that learning to master healthy conflict is the only way to have a healthy intimate relationship that lasts. Consistent with the messaging in the brilliant Somatic Abolitionist books *My Grandmother's Hands* and *The Quaking of America,* Resmaa helps us see that the only way we can stand for true, whole-hearted integrity (and hold our intimate partners accountable to their own integrity) is to condition our nervous systems to tolerate the heat of healthy conflict without collapsing to or bullying our beloveds. My partner and I ate this up and are already practicing being less monstery with each other. The best relationship book I've read in a decade."

Lissa Rankin, MD, *New York Times* bestselling author
of *Mind Over Medicine* and *Sacred Medicine*

• • •

"We live in a therapy culture, where the focus often is on nurturing, decreasing the heat, and eliminating conflict. In a manner similar to his bestselling books on healing racial trauma in a divided culture, Resmaa shines his bright light on intimate relationships and shows us how to go beyond standard approaches, grow up, and truly become our best selves. This is about becoming adults who can both give and receive love with a level of depth and clarity that is profoundly refreshing, bracing, and ultimately both life- and relationship-saving. An outstanding, unique contribution to our understanding of both the reality and the possibilities of deep intimacy."

Jeffrey Rediger, MD, MDiv, author of *Cured*

• • •

"Resmaa does it again! Shaking us up in all the necessary ways. *Monsters in Love* is an authentic, practical, no-nonsense guide to true, lasting love. It will ruffle your relationship up in all the necessary ways to bring it back to balance and health. Resmaa's approach is revolutionary, unfiltered, and bursting with love. Everyone needs these practices in their relationship toolbox."

Mariel Buqué, PhD, psychologist and generational trauma expert

Monsters in Love

Why Your Partner Sometimes Drives You Crazy—
and What You Can Do About It

Resmaa Menakem

Originally published as *Rock the Boat*.
Newly updated, revised, and expanded

CENTRAL RECOVERY PRESS

LAS VEGAS, NV

Central Recovery Press (CRP) is committed to publishing exceptional materials addressing addiction treatment, recovery, and behavioral healthcare topics. For more information, visit www.centralrecoverypress.com.

Publisher: Central Recovery Press
3321 N. Buffalo Drive
Las Vegas, NV 89129

28 27 26 25 24 23   1 2 3 4 5

Library of Congress Cataloging-in-Publication Data

Names: Menakem, Resmaa, author.
Title: Monsters in love : why your partner sometimes drives you crazy-and what you can do about it / Resmaa Menakem, MSW, LICSW, SEP.
Other titles: Rock the boat
Description: Las Vegas, Nevada : Central Recovery Press, 2023. | "Originally published as Rock the Boat. Newly updated, revised, and expanded"— Title page. | Summary: "A gritty and down-to-earth guide for real-life couples"— Provided by publisher.
Identifiers: LCCN 2022044521 (print) | LCCN 2022044522 (ebook) | ISBN 9781949481792 (paperback) | ISBN 9781949481808 (ebook)
Subjects: LCSH: Marital conflict. | Conflict management. | Interpersonal relations. | Emotions.
Classification: LCC HQ734 .M456 2023 (print) | LCC HQ734 (ebook) | DDC 306.872--dc23/eng/20220926 LC record available at https://lccn.loc.gov/2022044521LC ebook record available at https://lccn.loc.gov/2022044522

ISBNs: 978-1-949481-79-2 (paperback), 978-1-949481-80-8 (e-book)

Publisher's Note:
This book contains general information about marriage, other romantic relationships, trauma, racialized trauma, somatic healing methods, psychotherapy, and related matters. This information is not medical advice. This book is not an alternative to medical advice from your doctor or other professional healthcare provider.

Our books represent the experiences and opinions of their authors only. Every effort has been made to ensure that events, institutions, and statistics presented in our books as facts are accurate and up to date. To protect their privacy, the names and/or identifying details of some of the people, places, and institutions in this book have been changed. Some stories, and the people who appear in them, are composites created from multiple individuals and/or situations.

Author's Note:
This book is for informational purposes only. It is not intended as psychotherapy from a qualified counselor or a replacement for it. If you feel you can benefit from therapy, please contact a trained mental health professional.

Cover design by The Book Designers and interior design by Sara Streifel, Think Creative Design.

To all those who have gone before me,
I am humbled by your love and dedication.
Thank you.

This book is dedicated to the memory of

Dr. David Schnarch and Dr. James Maddock
Thank you for being my mentors.

Jodi Nowak
Thank you for being my friend.

Amelia Brown and Vesta Mason
Thank you for being my inspirations—
and now my ancestors.

Contents

Acknowledgments

I would like to first thank my mentors; I am grateful and privileged to stand on their shoulders.

The late Dr. David Schnarch was the author of *Intimacy and Desire, Passionate Marriage*, and *Resurrecting Sex*, and the founder of Crucible Institute (crucibletherapy.com). Some important terms, insights, and concepts in this book are his; other key concepts, and the diagrams in chapter 3, are partly based on his work. I could not have written this book without his mentorship. He combined a randy sense of humor, a sometimes-hard exterior, an engineer's mindset, deep insight into the human heart, and the ability to do amazing work with couples. I have never met anyone else remotely like him. Over the years, I grew to love and admire him deeply and trust him enormously. He often said to me—tweaking the words of Pierre Teilhard de Chardin—"We are energy having a human experience."

Dr. Schnarch died in October 2020, while I was working on the updated and expanded edition of this book. His death is a profound loss for the world, for the field of psychotherapy, and, of course, for me.

Dr. Schnarch did not do any of this work alone. His wife Ruth Morehouse, whom I respect and love immensely, was a close collaborator. Both of them were supported, assisted, and loved by their daughter, Sarah Morehouse. We never do this work by ourselves.

The late Dr. James Maddock—professor emeritus at the University of Minnesota, founder of the University of Minnesota Medical School's Program in Human Sexuality, and former president of the American Association of Sexuality Educators, Counselors, and Therapists— also taught me a great deal about how relationships really work. Dr. Maddock combined constant kindness and generosity with a complete refusal to tolerate bullshit. I've integrated some of his deepest insights into this book, which I could not have written without what he taught me. Doc Maddock began as a mentor and became an ancestor for me. He died fourteen years ago, and I still miss him terribly.

Dr. Joseph White, who is often referred to as the godfather of Black psychology, was instrumental in my thinking, and was deeply generous with his time in mentoring me. Joe was the first Black American to earn a Ph.D. in clinical psychology (in 1962). He died in 2017.

I am grateful to Dr. Ruth Morehouse (see above) and former Congressman Keith Ellison, later Minnesota's Attorney General, for their friendship and guidance.

My thanks to Beverly Dusso, executive director of Tubman Family Alliance in Minneapolis, whose friendship and guidance have helped me become a better person and a better professional. I'm also grateful to Antonia Drew-Vann of Asha Family Services in Milwaukee, whose commitment to working with communities of color helped shape my understanding of this important work.

I also owe much to other mentors and elders: Dr. Oliver Williams of the University of Minnesota School of Social Work; Dr. Noel Larson of Meta Resources; Mary Azzahir, known to the many people who love her as Mother Atum; her husband, Seba Akhmed Azzahir; and Mahmoud El-Kati. And I am deeply grateful for the love, presence, and support of my wife, Maria; my daughter, Brittney; and my son, Tezara.

This book would not have been born had it not been for the efforts of Scott Edelstein, my collaborator and literary agent.

I was not groomed to be a therapist, a writer, or a talk-show host. I was raised in a family that was both stable and chaotic. My father was sometimes violent, and for years he struggled with chemical dependency—though that life has been behind him for many years now, and I am immensely proud of him for it. My mother worked twelve-hour days to keep us fed. Both parents taught my brothers and me how to hustle and grind in different ways. I grew up in a lower-middle-class multiethnic neighborhood where neighbors and relatives watched out for me. Still, as a young adult, I was fearful, bitter, and naïve. It took me a long time to find my way. It seemed like everyone understood life long before I did.

As the novel *Frankenstein* begins, sailors in the Arctic spot a man on a fragment of ice. The man, Dr. Victor Frankenstein, is lost, confused, and suffering. The sailors see what bad shape he's in and they rescue and revive him.

In my teens and early twenties, I too was lost, confused, and suffering. Fortunately, the people around me came to my rescue and helped me come back to life. My mentors, ancestors, and elders all held me accountable without holding me up for ridicule. They taught me not to hurt or damage people, including myself. They encouraged me to grow up. I am deeply grateful to them all.

From One Monster to Another

Monsters in Love was first published in 2015, under the title *Rock the Boat*. Back then, Barack Obama was president of the United States; Hong Kong was a bastion of freedom and stability; Kim and Kanye were newlyweds; Jamie Foxx and Katie Holmes were a happy, recently-engaged couple; few people outside of Indiana knew who Pete Buttigieg and Chasten Glezman were; abortion was legal in all fifty US states; and marriage equality had just been made the law of the land.

I'm completing this new preface in 2022. Although many aspects of our world are vastly different now, nothing has changed about the essential ways in which we human beings act, react, think, experience, and relate to each other. So, although I've updated and expanded this new edition, its fundamental approaches and insights remain unchanged as well.

Over the past few years, my book *My Grandmother's Hands: Racialized Trauma and the Pathway to Mending Our Hearts and Bodies* was published and, I'm grateful to say, hit many bestseller lists. This led to my Somatic Abolitionism blog at www.resmaa.com/somatic-learnings, to the spread of Somatic Abolitionism, to my book *The Quaking of America: An Embodied Guide to Navigating Our Nation's Upheaval and Racial Reckoning*, and to many new opportunities for healing racialized trauma. That is currently the primary focus of my work—but it is not the only focus.

I'm a healer. My work involves helping people heal from trauma, grow closer, build discernment and resilience, and grow up. Today, some of my work continues to focus on couples in committed relationships.

Although I'm a healer, like you, I'm also a monster. (More about this in a few pages.) That's why I knew that it was important to create this new, expanded edition—and to give it a more accurate (and more compelling) title and subtitle.

Some of the experiences, practices, and concepts you'll read about in *Monsters in Love* also appear in *My Grandmother's Hands* (and in other things I've written). This is no accident. What can work to heal racialized trauma can also help couples to grow closer—and to grow up together. Some of these include:

- The **five anchors**. These can help you to slow down, stay present, and hold onto yourself when things start to cook in your relationship.
- Guidance for paying close attention to **what you experience in your body.**
- **Clean pain and discomfort vs. dirty pain:** pain that leads to healing vs. pain that creates more conflict and difficulty.
- How moments of conflict create both **peril and possibility.**
- How you and your partner can each **act from the best parts of yourselves.**
- Practices for **keeping your body healthy and alert.**
- How to **begin seeing other people as they actually are**, rather than how you wish, fear, or imagine them to be.
- How you and your partner, separately and together, can discover **unfolding purpose.**

If you (or you and your partner) are already doing some of the work of Somatic Abolitionism, then you may already be familiar with these experiences and concepts:

- **Life reps:** situations life presents you with that force you up against yourself and require you to choose either the clean pain and discomfort of growth or the dirty pain of harm.
- **Invited reps:** practices that you choose to practice and repeat, in order to condition and temper your body and mind.
- **Primal reps:** foundational body-centered practices that make you more aware of your body and the energies that move through it.
- **Geopathic stresses:** the cultural, social, political, institutional, and environmental stresses that weather our bodies, minds, and intimate relationships.

If you've read *My Grandmother's Hands*, or *The Quaking of America*, or my Somatic Abolitionism blog, you may discover that your experience has yielded insights, grounding, and discernment that can help you as you move through this volume.

I want to add a note on what I learned from rewriting parts of this book. Some of the original language I used had subtle negative overtones about race, gender, sexual orientation, and body image that I now regret. I am grateful for the chance to correct these items. (If I missed some others, please point them out to me. I continue to accept the challenges of my community to do and be better—not perfect, but emergently better.)

It's now been nine years since I completed the original manuscript of *Rock the Boat*. I'm still happily married to Maria, with whom I shared wedding vows back in 1997. Because we're a committed couple, we still drive each other crazy sometimes. But each year, that commitment has deepened. We are now both in our mid-fifties, and our kids (who sometimes drive us crazy, and vice versa) are adults. In less than a decade, Maria and I will both be seniors. While that prospect doesn't thrill us, we look forward to growing old together— and to continuing to grow up together.

I wish you and your partner (or future partner) this same growth— along with plenty of opportunities for deep sweetness, profound intimacy, sensational sex, and body-quaking laughter at your own shared monsterhood.

Resmaa Menakem
Minneapolis, 2022

Welcome to Monsterworld

Do you want your lover to rock your world? Good.

Do you want to rock theirs? Even better.

But rocking isn't always a thrill ride. Rocking creates conflict and discomfort, challenge and opportunity, peril and possibility.

Plus, there's much more to an intimate relationship than just rocking. In each new moment together, each relationship also has a direction, a charge, a weight, a speed, and a texture. Often these create discomfort. Sometimes they drive us crazy.

This book is about the reality of marriage and other committed, intimate relationships. It offers no comforting fantasies, false promises, or quick-and-easy fixes. Instead, it offers you and your partner a chance to make your relationship—and your lives—bigger and fuller.

This book challenges several common misperceptions about what makes for a successful partnership. It also rocks the boat of psychotherapy, calling out therapists who don't bring their best to their clients.

Every challenge in this book is based not on theory, or fads, or hopes, but on how relationships actually work.

Every challenge in this book applies to *all* committed couples, regardless of any member's gender identity (or lack of identity) or body configuration.[1]

Who am I to tell you how relationships actually work?

I'm a licensed clinical social worker, a divorce and family mediator, and a certified military family life consultant. For twenty-four years, I've worked with hundreds of couples, families, individuals, and organizations.

I've also served as behavioral health director for African American Family Services in Minneapolis and director of counseling services

---

1 It doesn't apply to threesomes and foursomes, open relationships, or casual relationships. These relationships rarely generate enough heat and pressure to enable important things to cook. Nor do they typically force people into emotional bottlenecks that lead to transformation.

for Tubman Family Alliance, a domestic violence treatment center also in Minneapolis, where I developed its holistic model and many of its violence prevention programs.

I spent two years working for a US military contractor in Afghanistan, designing and overseeing counseling programs for civilian contractors and managing the wellness and counseling services on fifty-three US military bases. As a certified military family life consultant, I also worked with members of the military and their families on issues related to family living, deployment, and returning home.

You may have seen me on *The Oprah Winfrey Show* or *Dr. Phil,* where I appeared as an expert on family dynamics and couples in conflict. If you live in the Twin Cities, you also may have listened to the radio show I cohosted for ten years with former US Congressman (and now Minnesota Attorney General) Keith Ellison, or my solo show, "Resmaa in the Morning," both on KMOJ-FM.

More recently, you may have heard me on podcasts such as Krista Tippett's *On Being,* Dan Harris's *10% Happier,* Gwyneth Paltrow's *Goop,* Sounds True's *Walking Together,* Sam Fragoso's *Talk Easy,* Malcolm Gladwell's *Revisionist History,* Eric Zimmer's *The One You Feed,* or Pilar Gerasimo and Dallas Hartwig's *The Living Experiment.*

This Is about Getting Real and Serious

Committed relationships can be gritty and in our faces. Sometimes they can seem dangerous. This is how they're meant to work. They're not always joyful or serene.

If you already know this, read on. If you're unsure but curious, read on. But if you're committed to avoiding grit or challenge or conflict, now is the time to step away (from this book, not from your partner).

Be forewarned: if what you strive for in your relationship is comfort, this book is not going to help you. Like committed relationships, this book is gritty and down-to-earth. It's 100 percent clinically sound. It's also 100 percent simple, straightforward, and bullshit-free.

If all you want is a pleasant and nurturing experience, put down this book and get a massage.

If you want a relationship that helps you and your partner grow into the people you most want each other to be, welcome aboard.

A lot of books about relationships aren't serious. This book is. I'm not saying other books have no value. A gardening book that only talks about weeding and mulching has some value, but it's not serious about the entire ecology of gardening.

You can buy a book that teaches you how to communicate better, or to understand cultural differences, or to learn men's and women's different needs and ways of thinking. Most of these books have some value, but they're not serious guides to the difficult, painful, and potentially transformative business of growing up as partners and as people.

If you're reading this book to get some new tools to add to your relationship toolbox, this book will shock the shit out of you. You and your partner don't need a toolbox. Instead, in this book, you'll open a *toybox* and take out some new toys—things to explore, investigate, and share with your partner.[2] But take careful note: these are toys for adults, not children. Each one will encourage you and your partner to grow up.

Just by being who they are, your lover forces you into making choices in which you either grow up or don't. By being who *you* are, you force them to make the same kind of choices. This happens over and over, day after day. Each time it happens, each of you has to choose to grow or not. You can't make your partner grow up, and they can't grow up for you.

When life (or your partner) pushes you into growing up, you usually won't want to do it. If you're like most people, your first impulse will be to take it personally and take offense. You may try to make the conflict into *their* problem, their pathology. Over time, you may grow rageful or even violent.

Just by being together, you and your partner will also shine light on each other's limitations. This is always painful at first.

If you're like most couples, you'll try to unwind each other's limitations. This can be terrifying—so terrifying that, at times, you lash out at each other.

Instead, both of you need to grow up.

This book is about choosing to grow up. That's what makes it serious.

Marriage—or any committed relationship—is not for the weak or timid. Each of you, without even trying, will naturally rock the boat of your relationship. Sometimes this will be uncomfortable or painful. Sometimes it will seem almost unbearable. *Yet this is exactly what is supposed to happen.*

---

2 My thanks to Dr. Leticia Nieto, who first made this important distinction.

We've all been taught that the best thing to do in relationships is not rock the boat. Leave things alone, don't push, and everybody will calm down, and your situation will become comfortable and familiar again.

With many small, daily issues, this is exactly the right thing to do. But a strong partnership isn't always about keeping your boat as stable as possible and keeping you and your partner aligned. It's also about staying present and upright when the wind and waves are tossing you around. When it comes to matters of integrity, there will be times when you need to rock the boat—or let it rock you. And sometimes, in the worst of storms, when your boat is being tossed about, trying to keep it stable can actually sink it.

Which is why, hard as it is, we're better off seeing our partners and ourselves as who we really are.

Welcome to the Monster Fairy Tale

Your partner is a monster. But you already know that.

You're a monster, too. And so am I.

Stay with me. I'll explain.

In the film version of *Frankenstein*, when the monster comes to life in the scientist's lab, he's curious and innocent, like a baby. Everything seems new and wondrous to him.

But of course he's not a baby. He's large and strong. He can control his limbs, but he doesn't know how much trouble they can cause. He doesn't understand many of his body's signals. He doesn't realize his power or how to control it. He's dangerous and doesn't know it.

He escapes from the lab and wanders off. He ends up by a lake, where he meets a small blind girl who gives him a handful of flowers. The girl and the monster toss the flowers into a lake one by one and watch them float. Both of them are happy until the monster runs out of flowers. Then he picks up the girl and throws her in the lake, thinking she can float, too, like flowers and boats. But she can't swim. She struggles and drowns. The monster is confused and miserable. From here his life goes from bad to worse.

In committed relationships, you and your partner—and your neighbor and their partner, and my wife and I—are all like Frankenstein's monster.

When you and your partner first got to know each other, you were curious about each other, you played with each other, and you focused on and responded to your similarities. Your relationship seemed new and open, and its possibilities appeared infinite.

At some point a commitment was made. Then, suddenly, life started to get more and more difficult. The two of you, just by being who you are, somehow created conflicts. You tried your best to be loving, but your efforts often led to disaster. At times, you may have been tempted to resort to manipulation or cruelty.

This didn't happen just once. It's happened over and over. The two of you became confused and miserable. It often seemed like you were drowning.

Now you sometimes look at your partner and think, *What the hell is wrong with you?* Your partner looks at you and has the same thought. Looking in the mirror, you sometimes think, *What the hell is wrong with me?* Your relationship, or your lover, or you, have become the thing you most fear.

But the reality is, *nothing is wrong. This is exactly how committed relationships work.*

We think that when people have a problem in their marriage, it's because of an issue. You and your partner don't communicate well. Or your different backgrounds and views of the world get in each other's way. Or your masculine energy conflicts with your partner's feminine energy. Or you're Muslim and he's Jewish. Or the two of you just grew apart.

This is most people's understanding of how the world works. This is also most *therapists'* understanding of how the world works.

But it's only part of the picture. If it were the whole picture, then gay, lesbian, and transgender couples who practice the same religion and who talk to each other regularly about their emotions would live charmed lives. But they're in my office, too, asking me, "What the hell is wrong with us?"

It's my job to tell them, "Nothing is wrong."

Couples typically look for The Answer as to why they're unhappy with each other. Often, they go to a therapist to assist them in their search. They hope that the therapist will help them explore beneath the couch cushions of their relationship and find the lost or missing keys. But this isn't how intimate relationships work. It's not how authentic therapy works, either.

Partners look for The Answer because they haven't yet conditioned and tempered themselves to move through the conundrums and emotional bottlenecks that are built into intimate relationships. This conditioning is vital for the health of their relationship. Encouraging this conditioning and tempering, and supporting people as they move into and through it, is therapists' most important job.

The Heart of Emotional Stalemates

If you're like most couples, you and your lover don't have a communication problem. You know perfectly well what your partner wants and doesn't want, what they care about and don't care about, what pisses them off, and what makes them happy. They know the same things about you.

Yes, you have issues and differences. Addressing these can reduce your day-to-day conflicts and smooth out your lives. But that won't necessarily keep you from being monsters to each other.

That's because, in marriage, we monsters naturally create one interlocking conundrum after another. These repeated crises—these *life reps*, as I call them—are built into intimate relationships. Each crisis challenges both monsters to stand in their own integrity, to grow, and, often, to face a horde of angry townspeople—family, in-laws, and friends—who want to burn up their asses. Each life rep forces the two monsters up against each other, grinding them together, pressuring and squeezing and pulverizing them, until they completely block each other's moves. This creates what is often called an *emotional stalemate* or *emotional bottleneck,* and it hurts like hell.

People will do almost anything to try to free themselves from this situation, including blaming their partners, manipulating them, trying to control them, having affairs, abusing drugs or alcohol or any of a hundred other things, gaslighting their partners, or even becoming violent. Over time, these tactics may even become part of the structure of the relationship.

All of us in committed relationships—including therapists, other healers, and spiritual leaders—experience these same temptations. But none of these tactics works to help us grow up. In fact, they all deepen the conflict.

What each of us needs to do is grow. We need to learn to become responsible for soothing the aches and pains of our own heart, rather than ask—or expect or demand—that our partner soothe them for us.

If you don't learn this, your emotional stalemate with your partner can continue for years, or even decades. You have been doing this dance for so long that it seems familiar and comforting, even though you both know something has to change. Yet you both also know that a split-the-difference compromise or find-a-middle-ground solution is impossible.

The process can lead the two of you to eventually reach critical mass[3]—the place where the pressure and stresses are so great that something has to give. Someone decides that they can't go on in the same way. Some spring-loaded energy that has been building up— perhaps for a very long time—is released. Often that energy has the power to metabolize the clean pain and transform the relationship.

And then something important changes. In a moment of peril and possibility, one of you makes a leap toward greater balance and integrity. Moments such as these test your resolve—and your limitations.

It would be great if the two of you could make the leap together. But this almost never happens. Usually one person makes the leap alone, while their partner shouts at them, "You're an idiot! I'm not leaping into the water with you! If you leap, you're leaping alone, asshole."

After the person makes this leap, their partner almost always demands that they leap back and return to the old status quo pattern— but they don't. Their spine straightens, their eyes brighten, and they hold their ground. They don't run away, but stand firm inside the relationship. They communicate to their partner, "I love you with my whole heart, but I'm not going back to things the way they were." This knowing and clarity, and the accompanying physical changes, is often called a *brightening of self.*

Now something else has to give. The other person has to either develop new emotional skills or shrink away.

Sometimes the other partner does leap. If they do, there is the possibility to create a stronger partnership and greater trust, intimacy, and respect.

Sometimes the other partner doesn't leap and leaves the relationship, only to come up against the same problems and limitations with their next partner, or someone else who gets close to them.

Sometimes they find a way to coax the partner who leaped to come back into the old, unsatisfactory arrangement—one involving

---

3 The terms *critical mass* and *brightening of self* (which you'll encounter in a few paragraphs) were first used in an interpersonal context by one of my mentors, Dr. David Schnarch. In a brightening of self, new neural pathways are carved—or existing ones widened and deepened— in the brain; at the same time, the person begins a process of building new social or relational skills. I'll discuss both of these terms in detail in later chapters.

great pain but also the comfort of familiarity. If the partner does let themselves get coaxed back, the partnership will have less trust, intimacy, and respect than before—and more anger, heaviness, and anxiety.

Like I said, marriage is not for the weak or the timid.

The process I just described—with a focus on emergence and transformation—is the subject of this book.

This book can help you create a stronger, deeper, more loving partnership—not through some magic formula, but by accepting the pain and growth that committed relationships demand of us.

You'll see this pain and growth illustrated in dozens of couples' stories throughout this book. All of these stories grew out of my clinical practice as a psychotherapist. Some, such as the story of Melissa and Kim in chapter 2, are adapted from actual encounters with clients in my therapy office. (I've changed names and multiple details to protect clients' privacy and identities.) Other stories, such as the story of Felicia and André in chapter 22, are composites of events in the lives of multiple couples. Still others, such as the story of Camilla in chapter 23, are fictional, provided solely to illustrate a key concept or process. When a story is purely fictional and illustrative, this will be clear in context.

In this book I use the words *partner, lover, spouse,* and *mate* to mean the person you're in a committed relationship with, whether you're married or not, whether you've been together one year or sixty, and whether you're straight, gay, bi, trans, or non-binary. I also use the words *marriage, relationship,* and *partnership* interchangeably.

Therapists Are Monsters, Too

In Part 4 of this book, we'll look at the role of therapy in working with conflict in your partnership. But we therapists are neither superior beings nor sages. It's vitally important to see us as human beings who face the same challenges and choices in our personal lives as everyone else.

I wish it were true that when we therapists hit emotional stalemates with our lovers, we always straighten our spines, make the right leaps, and stand our ground. The reality is that many of us don't.

Both my wife and I have gotten much better at this process throughout our twenty-nine years together. But there are still times when one of us says to the other, "If you think I'm leaping into the water with you, you're crazy." We've had fights and arguments about how and where to steer. We have kids, so we've lived through a couple of mutinies. But we have taught each other and helped each other to grow up. We learn the same lessons in the same way as everyone else.

I may be an experienced therapist, but I'm also a husband and father who sometimes makes mistakes—and who, like you, regularly faces the challenges of growing up. I often remind myself that when I was young and growing up in my parents' home, they were growing up, too. This recognition has helped me lean into the process of growth and play with the energies of living and relating with others.

Psychotherapy mirrors marriage in many ways. If therapists are both playful and strategic, if they understand what they are seeing, and if they are willing and able to calm their own anxiety, then they can provide couples in conflict with wise guidance, helping them navigate through emotional bottlenecks.

Unfortunately, this process scares the crap out of many therapists. They typically respond reflexively by calming everybody down. When one member of a couple starts rocking the boat big-time, the therapist tries to steady the boat. But what they need to do is let the conflict unfold—not into cruelty or violence, but into transformation.

This reflex occurs when therapists' own tolerance for conflict gets exceeded by the heat of the interaction taking place in their office. Sadly, while this process of temporarily calming things down makes *therapists* less anxious, it usually deprives their clients of the opportunity and heat needed to transform.

This dodge by therapists is especially likely when there has been some physical cruelty, with one partner grabbing or pushing or shaking the other. This kind of physical cruelty can be commonplace in committed relationships, but it is often mistakenly lumped together with life-threatening violence. Some therapists go so far as to refuse to work with any couple in which there has been physical cruelty, no matter how brief or small.

Instead, in critical moments, good therapists need to be present with their clients, keeping their own spines straight, standing firm as the hard truths begin to unfold. They need to soothe themselves and set aside their desire to be "helpful." Then they need to help the confrontation unfold without being scared off by it or drawn into it. Ultimately they need to help their clients construct a relational container that is large enough, strong enough, and flexible enough to navigate the turbulent waters of intimate relationships and life.

In short, like marriage, psychotherapy is not for the weak or timid—whether you're the client or the therapist.

Using therapy to strengthen your relationship with your lover often includes demanding the best from your therapist. Sometimes it means finding a different one.

In the strongest partnerships, whether with a therapist or your lover, both people consistently demand the best from each other and force each other to grow. This is never easy or painless. But it's way better than the alternative: making each other smaller, weaker, less adaptable, and more unhappy.

I wrote this book to help you and your mate create your own strongest partnership.

This book is partly about therapy—but it is mostly a book about healing and growing up. Therapy is personal. It involves individuals, couples, and family groups. In contrast, healing is both personal *and* communal. In healing we connect to energies that are always with us, in us, and around us. Healing radiates outward to other people and to the world, and reminds us of what we already are and what we always have been part of.

As for growing up, it hurts like hell. But the prospect and possibility of growing up are why you and your partner are together. And, although sometimes it may appear otherwise, growing up is what you and your partner most desire from each other.

One last note: at the end of each chapter, I've included a list of "compass points"—key ideas from that chapter that can help guide you, and point you and your partner in the right direction.

COMPASS POINTS

- This book offers no comforting fantasies, false promises, or quick fixes. Instead, it offers you and your partner a chance to make your relationship—and your lives—fuller than you ever imagined.
- In the strongest partnerships, both people demand the best of each other and force each other to grow. This is why marriage—or any committed relationship—is not for the weak or the timid.
- This book is a serious guide to growing up and handling conflicts as partners.
- You and your partner don't need a toolbox. Instead, in this book, you'll open a toybox and take out some new toys—

things to explore, investigate, and share with your partner. But these are toys for adults, not children. Each one will encourage you and your partner to grow up.

- In your partnership, both you and your partner may try to be loving, but your efforts often lead both of you into confusion and misery.

- When this happens, *nothing is wrong. That's exactly how committed relationships work.*

- Just by being who they are, your lover forces you into making choices in which you either grow up or don't. By being who you are, you force them to make the same kind of choices. This happens over and over, day after day. Each time it happens, each of you has to choose to grow or not.

- In partnerships, we naturally create one interlocking conundrum after another. Each crisis challenges both partners to stand in their own integrity and grow. It forces both people up against each other until they reach an *emotional stalemate* or *emotional bottleneck.*

- Eventually one or both lovers reach critical mass. At least one of them simply can't go on in the same way anymore. They may respond with violence or blaming, or by leaving the relationship. Or they raise their game, making a leap toward greater balance, integration, and adaptation.

- Now something has to give. Either the second partner makes a leap of their own, or the relationship ends or gets redefined. A transformation occurs. In the best of cases, both partners grow—and grow closer.

- To create the strongest, deepest, most loving relationship, both lovers must accept the pain and growth that committed relationships demand. How to do this is the focus of this book.

- In relationships and life, therapists face the same challenges as everyone else. In the face of these challenges, sometimes they choose to grow. Often they don't.

- Psychotherapy mirrors marriage in many ways. When therapists do their job well, they can help couples reach critical mass.

- When one person makes a leap and stands their ground, the other often freaks out. This scares most therapists, who respond by defusing the conflict. This deprives couples of the opportunity and heat needed to transform.

- Instead, in critical moments, a good therapist needs to be present with clients, standing firm as a crisis erupts around them and letting the crisis unfold moment by moment, without being scared off or drawn into it.

PART 1

How Relationships Really Work

1

Your Partnership Is about Transformation—Even If You Don't Want It to Be

Most of us get into committed relationships because they generate positive emotions. We become happy, or satisfied, or safe, or secure, or fulfilled, or energized, or socially accepted.

Some of us get into relationships even though they *don't* create positive emotions, because we hope they will later on. And some of us get into relationships because they're painful but familiar. Even though they hurt, they provide us with a sense of comfort or stability.

But rarely do any of us fall in love because we sense that our partner will help us grow up. Instead, we reach for the safety, comfort, and pleasure that we imagine the partnership will bring us. We get into each romantic relationship for reasons that are precisely the opposite of its actual purpose. As a result, in every committed partnership, everyone eventually gets the same wake-up call.

No matter what you do or who your lover is, eventually your partnership begins to hurt. Whether it takes a week, a few months, or five years, each of you starts having painful emotions you don't want to have. You start being confronted with your partner's and your own limitations and with the call for personal development. Confusingly, many of those limitations are couched inside your partner's and your own strengths, making them difficult to sort out and address.

If you're like most people, it seems like you've been ripped off. You think, *This isn't what I signed up for.* You experience it as the ultimate bait and switch, like you've been betrayed by the universe.

But you haven't. This is how committed partnerships are designed to work. Simple human caring, connecting, and relating are often draining. You're experiencing the pressure to grow.

The purpose of these relationships is to create the best in us by forcing us to grow up—and growing up is often uncomfortable or painful.

This pain drives many couples into therapy. They may tell the therapist that their problem is divergent communication styles or differing backgrounds or conflicting needs or diverse families of origin. These issues may be real. But most couples' primary message to therapists isn't about any of these issues. It's this: *We hurt. Please make the pain go away.*

In response, a courageous and skilled therapist doesn't offer emotional Band-Aids or pain pills; instead, they encourage each lover to grow up and learn to soothe themselves, right in the middle of the hate and love that show up in a tangled mess, with no sense of discernment or nuance.

This pain also drives many couples apart, because one or both are unwilling to tolerate it. They try to escape the pain through an affair, or with an addiction, or by finding a replacement partner, or by beating up their partner emotionally or physically. These may soothe the pain temporarily, but eventually the same pain and difficulties return, often in a more severe form—even if the person has tried to escape it by finding a new lover.

The conflicts you have with your mate aren't just about differing backgrounds or needs or communication styles or approaches to life. *They are about each of you becoming the person you want to be (or, at least, ought to want to be).* That's the opportunity of the relationship.

Committed partnerships are ecosystems[4] that are designed to force both people up against themselves and each other, over and over, day after day. Both partners get ground together in the same way that a rock gets polished into a jewel. Over and over, you and your partner have a choice: you can polish each other into jewels or you can grind each other to dust.

The pain you experience in your partnership isn't something to tamp down or medicate or avoid. You've already tried these, and they

---

4 One of my mentors, the late Dr. James Maddock, helped me see families and committed partnerships as ecological systems. Doc Maddock was a key figure in this ecological approach to therapy. His widow, Dr. Noel Larson, continues to be a prominent practitioner of this approach. For readers interested in this approach, I recommend their book *Incestuous Families: An Ecological Approach to Understanding and Treatment* (Norton, 1995).

don't work for very long. Instead, you need to work through the hurt. You have to get ground and squeezed to a point where, if you stay in the relationship, there is no choice but to grow up.

In choosing to stay and grow, you have the possibility of becoming the person you've wanted to be. If you take up that opportunity, it will naturally create the possibility for your partner to do the same. This work is done both separately *and* together.

If you keep having the same argument with your lover time after time, don't simply acquiesce, or tell yourself that it doesn't matter. Don't try to make your partner give in, either. Don't paper over your differences. And don't settle on a compromise that ultimately damages someone's values or safety. Any argument you keep having is an argument the two of you need to have. *Keep having it.* Come back to it regularly. Excavate, investigate, and interrogate those places in yourself and your relationship that you have avoided—or been unwilling to accept. Keep getting your reps in, while treating each other with as much love and respect as you can muster.

Do the things you need to do to grow up. (You'll learn what these are later in this book.) Do them frequently and consistently, as if you loved doing them—even if (especially if) they make you uncomfortable. Investigate yourself relationally, emotionally, physically, and culturally.

Eventually, through the argument that you and your partner keep having, over and over, you may reach critical mass and have the opportunity to transform.

In order to make it through this process, each of you needs to learn to hold on to yourself, to stay present, balanced, and connected in the midst of pain and uncertainty. You can do this by following some simple, down-to-earth practices that I'll describe in detail in chapter 35.

Growth always requires change. But it also requires transformation.

People can change—and even change for the better—without growing up. They stop doing something harmful, but they don't change the way they think or how they interact with other people and the world.

Transformation is more than mere change. It's visceral and elemental. When it happens to us, we experience it in our body. When it happens to someone else, we know it by the look in their eyes, or the sound of their voice, or the way they hold their body.

Growing up is a continuous process of one transformation after another.

Almost no one likes to grow up. We want *other* people to grow, especially our partner, but we want to stay just the way we are. If we're serious about growing up, however, this is not an option.

When most people grind against their lover and begin to experience the pain of growth, they look for a way to mitigate the pressure or blow off steam. They get involved with a hobby or interest or obsession. Or they leap into an affair or casual sex with strangers.

Most people don't turn to affairs and hookups because their partners are unimportant to them. They do it because their lover is *so* important that they're afraid to fully reveal themselves to them.

CARLOS

The person who Carlos hooks up with online doesn't really matter much to him. That is why he can comfortably show that stranger his freak side—his butt fetish or S&M fantasies or fondness for being spanked. But he's terrified to show his partner this hidden side of himself, because he's afraid his lover will say, "My God, you're a fucking freak! I'm outta here."

Sometimes both partners try to blow off steam together. They take long vacations, or schedule frequent date nights, or have lots of sex. These typically result in pleasant experiences, but they won't silence the call for growth.

Other folks try to lower the pressure by trying to turn their partner into their servant, or an obedient child, or their sexual plaything. Still others provoke their partners into fighting or blowing up or collapsing into a sobbing heap. All of these only heighten both partners' need to grow.

There's no sane or healthy alternative to growing up. And each of us has to grow up on our own. You and your mate can each grow up at the same time, but growing up is always a unilateral choice and a unilateral process.

Over time, when one person repeatedly chooses to grow and the other repeatedly refuses, the relationship usually ends. Couples often see this as a failure. But it's not. That relationship—including its demise—worked exactly the way it was supposed to. It served to transform one of the partners. Sometimes the ending of the relationship transforms the other partner as well.

Marriage is a capacity-building practice, but only if you allow it to be. If you're like almost everyone else, you got into a committed relationship without knowing how to handle all your anger, disappointment, anxiety, and fear within that relationship. The relationship itself will teach you these skills, by forcing you up against yourself, time after time, and providing you with one opportunity after another to grow, through life reps.

Growing up has nothing to do with whether you and your partner stay together or split up. Keeping the partnership going—or ending it—isn't the point. The point is doing and being your best, and becoming the person you most want to be.

In practice, this often means that you and your lover will each need to maintain your integrity *and* as much loving connection as possible. Each of you needs to honor and balance both.

In your own partnership, you and your mate will each be given a choice, over and over: *Are you going to be your best right now, or not?* That is the challenge, the value, and the promise of a committed relationship.

COMPASS POINTS

- Few of us fall in love because we sense that our partner will help us grow up. Instead, we reach for the safety, comfort, and pleasure that we imagine the partnership will bring us.
- We get into every romantic relationship for reasons that are precisely the opposite of its actual purpose. As a result, in every partnership, everyone eventually gets the same wake-up call. How each partner handles this wake-up call determines the trajectory of the relationship—and whether or not each partner grows up.
- The conflicts you have with your mate are about each of you becoming the person you most want to be. That's the opportunity of the relationship. Each of you needs to work through the pain and grow up.
- Over time, you and your partner have a choice: you can polish each other into jewels or grind each other to dust.

- If you keep having the same argument with your lover time after time, this is the argument the two of you need to have. *Keep having it,* while treating each other with all the love and respect you can muster. Interrogate the things that you have avoided or ignored in the past.
- One day, through that argument, you'll reach critical mass and create an opportunity to transform.
- In committed relationships, both partners are given this choice, over and over: *Are you going to be your best right now, or not?*

2

Conflicts Can Be Messy—
and Helpful

If you're like almost everyone else with a partner, you have a mental and emotional image of who they are—and that image is not 100 percent accurate. When your partner acts in a way that doesn't match your mental image, this can drive you crazy.

As you learn to deal with your partner as they actually are, your relationship will naturally turn up the heat, over and over. This can drive you crazy, too, until you learn to accept and tolerate the heat.

Over time, as you and your partner learn to support and lovingly challenge each other, both of you will change. The heat will get turned up in new ways, creating new difficulties—and new opportunities to tolerate that heat, grow up, and grow closer.

When you go crazy in any of these ways, nothing is going wrong. The craziness you experience is exactly what you need to go through. It's your body and brain and gut telling you, *This can't go on. Something has to change.* You're going to have to make choices.

This choice isn't one you want to make, or you'd have already made it. It's probably a choice you've been avoiding for a long time. It's a classic double bind. As Dr. James Maddock often phrased it: *You're caught between something you don't want to do and something you really don't want to do.* All of your options may hurt. But you still have to choose.

This is exactly what relationships are designed to do: create forced choices where you have to either grow up or stay emotionally young.

Couples show up in my office thinking they're screwed up because they have relationship problems. I tell them, "You're not screwed up at all. But a lot depends on the two of you. If you're both here to find a way to not have relationship problems, then you're screwed, because problems, and peril, and possibilities are baked into every long-term relationship.

"Actually, you guys are really fortunate to have gotten to this place. Your problems are important. The things you can't avoid—the things that keep coming up over and over—are the building blocks of your relationship. You've both gotten shaken and squeezed and pulverized to a point where there is no other choice—you have to either grow up or leave. You have to face both the possibilities and the peril."

This process is vital in every sense. Yet most people do everything they can to avoid it, even in therapy sessions.

Here's something else important that you need to know:

You and your partner will experience each of your conflicts and difficulties as personal and particular to the two of you. But, as you will see, each can also be a reflection of your culture, history, family, genetics, and a great deal more.

MELISSA AND KIM

Like many couples, when Melissa and Kim reached an emotional stalemate, they wanted me to show them the way out. "Resmaa, I just can't go on this way," Melissa told me. "This relationship doesn't seem safe anymore." A second later, Kim said, "And to me, it doesn't seem respectful. We're stuck, and it's driving us both nuts. Tell us what we need to do."

I said, "You're both looking for an answer or solution. You want me to tell you something like *Learn to use 'I' statements. Go on a date at least once a week. Have more sex. Do this; tweak that.* That's not how this works. There's no formulaic answer. There's no quick, easy, prefab solution. There's a *process*. You both have to live through the uncertainty, and each one of you needs to speak your truth. I don't think either of you has a problem doing that.

"Each of you already knows that your partner thinks you're small and not serious about changing. And each of you hates the fact that they think that about you. Each of you is in a *both/ and* situation. You must be willing both to speak your own truth *and* to tolerate the pain of hearing your partner speak their truth about you. You both are in a relationship with someone who has hurt you. Now you each have figure out how you're going to be in this relationship from this bright line forward."

Melissa was in tears. "But we don't know what to do. That's why we're here, so you can help us figure that out and make a plan."

I said, "The answer to the question *What are we going to do?* is not an idea or a plan or a foolproof strategy. It's a process of living through uncertainty, soothing yourself, and accepting some hard truths as they emerge. Some of these you can't see yet—not because you aren't looking, but because when you're in the middle of something, your vantage point won't always allow you to see all sides. And right now each of you has an emotional investment in protecting your current sense of self.

"This process of living into and through uncertainty is vital. If neither of you knows what to do, then for now just stay in *I don't know*, without running away. Take care of yourself without looking for your partner to take care of you. And when you can, reach out to your partner from the best parts of yourself. Over time, you'll develop some discernment around what the best and worst parts are. This is vital to helping you figure out what to do."

We look to our partner for harmony and safety and familiarity. A loving relationship provides these some of the time. But it also provides friction. Friction—not harmony or safety—is an engine of growth.

Most couples try to minimize friction and maximize harmony, especially early in their relationships. This works temporarily, but over time the friction keeps returning. And soon the effort to minimize the friction creates more friction.

This is when couples typically start dancing around conflicts. They try to reduce friction by avoiding difficult discussions and painful choices. This creates even more friction.

I tell couples, "You need that friction and the heat it generates, because it may be tied to your integrity. It's all about who you are as a person and how you're going to be in a relationship with the most important person in your life." The question is always, *Can I be the person I strive to be and still stay connected to the person who means the most to me?*

What couples actually need to do is not reduce the friction but reduce the cruelty in the partnership.

In committed relationships, cruelty is far more common than most of us realize or admit. This cruelty comes in many forms—physical, emotional, psychological, and spiritual. Nearly all couples practice it, at least occasionally.

In all types of this commonplace cruelty, we knowingly and deliberately hurt our partner—or eat their heart—to make ourselves hurt less. We enact this cruelty to either force temporary compliance from them or punish them for something they did (or didn't do). We also do it to avoid looking at what we need to do inside *ourselves* to grow up.

When there has been physical cruelty in a relationship, *temporarily* lowering the friction and providing boundaries and safety are very important to prevent further violence. But sooner or later the friction will come back, because that friction is not centered in the violence, or even in the individual partners, but in the very dynamics of relating.

Both lovers need to learn to tolerate that friction without slipping back into cruelty. If they focus only on keeping the friction down, then the violence may stop, but the couple will stay stuck.

Having a committed partner always creates friction and problems. Most of us want to keep the partnership and get rid of the friction and problems. That's a fantasy we need to grow out of.

Your relationship is about transformation. The friction you experience and the problems you face are the fuel for that transformation.

Each of us starts out as a lump of coal. A committed partnership is a vital and alchemical process in which a combination of heat, pressure, and time can transform us into a diamond—if we let it.

COMPASS POINTS

- Your partner drives you crazy in three different ways. You drive them crazy, too, in those same three ways:
  - ∗ You have a mental image of who your partner is, and that image is not 100 percent accurate.
  - ∗ As you learn to deal with your partner as they are, your relationship with them will naturally turn up the heat, over and over.
  - ∗ Over time, as you and your partner learn to support and lovingly challenge each other, both of you will change.

- When your partner makes you crazy, nothing is going wrong. You're experiencing exactly what you need to. You're experiencing an internal call for change.
- Relationships are designed to create forced choices where people have to grow up.
- You and your partner will experience each of your conflicts and difficulties as personal and particular to the two of you. But, each can also be a reflection of your culture, history, family, genetics, and a great deal more.
- When couples reach emotional stalemates, the answer is never a plan or a strategy. It's a process of living through uncertainty.
- The friction couples face is precious fuel for their transformation.

3

Not Hurting Is Not an Option

When you and your mate were first dating, you provided each other with blessed relief from the rest of your lives. The two of you created a bubble outside of the daily grind. In this bubble, you could enjoy each other and be safe and happy. When you and your lover were together inside your bubble, it probably didn't matter much that your job sucked or your relatives drove you crazy.

When the two of you chose each other, you both assumed that you'd naturally continue to enjoy this bubble. Whenever you needed a break, the two of you could slip into it and catch your breath.

But that's not what happened. Instead, *the bubble disappeared.* Suddenly, all your own issues and conflicts were in your face—and so were your partner's. Worse yet, many of your partner's problems made your own problems more difficult.

You thought that once you were married, the two of you would sail together in a single boat, navigating it through life as a team. Instead, you found yourselves in two separate canoes, side by side. Each of you has to navigate, steer, watch for rocks, and avoid the shallows. Each of you also has to coordinate with the other so that you stay close without colliding. Sometimes this is easy, but often it's frustrating or exhausting.

Welcome to the perils and possibilities of a committed relationship. The friction and frustration the two of you experience— and the betrayal, confusion, and grief that often accompany it—are just what you need to experience. All are potential sources of growth and transformation.

If you and your mate are like almost everyone else, you want a partnership that will ease your pain, not increase it. But in committed relationships, not hurting isn't an option. In fact, paradoxically, the only way to ease your pain is to accept it, work with it, and use it as fuel for growth. Only by leaning into your pain can you move through it and out of it.

In dealing with the inevitable pain of intimacy, you and your partner each have a choice:

You can accept the pain and use it to activate the best parts of yourself. We can call this *clean pain* (or *clean pain and discomfort*).[5] Clean pain gets metabolized when you make a leap and transform.

The other option is *dirty pain,* in which a person responds from their most wounded parts. They become cruel, or conniving and gaslighting, or violent—or, more commonly, they physically or emotionally run away. This prolongs the dirty pain and deepens the conflict.

Most people choose dirty pain most of the time, in part because they imagine that avoidance, or cruelty, will hurt less than leaping and transforming. But it always ends up hurting more.

Most people choose dirty pain most of the time for another reason: it's more familiar.

In dealing with the pain of intimacy, you and your mate can take either of two circular paths:

The first—the path of clean pain and discomfort—is the growth cycle. This cycle can create a new level of trust, understanding, and intimacy for both partners.

The second—a path of dirty pain that leads to distrust, harm, and, sometimes, violence—is the *commonplace cruelty cycle.* This cycle deepens existing conflicts and often creates new ones.

I call these sequences cycles, but what happens in each cycle doesn't always move smoothly and predictably, like the cycles in a washing machine. Sometimes it's just the opposite: you and your partner lurch forward, then stop, then lurch sideways, then stop, then inch forward. Sometimes you can seem totally in alignment with each other, and sometimes completely out of alignment—or even flip back and forth between the two.

However you move, the essential question facing you is this: *When the heat gets turned up, which cycle will you follow?*

---

5 The terms *clean pain* and *dirty pain* were popularized by one of my mentors, Dr. David Schnarch, and by Dr. Steven Hayer. Dr. Hayer defines and uses the terms somewhat differently, however.

Let's look more closely at the growth cycle.[6] A good place to begin is at the bottom of the diagram "Growth Cycle of a Relationship" (Figure 1) that follows.

As you and your partner go through life together, you find yourselves up against more and more of your limitations. This naturally creates ambiguity and adversity, turning up the heat under both of you.

If you're like most couples, you try to deal with the heat through accommodation, compromise, clear communication, and other such tactics. On little things, these often work, at least temporarily. But with the big things—things that matter to you, things that are tied to your integrity—all your efforts at accommodation and compromise fail. So do any short-term dirty-pain strategies, such as silently acquiescing, overriding your inner calls for integrity while privately burning with resentment, or bribing your partner with sex, attention, or other things they like. And so do withholding sweetness and regard, stonewalling, criticism, sending vibes of contempt, and acts of defensiveness. Instead, they make the conflict bigger and hotter. You and your partner keep coming up against the same issues, again and again.

The two of you grind against each other—for hours, days, months, or even years—because the conflict can't be resolved by some tactical decision or agreement. Your anxiety about the conflict increases. So does your partner's. One of you could simply acquiesce to the other, but that would mean violating your integrity—and you're not going to do that. Your partner is in exactly the same situation.

Eventually the two of you reach an emotional stalemate or bottleneck. Just by being who you are, each of you blocks the other's position. There seems to be no solution.

The conflict keeps growing until it reaches critical mass. One of you—possibly both of you—can't live with the way things are anymore. Something has to change.

This is a moment of both peril and possibility. It's a moment of peril because one or both of you may choose the commonplace cruelty cycle. It's also a moment of possibility, because both of you may choose growth. This means standing in your integrity and leaping

---

6 The concepts of the growth cycle and the commonplace cruelty cycle, as well as these diagrams, grew out of work I did with Dr. David Schnarch, as well as out of some of Dr. Schnarch's solo work. The diagrams, which reflect my own best thinking on the subject, are adapted from Dr. Schnarch's Crucible 4 Points of Balance™ Abuse and Growth Model, copyright 2007 by the Marriage and Family Health Center.

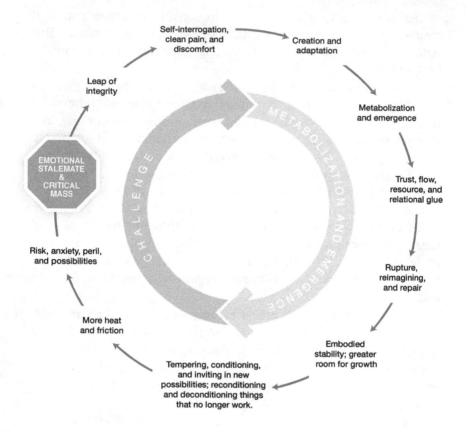

Figure 1.
Growth Cycle of a Relationship

As heat and friction between the two partners grow, the relationship is more seriously challenged. At the "emotional stalemate" stage, the partners reach a moment of truth. In a healthy growth cycle, they find a way to address the challenge by moving through clean pain and discomfort, ultimately transforming one or both partners and deepening the relationship. Still, this new status quo will face new challenges sooner or later, leading to more growth if they continue to choose clean pain and discomfort.

into the unknown. It also means having no idea whether your partner will leap with you or run away. And it means saying—to your mate, yourself, or both—"I'm not doing this anymore." More important, it means saying this from a calm, centered, anchored place inside you, no matter how hard your boat may be rocking.

In order to do this, you need to be clear with yourself about what's important to you and what you stand for. It means developing some discernment. It means paying attention to your body and to what arises in and through it. It means going through your growing edges, not around them. It means confronting yourself in a variety of ways (which I'll discuss in later chapters). It means holding onto yourself and regulating your emotions and behavior, so that you are firm and clear, but not threatening or violent or hysterical. It means being willing to accept and tolerate clean pain and discomfort.

And then something happens. Something shifts. This won't (or won't just) be a sudden cognitive realization. You'll experience an emergent shift that you will sense is right, and what you do next will seem at once solid and flexible.

The possibilities for this shift are infinite, but here are some typical examples:

- Your partner tells you about a difficulty they've been having that they've kept from you—and, partly, from themselves— for years. But they can't ignore it, or keep quiet about it, any longer.
- You tell your partner how worried you are that your daughter will never be able to make her way in the world.
- You say to your partner, "It scares the hell out of me whenever my Black son leaves the house alone. I'm afraid I'll never see him alive again. I'm tired of hiding that fear from you. Even though you're not his dad, I'd still like some support from you about this."
- You tell your mate that the next time his brother tries to pick a fight with you at a family gathering, you're leaving the event. He can either leave with you or stay behind; it's his choice.
- Your lover says, "I just can't stop spending money. I'd stop if I could, but I can't. I need to find a treatment and recovery program, and we need to figure out how to pay for it."
- Your partner tells you, "I don't care if you wash dishes at McDonald's or clean toilets in a sleazy bar. I don't care what you do to make money, so long as it's honest and legal. But

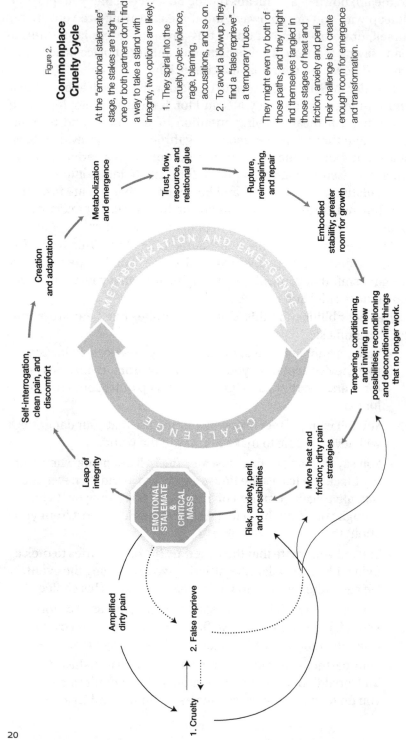

Figure 2.

Commonplace Cruelty Cycle

At the "emotional stalemate" stage, the stakes are high. If one or both partners don't find a way to take a stand with integrity, two options are likely:

1. They spiral into the cruelty cycle: violence, rage, blaming, accusations, and so on.

2. To avoid a blowup, they find a "false reprieve" — a temporary truce.

They might even try both of those paths, and they might find themselves tangled in those stages of heat and friction, anxiety and peril. Their challenge is to create enough room for emergence and transformation.

I am not staying married to someone who sells drugs for a living."

- You say to your partner, "I've always had some shame about the color of my skin. I've tried to grow out of it, but I just can't. I still think of myself as an impostor because I don't have white skin. Sometimes it seems like I'm an impostor in our relationship, too."

- You kiss your spouse on the forehead and say, "I'm going upstairs to let our son know that he doesn't have to attend your alma mater. If you truly think your family tradition is more important than the education he wants, then you come up with me and tell him to his face that I'm full of shit."

What happens next? You don't know. Your lover doesn't know. Nobody knows. That's what makes the moment so full of peril—and so full of possibilities.

But in that moment one of you has raised their game.

Now it's up to the other partner to make a choice of their own, to act out of their own integrity, and to accept their own clean pain and discomfort.

If they choose integrity, the entire relationship can shift. In most cases, the partners reach a new level of adaptation, integration, trust, commitment, and respect. The pain they experienced just moments ago may lessen. In their body, each person experiences greater balance, hope, and relief. The rocking of their boats begins to subside—or, at least, becomes more manageable.

There's no telling how things will play out when both lovers choose integrity. But here are the kinds of things I've heard my clients say to each other:

- "I'll tell you what—I have my doubts, but I'm willing to try. Let's follow your plan and see what happens. If things don't improve, we can work together to come up with a Plan B."

- "I had no idea you cared so much about my son. I thought you were just tolerating him. Are you telling me you're willing to be a stepdad and not just my boyfriend?"

- "You know what a shitstorm my parents will create over this, right? They'll treat us like we're the bastard children of Satan. But I'm in."

- "I'm scared to death. This will be the hardest thing I've ever done. But, okay, I'll do it."

- "I will *not* go through the hell of hormone injections and in vitro fertilization anymore. I'm never having another child. But *raising* another child—yeah, I can see adopting a baby."
- "You're right, we need the money. But I am *not* leaving the job I love in order to work for your mean-ass uncle, just because he'll pay me more. I'll find some other way to make more money. I'll ask for a raise and I'll take a job on Saturdays."

In all these cases, couples found their way to greater balance, awareness, and harmony. Meanwhile, the core issue—the situation that ground both lovers against each other for weeks or months or years—began to get worked through.

But another, very different outcome is also possible when partners reach critical mass and both stand in their integrity. They may see clearly that no resolution is possible. They realize that each partner's integrity blocks—and will always block—the other's.

This *also* leads to greater awareness: an awareness that the relationship may be over, because the only way it can continue is if at least one partner sacrifices their integrity. This hurts like crazy, but it is also a form of clean pain. For each partner, it is also a form of growth.

Any of these outcomes is possible when both lovers stand in their own integrity.

Sadly, much of the time, both people don't opt for integrity—or they don't both opt for it simultaneously. Under the heat and pressure of critical mass, at least one of them loses their mind and spirals into the commonplace cruelty cycle.

This can take all kinds of forms: rage, blaming, accusations, hypervigilance, panic, hyperanxiety, hard-and-fast demands, desperate attempts to control the other partner, or even violence. Sometimes it shows up as self-harm: drinking, drugging, other addictive behavior, or self-inflicted violence. All of these make the situation more difficult, more complicated, and more painful.

The commonplace cruelty cycle can lead to less trust, respect, intimacy, and mutuality. Instead of showing the best of themselves, one or both partners show the worst.

In a common variation of the commonplace cruelty cycle, both partners sense that any gaming is over, or soon will be. At least one of them needs to confront themselves and stand in their own integrity.

Critical mass is staring them in the face. This terrifies both partners, and (usually in unspoken agreement) they both back off from the conflict, finding a false reprieve. Desperately and reflexively, they grasp for comfort and safety by trying to ignore the conflict or put it aside.

But in doing so, they also set aside their own integrity. *This process inevitably creates conditions that further heat up the conflict.* Their attempts to create a false reprieve only create more dirty pain.

Meanwhile, both mates' anxiety about the conflict continues, and trust, respect, and intimacy continue to wither.

Figure 2 shows how the commonplace cruelty cycle can highjack the growth cycle. At the point of emotional stalemate, the partners have a choice: they can move into the commonplace cruelty cycle— or a false reprieve—or they can move into the growth cycle.

When faced with pain, our initial inclination is to try to make it stop, or to run from it. But there is great wisdom—and the possibility of transformation—in staying with that pain without overreacting to it, while being loving and respectful to both yourself and your partner. Much of the rest of this book explores how to do this.

When you and your mate hit an emotional stalemate, both of you will want to find ways to turn down the heat by compromising, or changing the subject, or letting the other person choose. With items that aren't important to either of you, this is fine—and even wise. But in situations that are tied to your integrity, you need to do just the opposite: keep the heat up and the pressure on. As you'll discover in later chapters, this may actually reduce both people's pain in the long run, because you may hit critical mass more quickly. As you'll also discover, even if you do succeed in turning down the heat of a conflict, the circumstances of your life will eventually turn it up again.

Heat can be uncomfortable. But every conflict needs heat in order to cook. When something is important to you or your partner, you need to learn to modulate the heat, not reflexively turn it down.

Every situation—like every recipe—is unique. There will be times when the best thing to do is let a conflict simmer slowly for a while. At other times, what's most needed is to bring that conflict to a boil. At still other times, the heat needs to be removed temporarily, so things can cool down.

Over time, you and your lover can learn how and when to best modulate the heat of conflict. You can also improve your ability to tolerate the heat and move through it together. This book will help you build both of these skills.

What *won't* help is reflexively turning down the heat when one or both of you gets uncomfortable. This deprives you of the opportunity to actually work through the conflict together and come out on the other side with greater trust, intimacy, and commitment.

In every committed partnership, the question ultimately becomes: *Which are you going to choose: clean pain and discomfort, or dirty pain?*

There's yet another angle to this. Every human body—and every important human relationship—gets impacted by a wide range of *geopathic stresses*. These are the many social, cultural, political, institutional, and environmental stresses that we all must handle, separately and together. Some of the most common geopathic stresses include noise, air pollution, bad weather, racism, sexism, ageism, clueless drivers, and obnoxious neighbors. These typically have both a weathering and a withering effect on our bodies, our communities, and, sometimes, our relationships. A full list of these stresses would easily fill this page.

Geopathic stresses can also be historical and collective—e.g., xenophobia, white-body supremacy, patriarchy, homophobia, anti-Semitism, and so on.[7]

Even when everything is going fine with your mate, these unrelated stresses may turn up the heat on you and force you up against yourself. And if a conflict is already simmering between the two of you, these stresses may suddenly turn up the heat to a boil. You may then want to lash out at your partner, or your children, or anyone else nearby.

In such situations, your choice is the same as always: clean pain and discomfort, or dirty pain. You can hold onto yourself, use the five anchors, which I'll discuss in chapters 5 and 35, and metabolize the clean pain of temporary suffering—or you can try, always unsuccessfully, to blow dirty pain through your partner (or someone else).

I live in Minneapolis. I'm writing this paragraph in February of 2022. The projected low temperature tonight is -9 degrees. A Minneapolis winter is full of geopathic stresses that can put pressure on any relationship.

---

7 I've listed some of the most common historical and collective stresses by name. They can also be listed by activity—e.g., land theft, religious or cultural persecution, genocide, conquest and colonization, etc.

In 2022 (which will be part of history by the time you read this), the United States is also suffering through what I call *collective drag*—a mental and emotional malaise. This is a widespread somatic response to the uninterrogated ferality, lawlessness, and budding autocracy currently sweeping through my country. Although these have all been parts of America's history, they are now rapidly rising together. As a result, for many of us, just getting through the day can sometimes seem like slogging through an atmosphere of oatmeal.

Also, I have a Black body. Every time I learn of another murder of an unarmed human being, this heightens my geopathic stresses. When that corpse is Black, the additional geopathic stress doubles or triples. I am hardly alone in this.

When my son Tezara was very young, on a cold day like this one, my wife Maria and I got up extra early and spent lots of time carefully making sure that he was dressed warmly enough. He fussed and protested as we wrapped him up, layer by layer, then led him out into the frigid morning and buckled him into his car seat. I put the key in the ignition and turned it.

The car wouldn't start. It was too cold for the battery to crank.

Maria and I had done everything right. Neither of us was angry or upset with the other. Yet the geopathic stress of the morning had made both of us angry and frustrated. We both wanted to scream—and, because we were sitting next to each other, we were each other's ideal targets.

But neither one of us chose dirty pain. I slumped in the car seat and said loudly, "*Fuck.*" Maria cursed under her breath. In that moment, we were both miserable. But because we each were able to hold onto ourselves, we did not make matters worse. We brought Tezara back inside, unwrapped him layer by layer, and began formulating a Plan B for our day.

COMPASS POINTS

- The natural friction in every partnership regularly creates discomfort and pain. In dealing with this pain, you and your lover each has a choice:
  - You can accept the pain and use it to grow up by activating the best parts of your resourced self. This pain—clean pain—goes away once you make a leap and transform. This is the *growth cycle*.

- * You can become violent, abusive, or accusatory. This creates dirty pain, which prolongs and deepens the conflict. This is the *commonplace cruelty cycle*.
- * In a variation of the commonplace cruelty cycle, you can physically or emotionally run from the conflict. This *also* creates dirty pain—as well as a deeper, longer conflict.

- When faced with pain, our initial inclination is to try to make it stop, or to run from it. But there is great wisdom—and the possibility of transformation—in staying in that pain without reacting to it, while being loving and respectful to both yourself and your partner.
- When a couple hits an emotional stalemate, both partners usually try to find ways to turn down the heat. They need to do just the opposite: keep the heat up and the pressure on.
- If one or both lovers do succeed in turning down the heat, the circumstances of their lives will turn it up again.
- Heat can be uncomfortable. But conflicts need heat in order to cook.
- The solution is never to reduce the heat. The solution is for both partners to improve their ability to modulate the heat, tolerate it, and move through it.
- Every human body, and every important human relationship, gets impacted by a wide range of *geopathic stresses*—the many social, cultural, and environmental stresses that we all must weather, separately and together. Even when everything is going fine with your mate, these unrelated stresses may turn up the heat on you and force you up against yourself. And if a conflict is already simmering between the two of you, these stresses may suddenly turn up the heat to a boil.

4

Double Binds in Committed Relationships

Committed relationships are naturally rife with double binds: choices in which all options seem to be risky, painful, and uncertain.

Each double bind forces both lovers to examine and reexamine what they consider important. It also tests their integrity in a real situation, in real time, with someone they care about.

Each double bind appears to present itself this way: *If I choose A, I'll be unhappy; if I choose B, I'll also be unhappy; and if I don't make a choice, I'll also be unhappy.* All choices appear to lead to pain. And often they will. But usually at least one choice involves clean pain and discomfort, which will help the person build resilience and discernment—and which may lead to greater freedom and intimacy on the other side of that pain.

LUANNE AND JACKIE

Luanne and Jackie have been together for six years and married for four. They regularly have discussions, debates, and sometimes arguments about money.

Both Jackie and Luanne want to work fewer hours, and both suddenly have the opportunity to cut back to thirty hours a week. But Luanne, who handles the couple's finances and who religiously saves a portion of every paycheck, worries that there won't be enough money to meet their expenses. Jackie tells her, "You're right; there won't be. We'll need to use some of our savings to make up the difference."

Luanne is horrified. "Our savings is for emergencies. It's our safety net. We can't just spend it on anything we choose."

"Why not?" Jackie asks. "It's our money. We're using it to buy more time to enjoy life and each other."

"We'd have the time, but I wouldn't enjoy it," Luanne insists. "I'll be worried sick about our shrinking savings."

"Then don't worry."

"I'm just being responsible."

"What if we compromise?" asks Jackie. "I'll drop down to thirty hours and you can keep working forty. We can still live on what we'll earn."

Luanne says, "If the point is to have more time together, it isn't going to work if only one of us cuts back. Anyway, why should you be the one who gets to take it easy? I'll be jealous and resentful in no time."

"Well, then, what do you suggest?"

"I don't know. Wait for a better opportunity, I suppose."

"A better opportunity?" Jackie asks. "Do you realize how lucky we are to both have the chance to work three-quarter time? We may never get a chance like this again."

"How is spending more money than we make an opportunity? It's a recipe for financial disaster."

"You worry too much," Jackie says. "Just like your mama."

Luanne replies, "And you expect other people to take care of you. Just like your daddy."

Jackie and Luanne are in a classic double bind. Luanne is standing up for the couple's financial security. Jackie is standing up for their mutual desire to spend time together. Both lovers want both things. Yet neither one can compromise without also compromising their integrity, so they keep turning up the heat on each other.

Double binds don't just go away on their own. The energy that fuels them either gets metabolized or continues to burn up both partners. Double binds force us to consider previously unexamined things in ourselves, and in each other. Double binds typically make us very uncomfortable. Nobody likes them. But when a double bind shows up, nothing is going wrong.

Jackie and Luanne have already reached an emotional stalemate, and critical mass may not be far off. If they keep snapping at each other, they'll enter the commonplace cruelty cycle, and all hell may break loose.

But if they can pull back from the insults and accusations, *while braving the heat and staying with the argument,* then heaven may shine through. For example:

Jackie says, "Let's leave my daddy out of this. We both know he can be a dick sometimes. What's more important to you? The extra time or the extra money?"

"The time would be extra. The money isn't. Not the way we're spending it."

"The way we're spending it? What would be another way to spend it?"

"We could spend less," Luanne says. "Way less. Do you know how much the Italy trip is going to cost us? Almost ten thousand dollars. And the bathroom remodel will cost us twice that."

"Wait. Are we arguing about the money we *make*, or the money we *spend*?"

"Both," Luanne says. "If you're going to balance a budget, you can't separate the two."

"Hold on," says Jackie. "Are you saying that if we ditch the Italy trip and stick with the funky bathroom, then you'd be okay with both of us working three-quarter time?"

Luanne is silent a long time before she says, softly, "Maybe."

Luanne's "maybe" is deeply important, because it suggests that there may be other things in her relationship with Jackie that they have not yet worked through, but need to. A major life rep may be about to appear.

Whatever this emerging piece is, it might be unique to this particular couple. But it might also be historical, or intergenerational, or institutional. These forces often create double binds for individuals and couples. Although such influences are broad and widespread, their effects are always experienced personally.

Our first impulse is to try to avoid double binds, or to fear them or dread them. But we need to do just the opposite and lean into them, because they are vitally important.

Any attempt to avoid a double bind—by acquiescing to your partner, or trying to bully or control them, or simply talking trash—always makes the bind tighter. This naturally increases your need to address it. (Think what would have happened if, after Luanne dissed Jackie's father, Jackie had replied, "At least my daddy knows what the hell caring is" or "Thank God my father isn't married to Ebenezer Fucking Scrooge.")

If you try to flee the bind by leaving the relationship, this *also* tightens the bind. It will reappear as part of the breakup—or in your next relationship, but with greater force and urgency.

The only way to loosen a double bind is to stand in your integrity and accept the potential for painful consequences—while continuing to love and respect your partner as much as you can.

Ultimately, double binds in committed relationships are not about happiness or unhappiness, pain or the avoidance of pain. They are about learning to stand in your integrity in all your interactions with your mate.

COMPASS POINTS

- Committed relationships are naturally rife with double binds: choices in which all options seem to be risky, painful, and uncertain.

- Each double bind forces both lovers to examine and reexamine what they consider important. It also tests their integrity in a real situation, in real time, with someone they care about.

- In a double bind, all options—including refusing to choose—appear to lead to pain. But at least one choice leads to clean pain and discomfort—and to freedom and greater intimacy on the other side of that pain.

- Our first impulse is to try to avoid double binds, or fear them, or dread them. But we need to do just the opposite and lean into them, because they are vitally important.

- Any attempt to avoid the bind—by acquiescing to your partner, or bullying them, or having an affair, or ending the relationship—always makes it tighter.

- The only way to loosen a double bind is to stand in your integrity and accept the potential for painful consequences.

5

Why Everyone Hates
Their Lover

Hatred exists in all loving long-term relationships. It's a part of how they work.

Everyone in a committed partnership has briefly hated their partner. *Everyone.*

Part of growing up is acknowledging this hatred. Most of us are afraid to admit this hate, because it isn't socially acceptable. So we hide it or pretend we don't experience it.

Therapists rarely bring up the subject of hate with their clients. But when I ask my clients, "Have you sometimes experienced hate for your partner?" nearly all of them say yes.

Denying this hate creates all kinds of problems. For starters, when it does pop up inside you, you don't know how to deal with it. Hiding from it or overriding it doesn't allow you to develop discernment or an awareness of nuance. So, instead, you may reflexively respond in a way that creates dirty pain. You might tell your partner, "There's something wrong with you," or you might say to yourself, *Oh shit, there's something wrong with me.* But there's nothing wrong at all.

If you don't acknowledge this occasional hate, it's going to come out in some other, nastier, unexamined form. You won't recognize the hate as completely normal—and you won't be willing to pause and stay with the constriction in your body, so discernment can develop, resources can deepen, and you can accept the clean pain and move through it. Instead, you're going to be cruel to your partner—and perhaps angry at yourself.

Actually, one part of you *always* hates your partner. In fact, the closer your relationship becomes, and the more vulnerable you become, the more it hates them.

When you and your lover were dating, before you made a long-term commitment to each other, you probably had an unspoken agreement that either of you could end the relationship. It would hurt, but each of you would be all right. Both of you had the option to leave.

But once you both said, "I choose you," or "Let's be exclusive," or "Let's move in together," your options shrank. Suddenly your actions and choices became bound up with your partner's actions and choices. The things you wanted started rubbing up against the things your partner wanted.

Your threshold of being able to tolerate differences immediately shrank. You couldn't blow off those differences anymore. "My lover wants children" became "We're going to have to negotiate compromises about children for the rest of our lives." Eventually this became a major bone of contention—not because someone is being unreasonable, but because the issue is important to both of you. That's why it kept coming up.

This happened with almost everything that affected both of you. Whatever bothered or worried you before about your partner was now in your face on a regular basis—and whatever bothered them about you ended up front and center for them.

In this process, the two of you became deeply vulnerable to each other.

From the time you moved into "I choose you," you had to consider your partner with everything you did and every decision you made. All the things you used to do to take pressure off yourself became things you had to negotiate. You couldn't quit your job, or move across town, or buy a new bicycle, or run up a big credit card bill just because you wanted to. This made you even more vulnerable.

When this happens, it drives people crazy. Suddenly the heat has been turned way up under them—and they can't easily lower the temperature. It's not just about them anymore. In every aspect of their life, it's now about *us*—them and their lover.

In my office, people tell me, "I don't know what happened. As soon as we got married, my partner changed." That's right. As soon as the two of you made a commitment to each other—either through a ceremony, a legal document, or an emotional choice—they changed, you changed, and everything changed. As soon as you said, "I do" or

"I'm yours," your options shrank and the pressure on you rose. Neither of you did anything wrong. All you did was choose each other. (Or one person chose the other, and that person went along with the choice. But the results are the same.)

Here's what's happening:

In your cortex, your thinking brain, you love your partner. But beneath your cortex, toward the back of your skull, is a part of the brain that we human monsters share with Godzilla. This back part of our brain—our lizard brain—only understands protection: fighting, fawning, fleeing, freezing, or annihilating.

Your back brain (and remember, your brain is very much a part of your body) loves whatever protects you and hates whatever makes you vulnerable. This part of your brain hates your lover because you're vulnerable to them. That same part of your partner's brain hates you for the same reason. To your lizard brains, your love for each other is an ongoing source of stress.

In immature relationships, hatred and resentment usually grow over the years. The closer you and your partner get, the more vulnerable you become to each other, and the more scared your lizard brain gets. Ditto for your partner's. Its logic goes like this: *I hate you for loving me and making me vulnerable. If you* really *loved me, you wouldn't make me vulnerable by loving me.* The fact that your partner makes you happy makes your Godzilla brain unhappy.

The paradox of intimacy is that the more important someone becomes to you, the less willing you may be to show all of yourself to them, because it terrifies your lizard brain. This is why people will sometimes tell their deepest secrets to a stranger in an airport or a bar but will hide them from their beloved partners.

This paradox is more than some people can bear. As a result, when the heat gets turned up under them and their partner, they may temporarily collapse into what's called *hypoarousal.* This is a state of numbness or withdrawal, or a sense of being disconnected from their own bodies. (As you'll see in later chapters, however, you can temper and condition your own body to hold the charge of this paradox, so that you don't collapse into hypoarousal.)

It's an act of deep integrity to show all of yourself—including all your warts, fears, dreams, and desires—to your partner. If you're able to do this, while standing on your own two feet and maintaining your own shape, something interesting happens. Whether your partner admits it or not, or is consciously aware of it or not, they develop trust and a deep respect for you. When they see you being honest and strong about your own stuff, they begin to think, *Maybe my mate can be honest and strong about other things, too—including me.* Deep down, this is what each of us most wants from our partner.

Let's turn this around. If your partner watches you refuse to take yourself on; or if they watch you recoil from things that you should take on and lean into things that you should not; or if you shrink from integrity instead of straightening your spine and embracing it—their trust in you contracts. *So does your trust in yourself.* That's a form of dirty pain.

Most of us feed our partners bullshit occasionally. It can be bullshit about why we didn't do what we promised, or why we've avoided some difficult task or decision, or any other variation on failing to stand in our own integrity.

None of us wants our partner to bullshit us. But when we bullshit our partner, in our heart *we don't want them to buy our bullshit*, either. We want them to have the presence and integrity to lovingly confront us—to say, "Hold on a second; that's not right."

That's what goes on in our heart. But our lizard brain operates on completely different principles. What makes our heart swell is precisely what makes our back brain tremble in terror.

Your lizard brain isn't wrong or bad. It's not some lowly part of you that you need to despise or dispense with. It keeps you alert, protected, and alive. Its messages also force you to learn to grow beyond mere survival and protection.

We all receive these messages from our back brains. As we grow up, though, we learn to not react to them. We accept the ambiguity that the more we care for our lover, and the longer we stay with them, the more frightened our lizard brain gets, and the more vulnerability we experience.

People with low self-awareness and low discernment don't realize where these messages come from. They don't understand the need to metabolize them, to turn them into caring for their partner and growth for themselves. They can't tolerate the ambiguity of *I love my partner; and, damn it, I hate my partner, too; so I need to keep loving my partner.* Instead, they just react to their own back-brain messages of fear and danger. This back-braining behavior is often what precedes a decision to seek therapy.

As adolescents and young adults, almost all of us live largely through our Godzilla brains, reacting reflexively to one perceived emotional threat after another. When kids in puberty mumble to their parents, "I hate you!," as they often do, they're back braining. Most parents understand intuitively that their adolescent child can sometimes both love and hate them. But we have a much harder time understanding this about our partners.

As we get older, however, we learn to tolerate this ambiguity and metabolize our raw hatred toward our partners. This isn't pathological. We all go through this, especially in our early romantic and sexual relationships.

This part of your brain is hardwired into you. It never stops telling you, *I'm vulnerable! I'm scared! Destroy Tokyo!* It takes time and effort to learn to metabolize the stress-response messages of your Godzilla brain and use your own situation as fuel for transformation.

I said earlier that people with low self-awareness and low discernment can get stuck in these messages. I don't mean just adolescents and young adults, or people living in violent or war-torn neighborhoods. I also mean you and me, when we're under extreme stress. If we're not careful, when the difficulties pile on, any of us can suddenly start back braining. I mean *anyone*—including Oprah and Stedman, or Dr. Phil and his wife Robin. None of us ever gets to a place where we can say to ourselves, "I'm never going to have to deal with this again." None of us is immune to the internal forces that can lead to emotional explosions—or even violence.

Anyone's skill set can get superseded, or at least challenged, by painful circumstances. If you're unbalanced and distracted at those moments when you most need to be centered and present, Godzilla could momentarily take over. Your partner says something curt or angry, and suddenly you're in fight, flight, or freeze mode[8]. You find yourself shouting at your partner and not knowing why.

Sometimes our body's sensations contribute to this process. This is common among service members and civilian contractors who return from an overseas conflict. It's also common among police and security guards who work in tough neighborhoods—and, of course, among the people who live in those neighborhoods. Because they spend a lot of their time in what they (rightfully) perceive as danger

---

8 Our reptilian brains can hijack us into any of five different emergency modes. *Fight, flee,* and *freeze* are the most common, but there are two others, one at either extreme: *annihilate,* a severe fight response that pushes us to destroy the source of our discomfort, or obtain a complete, scorched-earth victory over it; and *fawn,* in which we offer our total surrender and subservience (and, often, our abject flattery). If you or your partner flip into annihilate or fawn mode, your relationship is in serious trouble. One of you may also be in physical danger. Talk to a therapist or other counselor soon. If you do sense that you are in physical danger—or that you may physically harm your partner or yourself—put some physical distance (i.e., miles, not yards or city blocks) between the two of you. If necessary, call the police.

zones, their bodies become hyperaroused and hypervigilant. Their Godzilla brains are activated all the time.

In places where bombs explode and snipers may shoot at you, this is a good thing. The fight, flight, or freeze response often saves people's lives. But when these folks go back home to a supposedly safe place, it takes a long time for their hyperarousal to recede. When they walk in the door and their partner says, "You forgot to buy toilet paper," their lizard brain lights up like a neon sign. Even a strange look from their partner, or a negative vibe, or a sentence uttered in impatience or anger, can activate a stress response in the back of their brain and make them reflexively want to fight, flee, freeze, or annihilate. If hyperarousal becomes chronic, trauma responses can get stuck in their body—because, to their body, so much of everyday life has become tied to its survival. Over time, these trauma responses can begin to look like part of the person's personality.

Less severe disruptions to our normal bodily rhythms can also activate our dinosaur brains. When you've been grinding up against your partner for a long time, and your boat is rocking big-time, your body's energy may stay fixed and rigid. Eventually your body associates that rigidity with your partner, and you begin to see your relationship with them from that rigid place. Your lizard brain then senses potential danger in that rigidity and goes on high alert.

When your energy gets too rigid for too long, your job is to notice it and to use the five anchors described below. These can help you hold on to yourself and stay upright and balanced when your Godzilla brain has been activated. They also help you metabolize and transform hateful emotions toward your partner.

We primarily experience sensations in our bodies, not our minds. That's why, in order to process and work through any strong emotion, we need to first recognize it in our body. This recognition is not a place to stay; it is only a part of a larger process. It's like digesting food, or turning coal into diamonds, or the ancient practice of alchemy.

This internal process involves these five anchors[9]:

1. **Soothe and resource yourself** to quiet your mind, calm your heart, and settle your body.

2. **Pause, then notice and discern the sensations, vibrations, and emotions in your body** instead of reacting to them.

---

9 These anchors have many progenitors, most notably the Crucible 4 Points of Balance™ (crucible4points.com), which were devised by Dr. David Schnarch.

3. **Accept and tolerate the discomfort** instead of trying to flee from it.

4. **Stay present and in your body** as you move through the unfolding experience, with all its ambiguity and uncertainty, and respond from the best parts of yourself.

5. **Metabolize any energy** that remains.

In chapter 35, I'll explain in detail how to use these anchors. That material appears fairly late in the book because I first want you to understand how committed relationships actually function. But at whatever point you want to learn to use the five anchors—including right now—you are welcome to turn to chapter 35.

These anchoring practices can help you stay flexible, engaged, and loving. They can also help you stay aware of your environment, your bodily sensations, your emotions, and your thoughts. Most important of all, they can help you stay connected with your partner without getting hooked into anxiety, or fear, or a toxic pattern of thought or action.

You can support this process by caring for your body, mind, and spirit through good nutrition, fitness, and mindfulness, using some of the practices described in chapter 37. You can also support it by loving yourself.

COMPASS POINTS

- Hatred exists in all loving long-term relationships. Part of growing up is acknowledging this hatred.

- If you don't acknowledge the occasional hatred, it will show up in some other, nastier, unexamined form.

- There's a part of your brain that you share with lizards, dinosaurs, and Godzilla. When this part of your brain is activated, it gives you a message to fight, flee, freeze, fawn, or annihilate.

- Your lizard brain loves what protects you and hates what makes you vulnerable. This part of your brain hates your lover because you are vulnerable to them. The closer you and your mate get, the more frightened your lizard brain becomes.

- It takes time and effort to learn to metabolize the messages emanating from our Godzilla brains and to use them as fuel for transformation.
- To help you stay balanced and upright as everything rocks around you, use these anchors: (1) soothe yourself; (2) notice the sensations, vibrations, and emotions in your body; (3) accept and tolerate the discomfort; (4) stay present and in your body while coming from the best places in yourself; and (5) metabolize any remaining energy.

6

Peril and Possibility
Are the Same

In your relationship, every moment is a moment of potential peril and pain—as well as a moment of potential growth and transformation.

There are never any guarantees in any relationship. No one ever knows how their partnership will turn out. Even the strongest and closest relationship can be torn apart—by death, illness, deceit, poverty, trauma, or bad luck. And a relationship that begins on shaky ground can blossom into deep love and respect and last a lifetime.

We'd all like to believe that love, caring, and commitment will ultimately overcome everything. And sometimes they do. But other times, life tears people and couples apart. I know of loving relationships that ended because one partner was killed by a drunken driver or a stray bullet. I know of sane, loving, devoted spouses who divorced because of sociopathic in-laws. I've seen marriages destroyed by war, natural disaster, illness, bad investments, and hospital bills.

Life is always full of peril.

But peril is not always what we imagine it to be. We think that peril holds us back. When we hurt, we want to experience some safety and security in order to be able to take a risk. But life doesn't operate that way. In fact, it's just the opposite. Security and safety come *after* taking a risk, not before.

Think of the first time you asked someone out—or went on a date. Think about your first kiss. Your first job interview. The first time you had sex. There was *never* any safety first. There was always risk and the potential for peril.

Life is also always full of possibility. I've seen loving relationships created in the midst of—and even because of—war, natural disaster, illness, and other tragedies. I've seen couples respond to tragic events by deepening their connection and strengthening their trust and commitment.

Most of us have very little tolerance for anxiousness, ambiguity, and uncertainty. Instead, we naturally gravitate toward whatever is familiar to us, even if it's painful, because we're desperately afraid of what we don't know and can't predict.

But in life nearly *everything* is uncertain and unpredictable.

Despite their multimillion-dollar technology, weather forecasters still aren't very good at predicting the weather. We all know we're going to die, but unless we're already very ill, we have no idea when. Accurately predicting the winner of most sports championships is notoriously difficult.[10]

Can you accurately predict when your lover will be in a good mood? When *you* will be in a good mood? When you'll next get sick? When your car will next break down? What you'll want for dinner two weeks from today?

How many times in the last month did your day not go the way you expected it to?

Our reflexive emotional response to uncertainty is to either try to wrest control over the unpredictable events in our lives or flee from them into more familiar, seemingly less perilous territory. These impulses parallel our desire to manipulate or bully our partner into doing what we want, or to flee from conflict altogether.

Neither of these responses works. Both only make our conflicts larger and more painful.

The only way to grow up is to accept the uncertainty and ambiguity in our lives—and our own anxiousness about them—and move forward in the face of them.

This is particularly true in our relationships. Simply becoming someone's committed partner automatically creates peril: the painful possibility of losing them. (This is why casual sex is so seemingly attractive. It appears to offer the possibility of pleasure without the risk of loss. But, in fact, casual sex is awash with perils, including sexually transmitted disease, emotional and spiritual

---

10 At least for human beings. A German octopus named Paul did very well for years, correctly predicting the winners of soccer championships 85 percent of the time. Seriously. Google it.

emptiness, and the possibility of hooking up with someone who is violent or mentally ill.)

Becoming someone's committed lover always creates possibility as well: the possibility of both of you transforming into the people you most want—and want each other—to become.

When couples hit emotional stalemates, they naturally want answers. This is when they typically ask us therapists (and each other), "What should we do now?" This question is an invitation, not a punishment. If all of us pause, and examine and interrogate this question together, other possibilities may emerge.

This an important question, but the answer is almost never tactical, like *Sell your house and retire* or *Send your daughter to boarding school* or *Have a date night once a week*. If the answer were that simple, the two of you would have already found it.

Finding good answers to tactical questions is important. But growing up is not about finding answers to tactical questions. It's about going through a process together—about moving willingly into peril, pain, possibility, and the unknown.

Couples open up a world of possibilities when they say to each other, "Honey, I don't know what to do. What I do know is that something has to change. I don't even know what that change is. But I'm not going to keep doing the same thing in the same way anymore. And I accept all the pain I'm experiencing right now."

This not knowing isn't a sign of weakness or stuckness. It's a necessary part of growing up.

When couples stand respectfully and lovingly together, in the middle of pain and uncertainty, eventually something can shift. A way forward can appear, and their relationship can deepen and transform.

Every loving partnership is built on compassion and accountability. Each of us needs to offer our mate empathy, respect, and compassion—without giving them a free pass to attack us, or treat us like shit, or run away. We need to hold them in our heart and stay present with them, while also holding them accountable for their speech, actions, and choices.

When both lovers do this, perils often transform into possibilities.

COMPASS POINTS

- In your relationship, every moment is a moment of potential peril and pain—as well as a moment of potential growth and transformation.

- Most of us have little tolerance for anxiousness, ambiguity, and uncertainty. We naturally gravitate toward whatever is familiar to us, even if it's painful. But in life nearly everything is uncertain.

- The only way to grow up is to accept the uncertainty and ambiguity in our lives—as well as our own anxiousness about them—and move forward in the face of them.

- Becoming someone's lover always creates peril: the possibility of losing them. It also creates the possibility of both of you transforming into the people you most want—and want each other—to become.

- Growing up is not about finding answers. It's about going through a process with your lover in which you move into and through peril, pain, and the unknown.

- When we hold our partner in our heart and stay present with them, while also holding them accountable for their speech, actions, and choices, peril often transforms into possibility.

7

You Can't Choose
Not to Choose

When we need to make important choices, there's always the potential for loss. This scares us, and can make us want to fight, flee, or freeze.

One common form of freezing is refusing to choose. In couples, this often happens when there's a recurring conflict or emotional bottleneck. At these times, all choices lead to difficulty and serious pain, and both lovers know it. But some choices create dirty pain, which can be paralyzing, while at least one can travel into and through clean pain and discomfort. Each lover can choose clean pain or dirty pain, but they can't avoid choosing.

Refusing to choose is itself a choice. It's choosing to dodge, to try to flee from responsibility, to refuse to grow up. This works only up until one of you decides you want something better.

By refusing to choose, people hope to avoid being vulnerable—or responsible for a painful outcome. By default, they force the choice onto their partner. This only worsens the conflict, and usually creates even more difficulty and pain. It also reduces their partner's trust and respect for them, because in committed partnerships every important choice is about growing up or not growing up.

When you're faced with such a choice in your partnership, and all your options scare you, ask yourself these questions: *What am I afraid to go through? What haven't I confronted? What needs to be examined and interrogated more fully? Will I die if I do this examining and interrogating? What do I keep overriding and/or avoiding?*

Sometimes people are afraid to choose because they simply have no idea what to do. But not knowing isn't wrong or shameful or abnormal. If you don't know what to do, stand in your integrity and say to your partner, "Honestly, I don't have any idea what to do." Then pause—and notice what emerges, both inside you and in the unfolding interaction.

And you might not need to have an idea about what to do. Instead, look to your body. It may give you an answer or direction that the cognitive parts of your brain can't.

What are you *physically* sensing in your body, and where? Does a particular choice or action make your gut hurt, or your stomach tighten, or your jaw clench? That could be your body saying *no.* Is there a choice that tingles the back of your neck, or widens your eyes, or makes energy zing up your spine? That might be your body saying *yes.*

By leaning into each sensation, you slow down the process of sensing and experiencing. This gives you the time and the opportunity to metabolize what you experience. Over time, and after enough life reps, you will become better at discerning what supports you and what thwarts you.

One common form of not choosing is not asking your partner for something you want from them. You already know that if you don't ask, you won't get it; that's why you need to ask in the first place. Yet asking makes you vulnerable, because your partner's answer may be *no.* It may even be *hell, no*—or *hell, no, you crazy freak.* Then you not only don't get what you want, but you're hurt and disappointed.

To avoid these painful emotions, many of us don't ask our partners for what we desire. This all but *guarantees* that we don't get it—and we end up hurt and disappointed. By trying to protect ourselves, we bring on exactly what we'd hoped to avoid.

In relationships, some lovers are so afraid of potential loss and disappointment that they avoid making choices of any kind. Have you ever met a couple where one person usually says, "Oh, I don't care; you choose" or "Whatever you want is fine"? But, in fact, they care very much. They care so much that they're terrified to ask for what they want.

When someone repeatedly chooses not to choose, they withhold a part of themselves from their partner. Their lover, sensing this keenly, reaches out and tries to connect with their partner. Out of fear, the other partner withdraws further. Soon both people are caught in a dance in which one partner is always pursuing, the other always fleeing.

GARY AND YUMIKO

Gary first came to see me because he was troubled by anxiety. As often happens with people with anxiety or depression, much of his suffering involved his partner.

Gary and Yumiko had been together for seven years and lived together for the past five. From the beginning, Gary worried that Yumiko might leave him at any moment.

"What gives you the impression that she'd do that?" I asked.

"She travels a lot for her job," Gary said. "It would be easy for her to have another boyfriend somewhere else. Unless she told me, I'd never know it."

"Has she given you any indication that she might have someone else on the side, or might want to?"

"No. But she's a very private, quiet, discreet woman. If she wanted to keep something from me, she'd be able to."

Gary's strategy for dealing with his anxiety was to treat Yumiko like a princess whenever she returned home. He'd make special meals for Yumiko, do whatever she wanted to do, and accommodate whatever requests she made, all in a quest to prevent her from straying.

As Gary and I talked, it became clear that he wasn't doing any of this out of love, connection, or generosity. It was manipulation, like using treats to train a dog. His actions came not from what was best in him but from what was weakest. It was a strategy of preemptive appeasement.

In any committed relationship, when one partner acts inauthentically, the other partner eventually senses it. For a while they might swallow it, but eventually they sense that something is off, even if they can't articulate it.

At first Yumiko appreciated Gary's pampering. But the thrill had worn off long ago. "Now when she comes home from a week away," Gary lamented, "she'll spend a few hours with me, then take off to see her friends."

"What does she say when you do all the things she likes?"

"She smiles and thanks me. But it seems hollow."

"Does she say why she wants to hang with friends instead of you?"

"Not really. She just tells me where she's going and who she's seeing, and then she kisses me and goes. When I ask her to stay, she squeezes my arm and says, 'Honey, I'll be back in a few hours, I promise.' And she always comes back when she says she will."

"Have you talked to Yumiko about this?"

"No."

"Why not?"

"I'm afraid to."

Gary and Yumiko had created a dance in which Yumiko was always fleeing and returning, and Gary was always pursuing.

Gary wouldn't confront himself about his own anxiety and fear. For her part, Yumiko knew that her partner wasn't being authentic—but instead of confronting Gary about his actions, she accepted the royal treatment with a smile, then slipped away to join her friends.

The more they repeated this dance, the more both lovers lost trust and respect for each other.

Gary needed to take himself on around his own fear and anxiety, which were about himself, not his partner. Then he needed to sit Yumiko down and say, "Yumi, I need to tell you what I've been doing and why. A lot of it has been bullshit, and I'm truly sorry for it. But I'm done with the bullshit. Now I need to talk to you about how—and if—we're going to be together."

Doing this would require Gray to up his game, build greater discernment, and strengthen his ability to examine and interrogate himself.

It took some months before Gary got enough conditioning and tempering through life reps to make a move. But eventually he did, and Yumiko started coming in with him to see me. Now, at last, the two of them had an opportunity to share their strengths instead of their limitations—as well as a chance to grow up.

We assume that in couples, both partners chose each other. But often that's not the case. Often at least one partner *didn't* choose the other.

Many people get married or form long-term partnerships not because they want to spend their life with that person, but to get something specific out of the relationship. That "something" might be money; sex; companionship; a stable home; emotional or financial security; career advancement; the approval of one's relatives; social, financial, or political connections; higher social status; the chance to have a baby or raise a family; or the opportunity to get out of an abusive situation.

In other cases, people get involved with their partners simply to follow a familiar, comforting script. Usually the person is unaware of the script, and almost always it's not unique to the person following it. Instead, it was written by their family or religion or culture or tribe.

Sometimes the script is as simple as *Do whatever you see the people around you doing.* I can't tell you how many people I've known who are dead, or went to jail, or got addicted to drugs or alcohol, or became parents at a very young age, for no reason other than they copied what they saw around them.

In these cases, the person never really chose their partner; they just used their partner as a means to an end, or as something to fulfill a role in their life.

This can easily create problems in the relationship. It may take months or years or even decades, but eventually at least one partner begins to sense that something is missing.

When one partner hasn't chosen the other, both partners always know it in their bodies—even though they don't always admit the truth to each other.

When *both* partners haven't chosen each other—if their marriage was arranged by their parents or if one partner married for money and status, the other for sex and companionship—the conflicts usually go much deeper. On the surface, there seems to be a tit-for-tat balance, a kind of business deal; but over time, both partners typically become more and more unhappy with their relationship.[11] Typically, the withholding of sweetness becomes an unspoken, ongoing part of their relationship.

OLYMPIA AND DEREK

Olympia and Derek married when he was twenty-two—a senior in college—and she was thirty-seven, a multimillionaire entrepreneur. They had met a year earlier at a mutual friend's wedding. Although Derek originally planned to be a teacher, he dropped out of college in his final year to marry her. Within two years they had a daughter and, two years after that, a son.

Money was never an issue. Whenever either of them wanted something—a car, a boat, travel to an exotic locale—the money for it was always there.

They hit their biggest emotional stalemate in their tenth year of marriage, when Derek wanted to start a small retail business with a friend. Because Olympia normally said yes to his requests, he assumed that she would be happy to back him. "It's

---

11 The exceptions are partnerships that are business deals *and* total shams from the beginning, such as the famous (and gay) Hollywood leading man married to the blonde (and lesbian) bombshell, or the brilliant engineer from Guatemala who marries her distant American relative to get a green card, so she can move to Silicon Valley and work for Apple.

an ideal situation," Derek told his wife. "Both kids are in school, and we have someone to watch them when I can't; we don't have to borrow money to get the store up and running; we don't have to buy a building; and the initial investment is relatively small. The start-up money is only two hundred thousand dollars, so we don't have to take much risk, and it's not like we have to mortgage the house for it. I'm really looking forward to finally doing something useful with my life."

But instead of being supportive, Olympia was baffled and ticked off. "Why the hell would you want to run a store?" she asked him. "You already have everything you could want. All you have to do is ask for it."

"I *am* asking for something. I want to start this business. All I need is the start-up money and your support."

Olympia looked at him accusingly. "The answer is no. This isn't what we agreed on when we got married."

"What the hell do you mean? Or did you think I signed my life away when I married you?"

Although Derek didn't sign his whole life away when he and Olympia got married, he did bargain away a piece of it. People routinely bargain away parts of themselves at the beginning of committed relationships—without even noticing that it's happening. But any part that gets bargained away at the beginning will always reappear later on and demand to be addressed.

When Derek first asked Olympia out, he was awestruck by her wealth, her success, and her natural comfort with money, status, and influence. In fact, he was surprised when she said yes to his invitation. He also found her sexy and charming, despite their age difference. For her part, Olympia was delighted by Derek's youth, intelligence, good looks, and sexual stamina—and his unabashed appreciation for her.

When Derek left college to marry Olympia, he assumed he would be able to work or return to school whenever he wanted. After all, money wasn't an issue. Olympia routinely bought him anything he asked for, within reason. He couldn't understand why she thought that starting a business wasn't within reason.

Meanwhile, Olympia assumed that when Derek married her, he was permanently leaving behind the worlds of school and work. He would be her companion for travel and sex and fun; the father of her children; and the point person at home. Now, suddenly, he didn't want that life—or, at least, only that life—anymore.

To each spouse, this seemed like a betrayal. They each thought their partner was violating the basic bargain they had made when they said, "I do."

The underlying issue was that they had approached marriage as a bargain in the first place. Marriage is a repeated commitment, not a bargain.

Spouses make all kinds of bargains with each other. These can be clean (you walk the kids to school while I do the dishes) or they can be dirty (don't hassle me about my drinking, and I won't bother you about your gambling). But beneath those bargains is a simple, all-in commitment: *I choose you. Not your money. Not your family. Not your status. Not your lifestyle. You. Which makes me more vulnerable.*

But Olympia and Derek hadn't chosen each other.

Eventually they decided to go to therapy. But in therapy sessions, when each spouse had the opportunity to take themselves on, they backed away. Instead, they took on each other. They blew their anxiety, disappointment, and fear through one another. They hurled blame back and forth. They fought over money and responsibility and past agreements.

But each partner never looked closely at themselves. Neither one made the choice to grow up. As a result, neither mate was able to genuinely choose the other.

Eventually they divorced.

COMPASS POINTS

- When couples face conflict or emotional stalemates, all their choices may be painful. Each lover can choose clean pain and discomfort or dirty pain, but they can't avoid choosing.
- Still, when faced with options that are all painful, some people refuse to choose. But this is itself a choice: they choose to force the act of choosing onto their lover.
- People try to not choose because they don't want to be vulnerable, but not choosing makes them even more vulnerable—and creates more conflict and pain.
- In committed partnerships, every important choice is a choice between growing up and not growing up.

- When you don't know what to choose or what to do, stand in your integrity and say to your mate, "I don't know."
- When your head doesn't know what to do, look to your body.
- When someone repeatedly chooses not to choose, they withhold part of themselves from their lover. This can create a dance in which one partner is always pursuing, the other always fleeing.
- Often at least one partner didn't choose the other. They use their mate as a means to an end—money, sex, status, refuge, etc.—or to fulfill a role. This eventually creates serious conflict, because at least one partner begins to sense that something is missing.
- When one partner hasn't chosen the other, both partners always know it.
- Eventually both partners have to choose each other. If they don't, the relationship may shrivel up and die—or one partner may leave.

8

The Dynamics of
Critical Mass

Critical mass is the place where at least one member of a couple can no longer continue with the status quo. For them, something *has* to change.

Couples often reach critical mass around things that are finite or scarce, such as money, time, or physical or emotional energy. More importantly, critical mass nearly always involves a challenge to at least one partner's values and integrity.

Critical mass isn't a position or a decision or a demand. It isn't strategic. Often it's not even cognitive. It's an unequivocal, undeniable sensation in your body. You *know* that the game is up.

The process of critical mass mirrors the process by which coal is transformed into a diamond. Sustained heat and pressure eventually create the conditions for a potential transformation.

When couples reach critical mass, both lovers face the possibility of losing something or someone important. They have also reached a point where at least one of them can't compromise their integrity.

Each partner now has to choose: they can grow up, and potentially transform (or end) the relationship, or they can stay stuck and worsen the problem.

This choice usually involves an ultimatum—not to your partner, but to yourself. That ultimatum is usually experienced in your body, as well as in words, concepts, and actions. The central message of this ultimatum is: *Things are different now. I'm different. I don't know how things will end up, but I'm doing something different, starting right now.*

In order to avoid the commonplace cruelty cycle, that "something different" has to come from your integrity, from the best part of you—not from an old wound. Lovingly and respectfully, you need to stand before your partner and say, in essence, "I'm not doing things this way anymore. I'm no longer willing to give myself up for you—or for some goal or purpose that isn't serving us. I need to do this. Now you do what *you* need to do."

This sounds like you're confronting your partner, but actually you're confronting yourself. You're challenging yourself to continue to stand in your integrity, no matter what happens next. You need to be able to hold on to yourself, soothe yourself, and not fly off the handle if your partner pushes back, or withdraws, or treats you with indifference or contempt.

When you experience critical mass, it usually seems like everything is going to hell or falling apart. But *exactly the opposite is happening.* The contours of the relationship are pushing both you and your partner to grow up.

Moving through critical mass is always about integrity, about becoming the best person and partner you can—even if your choice ends the relationship. It always means making a leap—and not knowing what the consequences of making that leap will be.

MYRON AND ISABELLA

Myron was the CEO of a large multinational accounting firm. He had reached his fifth decade without ever having a romantic relationship that lasted more than a year. But now, at age fifty-four, he was in a partnership that looked like it would stick. He and his fiancée, Isabella, had been together for three years and had lived together for seven months. Her three adopted kids lived with them, and Myron was learning to be a stepdad. "It's tough," he told me. "Everyone knows the household rules except me. I'm having to learn them—and sometimes negotiate them—one by one. Our five-year-old thinks I'm a bumbling idiot because she knows all the household norms, but I don't." He laughed. "Sometimes she lectures me about them."

When Myron began therapy with me, he was working very long hours, helping his corporation navigate a merger with a larger competitor. This meant some very frank—and occasionally confrontational—negotiations. "Each day I have to deal with three completely different cultures," he told me. "There's my company, the acquiring company, and Isabella's family—which is now my family, too. At every turn—whether it's retirement benefits or figuring out who walks the dog—I have to negotiate everything."

Isabella was a very focused, detail-oriented woman. She *had* to be to run a three-child, single-parent household for years. She would look a child—or her husband-to-be—in the eye and say things like, "Here's what I need you to do, and I need it done before I leave for work." She wasn't mean or overbearing, but she was good at mobilizing people and getting things done.

One night Myron got home late after a marathon session of haggling over the makeup of the new corporation's management team. He was exhausted, hungry, and eager for some loving company.

When he opened the front door, he found a dog barking in anxiety, two children crying, a third shouting at his mother, and a fiancée with her hands on her hips shouting back, "RIGHT NOW YOU NEED TO HELP ANDY GET READY FOR BED." As Myron put down his bag, Isabella turned to him and said, "Just in time. Roll up your sleeves and help me out here."

Myron could sense his fight-or-flee instinct getting activated in the back of his brain. First he took a step toward Isabella, to tell her to back off. Then he took two steps toward his bag, ready to grab it and run. Then he caught himself. Instead of back braining, he took three deep breaths. Then he said, "Okay. What needs to be done first?"

A few days later, in my office, Myron told me, "I made it through, but just barely. Next time I might not be able to keep it together." It was clear that Myron and Isabella had reached an emotional bottleneck, and Myron was nearing critical mass.

I said to him, "You're going to come home to something like this for years. You can't rely on any quick fixes. So what are you going to do to help make things work for you at home?"

He nodded thoughtfully and said, "I've been talking to one of my colleagues. He told me that he and his wife used to fight all the time, but now things are better. He found a way to deal with all the stress. He found someone on a dating site to have an affair with—very discreet, from an old-money family. They hook up when he travels. He says it's balanced out everything for him. He told me that she has some beautiful friends." Myron pointed at me. "Before I do this, though, I wanted to see what *you* thought."

I started laughing. "Dude, are you serious?"

"Hell, yes. My colleague says he and his wife aren't fighting anywhere near as much anymore."

"If it's working out so great," I said, "why doesn't he tell his wife about it? He should let her in on his strategy."

Myron started laughing. Some part of him understood.

I said, "You think the secret to dealing with your fiancée and your future stepkids is to bring in another person to fuck? You really think that's the missing puzzle piece?"

He frowned. "Resmaa, you're a guy. You get where I'm coming from. Anyway, Isabella and I haven't tied the knot."

"Yeah, but you're living in same house, raising kids together. A commitment has been made. That's why this shit is happening—and why it hurts so much. The simple act of choosing Isabella is creating this critical mass. If you hadn't said to her, 'I choose you,' you would have been out the door a long time ago. Right?"

"I suppose." He thought for a few seconds. "Yes."

"Look, man," I said. "You can do whatever you want. But having an affair on the side is not going to get you around the issues. And when Isabella finds out—because you know she will—do you really think she's going to say, 'Good decision, honey. That was way smarter than talking to me'?"

He laughed. "This is why I wanted to run the idea past you first."

"Myron, it's like this: either you're going to grow up and move through this—with all the risks, and the pain, and the kids, and a fiancée who won't automatically do whatever you say—or you're not going to grow up. That's the call. That's what's on the table right now."

To Myron's credit, he chose growth. He finally started to take himself on—something he never would have done before. With Isabella, for the first time in his life, what he did or didn't do in a romantic relationship *mattered*. That's what led to his critical mass.

What eventually popped loose from the crisis was fear. Myron was afraid of Isabella, and of all women who weren't subservient. That's part of why he'd never had a long-lasting relationship before. Myron could tell a subordinate what to do, but with Isabella, everything had to be on the table, and they had to negotiate each piece as equals.

When Myron finally confronted his fear, he was able to unhook it and move through it. He never had the affair, and he accepted the clean pain and discomfort of learning to be part of a loving, imperfect family.

Getting through critical mass is about integrity, not strategy. In fact, strategy usually creates more dirty pain.

At first this seems counterintuitive to people (like Myron) whose jobs involve negotiation—people like lawyers, mediators, and agents. When these folks get to critical mass with their partners, their first impulse may be to try to negotiate a settlement. Or they may attempt to head off the conflict by proactively offering a strategy-based solution. ("I can see that we're going to fight about which stepkids to invite. So let's spare ourselves the misery and not invite any of them.") Then they're hurt and bewildered when this only deepens the conflict. That's because growing up is never a business deal. Committed relationships don't operate according to the rules of dispute resolution.

It's possible that you and your partner may end up proposing alternatives or hashing out a course of action together. But if you make those your operating principles, your lover may hit the roof—without even understanding why. (One sure way to dump a truckload of dirty pain on the two of you during critical mass is to say to your partner, "I'm just trying to be reasonable. Why can't you?")

Another way to make things worse during critical mass is for both of you to back off; go to your separate, safe corners; stay there for a while; come out and pretend that nothing happened; and go back to your old, familiar dynamics and interactions.

Next time, don't. Raise your own game instead. Go to your separate corner for a time to lick your wounds, if you need to. But when you come out, say to your partner, "We've done this the same way time after time. No more. I'm done with business as usual. It's time for us to deal."

In the heat of critical mass, each partner needs to hold on to themselves and keep their spine straight in the midst of pain and uncertainty. They can't look to their partner to do it for them.

Or even with them. Keeping your own spine straight doesn't mean your mate will do the same. If they meet you with love, respect, and integrity, that's great. But they might slink away, or push back with hurricane force, or go completely batshit. There's no way to know until it happens.

In critical mass, all kinds of possibilities present themselves. All the built-up energy behind the emotional bottleneck can explode—or become fuel for transformation.

As critical mass nears for you and your partner—or when you find yourselves in the middle of it—shaking or quaking may emerge in your body. This might happen once, or multiple times, or repeatedly.

Shaking is clearly visible to anyone watching you. It's so visceral and visible and overt that no one can deny or ignore it. In contrast, quaking is internal—you experience it, perhaps profoundly, but no one else can see it.

As I wrote in *The Quaking of America:*

> Although this quaking [or shaking] might seem frightening and unfamiliar at first, consider it a very encouraging sign. It tells you that something significant is happening in your body. It may also begin to reveal to you what is possible— or what you need to do....The first time your body quakes, you may become afraid and have a reflexive urge to grasp for comfort. This urge is normal. But following that urge inhibits growth. So, instead, be as curious about the fear as you are about the quaking [or shaking]. Stay with what your body experiences. Notice what it does when you don't respond reflexively. If necessary, remind yourself that both the quaking and the fear are temporary....Let your body do whatever it wants or needs to do (so long as it doesn't harm you or another body). Open yourself to the experience. And pay attention to your body's movements and energies.

Visible shaking might frighten or upset your partner. But it's a normal response to strong, unexpected energy. Hold onto yourself using the five anchors. Remind yourself that you and your partner will need to take a leap of emergence.

Quaking or shaking can be a response to something that affects you (or you and your partner) personally. But it can also be a response to something larger and less personal, such as historical trauma, a sudden widespread cultural shift, or collective danger.

Novelist Louise Erdrich wrote, "Life will break you. Nobody can protect you from that, and living alone won't either, for solitude will also break you with its yearnings. You have to feel. It is the reason you are here on Earth. You are here to risk your heart."

When life breaks you in the heat and pressure of critical mass, it can break you open into something larger.

Each time you choose clean pain and discomfort while going through critical mass with your partner, you make a little more room in your body for growth and healing. And each time *both* of you choose clean pain and discomfort while moving through critical mass, you create a little more relationship glue.

This process can compound over time, with each journey through critical mass creating more room and more glue. This makes it a bit easier to get through the next critical mass the two of you encounter together.

Eventually, you and your spouse will both sense in your bodies when you reach (or are about to reach) an emotional stalemate—and the process will seem familiar. *This won't be fun,* your bodies will tell you, *but we've been through it together many times before. We'll hold onto ourselves, stay with the clean pain and discomfort, and get through this together.*

RIAZ AND MARTA

In nearly every couple, one lover is very concerned about being on time, while the other is more relaxed about it.

Marta and Riaz are a classic example. Riaz always wants to get to the airport (or appointment or restaurant) early, to allow for mishaps and unexpected delays. Marta keeps tabs on the time and doesn't typically run late, but she doesn't see a need to be so careful.

From the early days of their relationship, this created an ongoing conflict. Every time they got ready to go somewhere together, Riaz would be ready first, keys in hand, while Marta was still getting dressed or putting on makeup or packing her suitcase. When they didn't leave as early as Riaz wanted, he would get anxious.

In their first few years together, Riaz would sometimes blow this anxiety through Marta. He'd say, "You're going to make us late," or "Hurry up, please," or "It's almost 5:30."

Understandably, none of these would sit well with Marta, who would respond with "Back off and chill; we've got plenty of time" or "I know what time it is—time to get off my back."

Occasionally, Riaz would get them somewhere very early, which would annoy Marta. Once in a while, Marta would make the couple late, which would bother Riaz.

Each partner needed to grow up and confront themselves about this conflict. It took a while, but each of them did.

Today Riaz and Marta still have the same values and priorities around time. But they've created some wiser and more compassionate dynamics around those differences.

First and foremost, Riaz stopped trying to blow his anxiety through his wife. He still sometimes gets anxious about arriving on time, but now he'll dry and put away the dishes, or answer a few texts, instead of breathing down his wife's neck. Or he might say—out of generosity, not impatience—"Is there anything I can help you with?"

Marta has made positive moves of her own. If Riaz is ready before she is (which is most of the time), she'll say, "Oh, you're ready. Cool. I'll be ready, too, in fifteen minutes." Her giving Riaz a specific departure time helps him be less anxious.

Through these seemingly small actions, they send each other this vibratory message: *I love you, care about you, and respect how you deal with time. While I won't sacrifice my own values around time, I'll make things a little easier for you.*

COMPASS POINTS

- Critical mass is the place where at least one member of a couple can no longer continue with the status quo. For them, something has to change.

- When couples reach critical mass, both lovers face the possibility of losing something or someone important. They have also reached a point where at least one of them can't compromise their integrity.

- Each partner now has to choose: grow up and potentially transform (or end) the relationship, or stay stuck and worsen the problem.

- Choosing to grow always means making a leap—and not knowing what the consequences of making that leap will be. This choice usually involves an ultimatum—not to your partner, but to yourself.

- In the heat of critical mass, each partner needs to hold on to themselves, soothe themselves, keep their spine straight, and not fly off the handle in the midst of pain and uncertainty. They can't look to their partner to do it for them—or even with them.

- In the heat of critical mass, it usually seems like everything is going to hell or falling apart. But exactly the opposite is happening. The contours of the relationship are pushing both lovers to grow up.

- Getting through critical mass is all about integrity, not strategy. Strategy never creates transformation and usually creates dirty pain. Integrity means becoming the best person and partner you can.
- In critical mass, all kinds of possibilities present themselves—and the built-up energy behind the emotional bottleneck can become fuel for transformation.
- As critical mass nears—or when you find yourself in the middle of it—shaking or quaking may emerge in your body. This tells you that something significant is happening. It may also begin to reveal to you what is possible—or what you need to do.
- When life breaks you in the heat and pressure of critical mass, it can break you open into something larger.
- Each time you choose clean pain and discomfort while going through critical mass with your partner, you make a little more room in your body for growth and healing. And each time both of you choose clean pain and discomfort while moving through critical mass, you create a little more relationship glue.
- Eventually, you and your spouse will both sense in your bodies when you reach (or are about to reach) an emotional stalemate—and the process will seem familiar.

9

Integrity Appears at the Most Difficult Times

Committed relationships force each of us to develop integrity—or to flee from it—in the context of being connected to someone we care about.

Most of us don't understand how integrity works. We think it's about respectfully confronting someone else—our lover, our boss, our family, our culture, our government, or our religion.

That's only looking at integrity's most visible pieces. Much more goes on beneath the surface.

When people get a glimpse of the Loch Ness Monster, all they see is its head and neck. Yet most of the creature is actually under water, keeping it upright and balanced.[12] Integrity is similar: its less-than-obvious (and often unseen) aspects are what give it its transformative power.

Integrity emerges from the energy of creation itself. This emergence and expression through us is a natural process. Often, however, there are energies stuck in our bodies—and in our larger culture, systems, and structures—that thwart integrity's emergence. Yet this thwarting can have its own purpose and value: it can push us into critical mass and double binds, so that integrity can emerge. This is an unpredictable but elegant process—and, when it unfolds, nothing is going wrong.

---

12 I'm basing this metaphor on the reported sightings of Nessie and on the design of simi-lar-looking creatures. The Loch Ness Monster may of course turn out to be mythical or a hoax.

In your partnership, integrity is mostly about confronting *yourself.* It pushes you up against your own fears, issues, and limitations, and challenges you to deal with them. No matter what moves you make with your partner, and no matter why you make them, your interlocking issues will force each of you to make a choice: respond from the strongest parts of yourselves or from the weakest, damaged parts.

Integrity appears when there is conflict or stress. It doesn't take integrity to do the right thing when nothing stands in your way. Boycotting Walmart doesn't require any integrity if there's a Target next door. Staying faithful to your partner is easy when you're getting along well and having lots of good sex. But when your lover tells you, "Don't even *think* of screwing me until you start acting like a father to your own kids," it takes integrity to stay faithful—and to stay connected and calm in the heat of the moment.

Integrity shows up at those times when it's difficult or impossible for you to compromise, because the things that you're asked to compromise are important to you—and closely tied to your sense of who you are.

Integrity appears when you do the right thing in the face of serious trouble or opposition. And integrity always has a cost.

Instead of confronting ourselves, many of us try to blow our issues or painful emotions through our partners. We usually do this through blame, or manipulation, or coercion, or even violence. None of these ever works; they only deepen the problem, often creating new ones and producing dirty pain.

JATY AND ADA

Jaty is afraid that her partner, Ada, will leave her. But instead of saying to her, "Ada, I'm scared; can we talk?" Jaty tries to blow her fear through Ada by accusing her of flirting with her assistant. Ada responds angrily, "After all these years, don't you trust me?" Jaty huffs, "Don't you *dare* make this my problem!"

But, in fact, it *is* her problem. She's unwilling to confront herself about her own fear, express it to Ada, and make herself vulnerable to her partner. By refusing to stand in her integrity and talk about her emotions—and by not attending to the stirrings and quakings she experiences in her body—she creates a new conflict around trust.

Meanwhile, below the surface, Jaty leaves an important issue unaddressed—one that has little to do with Ada. Deep in her body, Jaty senses that she is somehow inherently inadequate or defective—not up the basic standard of humanness. She experiences herself as an impostor, faking her way through life. Jaty is terrified that if Ada discovers her impostorhood, she will pack up and leave.

Of course, Jaty is anything but an impostor. She's as fully human—and as fully equipped for human life—as you or me. Also like you and me, she's flawed. But these flaws are aspects of her humanness, not aberrations.

Therapists often call this an issue of *self-image* or *self-esteem*, as if the problem is a cognitive assumption or idea. But it's not. For Jaty (and for many other human beings), it's an ongoing *experience* deep inside her body.

In Jaty's case, this sense of being inadequate was passed down to her energetically by her parents, both of whom also experienced themselves as impostors.[13] If she can learn to pause, lean into the stirrings and discomfort in her body, and interrogate what's behind them, she may be able to unhook and release the energies behind her fear.

KWAME AND KIMBER

Kwame and his lover, Kimber, have not had sex for several weeks, and Kwame has no idea why. The situation makes him very anxious, but Kwame is unwilling to confront himself about his anxiety.

Instead, he tries to blow his anxiety through his partner. Over dinner he suddenly says, "You think I've gotten old, wrinkly, and ugly, don't you?"

Kimber looks bewildered and says in jest, "Have you started smoking weed again, man? You promised me you'd stop. It makes you paranoid."

Because Kwame won't stand in his integrity around sex, Kimber questions his integrity around staying clean and keeping promises. His question is intended as affectionate ribbing rather than confrontation—but Kwame's integrity issue nevertheless remains unaddressed.

---

13 This sense of being an impostor is quite common. There's even a name for it: *impostor syndrome*. Although any human being can experience impostor syndrome, it's especially common among bodies of culture—i.e., bodies that are not white and Christian. In a culture that has absorbed white-body supremacy—the sense that the white body (or the white Christian body) is the supreme standard by which all other bodies are measured—it's not surprising that impostor syndrome has become widespread.

As you can see, the real issue is not how often the two partners have sex. But the temporary lack of sex creates enough heat to force Kwame up against his limitations. It also gives him an opportunity to stand in his integrity in his relationship with Kimber. If he takes this opportunity, he can ask Kimber about their lack of sex and what, if anything, might be behind it. This gives Kimber an opportunity to respond honestly, from his own integrity.

Think how differently this dinner would go if Kimber responded to Kwame with, "Wow. And I was thinking that you were starting to lose interest in *me*. Get your ass over here and kiss me right now." Or if he were to nod and say, "Yeah, I've been meaning to talk to you. My testosterone level's gone way down. I just got back the test results this morning. It's half of what it ought to be." (In this case, something *would* be going wrong: Kimber's testosterone level. But his and Kwame's relationship would be going very right.)

In committed partnerships, we often have to choose between integrity and equilibrium. Over time, many relationships evolve into an unhappy equilibrium that both lovers choose to tolerate. Neither one likes the situation, but neither one is willing to say to the other, "I'm not doing this anymore. I want something better."

Lovers choose equilibrium over integrity for all kinds of reasons. They might believe that they don't deserve better, or that nothing better is even possible. They might be afraid of being alone. They might simply be patient or stoic to the point of neurosis.

Usually, though, both partners are afraid of change or conflict—or, most of all, loss. They worry that if they rock the boat and disrupt the painful but tolerable (and familiar) equilibrium, all hell will break loose. They're not willing to take that risk.

In some cases, all hell *will* break loose. That's why standing up and saying, "I want something better" requires integrity. The only way to create the possibility of something better is by accepting the peril of losing not only the equilibrium and the uneasy calm, but the relationship itself—and perhaps much more as well. Integrity always requires a willingness to step into uncertainty and the unknown.

Integrity trumps protection. It trumps survival. It even trumps the relationship. Integrity puts everything on the line. It appears at the most difficult times because those are the times when everything is at stake. And no committed relationship can survive without it.

COMPASS POINTS

- In your partnership, integrity is mostly about confronting *yourself*, not your partner.
- No matter what moves you make with your partner, and why, you're going to get pushed up against your own stuff.
- Integrity appears in times of stress or conflict. It doesn't take integrity to do the right thing when nothing is in your way and nothing is at stake.
- Most of us try to blow our issues or problems or painful emotions through our partners—through blame, or manipulation, or control, or even violence. This only deepens the problem, and often creates new ones—as well as lots of dirty pain.
- In committed partnerships, we often have to choose between integrity and equilibrium. We worry that if we challenge our partner and the equilibrium, all hell will break loose.
- In some cases, all hell *will* break loose. That's why standing up and saying, "I want something better" requires integrity.
- Integrity always requires a willingness to step into uncertainty.
- Integrity trumps protection. It trumps survival. It even trumps the relationship. No committed relationship can survive without it.

10

Continuous Improvement
in Relationships

There's much more to be said—and I'll say it in later chapters—about integrity, critical mass, and the dynamics of transformation.

But I don't want to give you the impression that in committed partnerships, growth *only* happens when couples reach critical mass and someone changes the game. It's also about continuous, incremental improvement. This improvement usually follows a clear sequence.

First, both partners need to create stability in their relationship. This is a goal that most couples naturally seek, because it seems safe, like a boat that's properly anchored. Without stability—and the trust and respect that stability helps to build—incremental improvement is impossible.

What happens next, though, often catches lovers by surprise: *the very act of stabilizing the relationship naturally brings forward difficulties and problems.* Because the partners no longer have to focus on creating this basic stability—and because this stability supports trust, connection, and communication—they can begin to work through these difficulties together.

In turn, the process of working through problems can create greater empathy, less rigidity, a better flow of energy, and more relationship glue between the two partners. Over time, a positive feedback loop can emerge. Issues will continue to pop up, but the partners will now be more comfortable with addressing them. They will also have created an informal alignment process for handling them, as well as some norms, standards, and agreements. In essence, the partners say to each other, "We're going to tolerate conflicts and work them out. This is how we're going to do it, and here's what we can expect from each other." All of this creates more stability, and the cycle of continuous improvement tends to build on itself.

KATARINA AND BEATRICE

I recently worked with Katarina, a client whose early life was extremely painful. Her father often beat her, and as a teenager she was sexually abused by a family member.

Before she was twenty, she was arrested for beating up her girlfriend. As part of her treatment, she was assigned to a group of domestic violence offenders I worked with. After a few months in the group, she moved on and I lost track of her.

A few years later, she called and asked to work with me one-to-one. She told me that she'd been in and out of relationships all her life and that all of them had been full of conflict. Now she had a new partner, Beatrice—a young woman about her age. The partnership wasn't going any better than her previous ones.

She and Beatrice were homeless. Bea had a job, but it paid just above minimum wage, and Katarina didn't work at all. They usually stayed in a motel two nights a week, and slept in their car the other five.

Katarina and Bea fought almost constantly. Their relationship was always in crisis, always on the verge of breaking up. Each lover would set off the other. "Yesterday I accidentally broke a mug," Katarina told me in my office. "Bea said, 'I hate it when you're clumsy. Forget about sex tonight.' It was going to be our last night in a motel for a week, so I said, 'Fine. I'll go to the Pony Club and find somebody there to fuck.'"

They finally reached critical mass when, in the middle of an argument, Katarina suddenly clenched her fists and advanced on Beatrice. Bea ran to the bathroom, locked the door, and called her cousin Chauncey.

Chauncey arrived half an hour later. He was tall, muscular, and serious looking. "You're Katarina?" he asked softly through the motel window. "Is my cousin okay?"

Katarina opened the door and let him in. She and Bea were both crying. "I'm all right," Bea said. "She never touched me. I just got scared."

Chauncey nodded. "Katarina," he said in the same soft, slow voice, "would you mind taking a walk with me?"

This is it, Katarina thought. *I'm being set up. He's big, but I'll go straight for his balls and eyes.* "Okay," she said. "Let's walk."

As soon as they got around the corner, Chauncey stopped. He looked at Katarina and said softly, "My cousin has ovarian cancer, and it's getting worse. Has she told you?"

Sitting on the couch in my office, Katarina blinked back tears. "Resmaa, I swear, I didn't know what the hell to do. Of course she hadn't told me. I just sat on the curb and started crying."

"What did you do after that?" I asked.

"I turned to her cousin and said, 'Chauncey, all I know how to do is fight.'"

Through tears, Katarina told me the rest of the story. "Chauncey asked me, 'Do you know why she didn't tell you?' He didn't even wait for a response. He said, 'Because she thought that if she told you, you'd leave her.'"

Katarina and I spent some time focusing on the emotions and sensations Katarina was experiencing in her body. Then I said, "You and Bea reached critical mass that day. Now you have a chance to figure out what it's going to take to grow in a way you never have before. This is your bright line. This the opportunity for the two of you to answer the question, *What now? What do we want this relationship to be?*

"You've hurt and been hurt by this person you love, and who is in a relationship with you. So this is also the time to ask yourself, *How will I be different now?*"

Then I said to Katarina, "Maybe you and Bea can get through this together, but you're not going to be able to do it living in a car and motel rooms. If you want to be with this woman, be with her. But it can't be on the same old terms. Your current lifestyle is not workable for someone with ovarian cancer. The question is, do you have the capacity to do this? I believe you do, because you've been able to survive some serious shit to make it to where you are now.

"You get to choose. You can start working toward stability, or you can leave, or you can try to blow all your problems through your partner who has cancer."

Three days later, Katarina went to a temp agency. The next day she started working temporary jobs regularly. That's when the continuous improvement began.

She and Beatrice went on the insurance exchange and bought health insurance, so some of Bea's medical treatment, and 90 percent of her medications, were covered.

Three months later they got an apartment together.

One of Katarina's temp jobs turned into an offer of a permanent part-time job. She took it, and now she's trying to increase her hours.

Slowly, Katarina and Bea are learning how to be a caring couple.

It's not easy for either of them. Bea is often tired and in pain. Katarina does most of the housework and cooking, so she's tired most of the time, too. They argue sometimes, like any couple. But they're no longer a couple in crisis. Step by step, challenge by challenge, day by day, they're continuously improving and building a life together.

The greatest continuous improvement takes place when both lovers are committed to growing up. But even if only one partner makes that commitment, the relationship can improve—or else it will end.

Two different types of energy can improve an intimate relationship: *reparative* energy and *building* energy. A committed relationship requires both of these energy streams in order to grow and deepen.

Reparative energy is vital when a relationship needs immediate attention. When you say to your partner after they get laid off, "Let me talk to my boss; I'll see if she can assign me some overtime hours for the next few months, while you look for a new job," that's reparative energy.

Reparative energy focuses on the present and the near future—on what is in front of you and your partner, and on what is on your horizon. Reparative energy can keep a relationship from going off the rails in times of great stress or challenges.

Building energy is visionary and future-focused. It looks at what can and might be. Building energy would prompt you to say to your partner after they get laid off, "That's the second time you've been laid off in eighteen months. I've been thinking that the same thing could happen to me. Maybe it's time that both of us train for new careers. Or maybe we can start our own business together."

These two energies are complements, not opposites. It's both inaccurate and harmful to think, *I'm a builder and my partner is a fixer,* or vice versa. That's like saying *I'm an inhaler and my partner is an exhaler* or *I'm an eater and my partner is a crapper.* When it comes to relationships, each of us needs to learn to work with both types of energy.

The more you and your partner can each practice working with both, the more each of you can contribute to improving your relationship—and the more relationship glue you will create together.

COMPASS POINTS

- In committed partnerships, transformation isn't only about reaching critical mass and changing the game. It's also about continuous, incremental improvement.
- For this to occur, both partners first need to create stability in their relationship.
- The very act of stabilizing the relationship will naturally bring forward difficulties and problems. But because the partners no longer have to focus on creating basic stability, they can begin to work through these difficulties together.
- The process of working through problems creates greater empathy, less rigidity, and a better flow of energy. The lovers will also have created an informal process for handling them. All of this creates more stability, and the cycle builds on itself.
- For a committed relationship to improve, deepen, and grow, it requires both reparative energy and building energy.

11

Rocks and Holes

Most of us think that the success or failure of a committed partnership largely depends on personality—people's backgrounds, politics, religion, likes and dislikes, interests, senses of humor, quirks, and so on. But these elements only speak to *compatibility*. And compatibility doesn't get at the purpose and opportunities of a committed relationship.

Compatibility is what supports a pleasant and comfortable *friendship.* The dynamics of a committed relationship are entirely different; they involve *fit.*

Fit has to do with the mental templates each partner uses to live their life and negotiate the world. My wife and I have very different personalities. But, as I've learned over the years, we're a perfect fit.

In every couple, both partners' strengths, weaknesses, traumas, fears, hopes, and desires fit together and are interlocked. This fit is why the two people have come together. It's also why they keep sailing into emotional bottlenecks.

If you look at a couple and wonder, *Why the hell are they together?* or *What in the world do they see in each other?,* it's because of those things that interlock. But that might not be visible to a casual observer.

As Dr. James Maddock used to say, the rocks in one partner's head always fit perfectly into the holes in the other's.

This is no accident. It's how committed partnerships work.

There's another aspect of fit: the lived experiences that you and your partner bring to the relationship.

Year by year, each of us lives out multiple stories—some purely personal, some persistent and institutional, some historical, some intergenerational. Some of these are stories of hope and success; others are stories of loss and harm. As we grow and age, we can choose to repeat certain stories, to stop repeating them, or to rewrite them.

Here are some examples:

- You often have to fight to be heard, or to have your presence recognized.
- You are consistently rewarded for your minor achievements, while your major ones sometimes get overlooked.
- You regularly find yourself stepping in to calm out-of-control kids.
- You advance quickly in most of your jobs, but within two to three years reach a place where no more advancement is possible.
- You often injure yourself while playing sports.

Similarly, over time, through repetition, certain energies can come to inhabit your body. Your belly constricts when you sense that you are being evaluated. You reflexively brace yourself for a fall when someone else's body gets within a foot of yours. Your chest tightens when someone you care about gets angry. You experience a whole-body surge of excitement when you dive into the ocean.

I call this unique set of stories and energies your *somatic throughline*. (*Somatic* simply means *body-centered* or *related to the body*.) When two people's somatic throughlines line up especially well, this is another classic form of fit.

HOLLY AND AARON

Holly, the daughter of an Air Force lieutenant, grew up moving from place to place every few years. When she falls in love with Aaron, an actor who makes a living playing minor film roles, her body experiences his constant traveling as comfortable and familiar. Because Aaron was raised in a tightly controlled and highly scheduled household, *his* body experiences Holly's flexibility and adaptability as deeply supportive. In these and other positive ways, Aaron's and Holly's somatic throughlines dovetail beautifully.

But dovetailing isn't only positive. In any couple, each person's somatic throughline includes unresolved issues and dirty pain. These typically line up perfectly, so that the rock of your unresolved issue or limitation fits perfectly into the hole of your partner's issue or limitation. This causes conflict, friction, and, often, pain and confusion.

When this happens, nothing is going wrong. It's exactly what is supposed to happen.

The positive and pleasurable aspects of dovetailing usually show up early in a relationship—and they help the relationship to grow. But eventually—after weeks, months, or even years—the dovetailing of limitations and issues shows up as well.

When this happens, most couples initially see their situation as surprising and tragic—maybe even as a betrayal. But it's actually a huge opportunity.

When one of your limitations or issues lines up with one of your partner's, it's a call for both of you to grow up. It's also an ideal chance for each of you to support the other's growth.

If the only thing bringing you and your partner together is compatibility, it's similar to hooking up with someone because they have a nice smile, or a sexy walk, or a talent for making you laugh. It may support some brief good times, but it won't provide a foundation for a long-term relationship.

If all you want is a summer fling or a week of sex and partying while you're on vacation, then finding someone who's compatible will probably do. But if you want a real relationship with another human being, you're going to be motivated by *fit*, whether you realize it or not.

Here are two real-life examples of fit (with some details changed to protect people's privacy).

CRAIG AND GRETA

Craig is a very laid-back, easygoing, no-drama guy. When he's faced with a problem, he says, "Okay, let's work on it," and deals with it without complaining. When things are going well, he's naturally relaxed and content.

Craig likes to lounge on the sofa and read, or watch videos, or simply think. He's a big-picture, systems thinker, so his job as an interior designer is perfect for him.

His wife, Greta, is extremely organized and task oriented. She always has a list of things to do, and she goes through her day completing them and checking them off. Her job as an executive assistant is equally perfect for her.

When people first meet Greta and Craig, they think, *How in hell did these two get together? He's a sloth on LSD, and she's a high-strung bulldog.* But if you get to know them, you begin to see that neither impression is accurate, and that the two have a nearly perfect fit.

At home, Craig has no idea where his shoes are or whether the family needs to buy toothpaste. But Greta knows exactly where every pair of shoes is; when they'll need to buy more toothpaste; when Craig needs to take their son, Jason, to soccer practice; and five hundred other household details. Her organizational abilities make their lives manageable. When she says to her husband, "You need to pick up Jason now," he knows she's carefully thought through the timing, so he immediately puts down his magazine and grabs his car keys.

Craig also makes life more manageable for Greta. At the end of a long, busy day, when she gets into bed, he massages her feet and back. When she's especially tense, he hums her a lullaby, which makes her laugh. When she's flitting about like a hummingbird, he'll sometimes grab her gently, pull her down into his lap, and say, "You're even more beautiful when you're sitting still."

Their relationship wasn't always like this. During their first year of marriage, they nearly drove each other over the edge. Greta would say to Craig, "Time to pick up Jason," to which he'd say, "Sure, in five minutes." Then she'd tear the book out of his hand, throw it across the room, and say, "I'm not your goddamn snooze alarm." When Greta rushed about at ten o'clock at night and Craig pulled her into his lap, she'd push herself back off and say, "Hands off, buddy, until my list is *done*."

But over time they learned to appreciate how they fit together. They both leaned into that fit, using it to deepen their intimacy and support their life together. Each partner also learned to use the five anchors (from chapter 5, and described in more detail in chapter 35) to stay balanced and present when the heat was turned up under them.

Here's another example of fit.

ROSEANNE AND BART

My client Roseanne is an emergency room doctor at a big urban hospital. Her work in the ER is fast-paced, unpredictable, and chaotic. Her shifts can run from eight to fourteen hours, and her schedule can change from week to week. Roseanne comes from a well-educated, upper-class family; both her parents were university professors. When people first meet her, the first word they often think is *professional.*

Her husband, Bart, is a mechanic who owns his own repair shop, which he inherited from his dad. He's a hard worker, a good father to their daughter, Alexandra, and extremely reliable. When people first meet Bart, the words they often think are *salt of the earth.* Bart isn't particularly educated—he has an associate degree in small business—and he's visibly uncomfortable in a suit.

When people see the pair having their breakfast together in a coffee shop—Bart in his coveralls, Roseanne in her medical attire—they wonder how this marriage can possibly work.

But their friends and relatives know better. They see it work every day.

For starters, Roseanne and Bart are intellectual equals. Although his background is working class, Bart is extremely bright and well read. He can hold his own with Roseanne in any discussion about politics, religion, or social issues. Bart can't have these kinds of discussions with his parents or siblings, so he appreciates Roseanne's erudition and worldliness.

Roseanne equally appreciates the great stability that Bart brings to the marriage. His repair shop earns a good, consistent profit. Also, no matter how chaotic things get in the ER, and no matter how crazy Roseanne's own day gets, Rosanne knows that Bart will be in the shop, keeping his regular hours.

I'm told that in the bedroom, things get especially interesting. Roseanne relaxes and discards her veneer of professionalism, and Bart reads classic love poems to her. He's also as reliable a lover as he is a dad.

What is behind this interlocking of rocks and holes? Partly it's the vibes we send out to others—and the ones they send out to us. (I'll talk about vibes in detail in chapter 15.)

But the process of rocks and holes fitting together is far more mysterious than vibes alone can explain. Many of the interlocking dilemmas couples face aren't created by vibes at all. Here are a couple of examples.

EDWIN AND CHERISE

Edwin and Cherise meet, fall in love, and, after dating for a year, decide to move in together. They rent an apartment from

Antonio, a very demonstrative Italian. Just by being who he is, Antonio activates Cherise's fear of aggressive men and Edwin's urge to get violent with potential rivals. It's a perfect rock-and-hole setup, but it was obviously created by the circumstances of their life, not by some vibratory messages the lovers sent to each other.

MICKIE AND SVI

Mickie and Svi have been together for more than fifteen years. For all of those years, sex has been easy and pleasurable for both of them. But even though they've grown emotionally closer over the years, their bodies are beginning to change in opposite directions. Svi often experiences his body as too warm—and when he's too warm, he can't maintain an erection. Mickie is often cold and keeps turning up the thermostat. But *any temperature that makes Svi comfortable makes Mickie uncomfortable,* and vice versa. Soon this begins to affect their sex life. A warm temperature is a big turn-on for Mickie, and a huge turn-off for Svi. He tries to accommodate Mickie, but his penis simply won't cooperate. It's another classic rock and hole conundrum.

When talented therapists work with couples, they look for these metaphorical holes in each client's head (or, in Svi and Mickie's case, their bodies). Whenever they see one, they look for the matching rock in the head (or other parts) of the person's partner. As they discover these matches, they can begin to understand the dynamics of the relationship ecosystem—and they can better help both lovers grow.

Sometimes when couples divorce or break up after years together, at least one of them says, "We just fell out of love, I guess" or "We were never really that compatible in the first place."

Both of these explanations miss the point. If you're together for that long, it's because there was a mental and emotional fit. What usually happens is that, after two people have lived through the butterflies and lollipops stage of the relationship, they begin having to deal with each other for real. This may scare the hell out of them, because now they have to grow up.

Or, one of them may freak out because they *want* to grow up, and their partner may not. They may say to their lover, "You know what? I've had enough of us serving up mother's milk to each other. I want something more than just giving each other what we want. I don't want to be your mama anymore, and I don't want you to be my daddy."

Fit naturally creates opportunities for both clean pain and dirty pain. When people are committed to growing up together, they can use their fit to sort things out and work their way through emotional stalemates. But couples can also use fit to keep each other stuck in dirty pain.

My grandmother and grandfather stayed together for more than sixty years, until my grandfather died. They slept in the same bed and raised six kids together. They were a classic example of fit. But it was a dirty fit. They couldn't stand each other. Everybody around them knew it and sensed it. They used their fit to keep themselves stuck instead of helping each other grow.

Let's look at Edwin and Cherise again.

One afternoon, as Antonio is repairing their air conditioner, Cherise walks into the apartment. Antonio is noisily packing up his tools, almost hurling them into the toolbox. He looks up at her, grimaces, and half-shouts, "Why do people even live in Houston? You might as well live in a sauna." He points a finger at her and begins waving his other hand in circles. "You grew up here, *signora*," he says loudly, taking a step toward her. "How did you survive, summer after summer?"

Cherise's stomach tightens in fear. Her first impulse is to flee into her dirty pain by running into the bedroom and slamming the door. But she immediately recognizes this as her lizard brain's stress response. So, instead of running, as the back of her brain tells her to do, she begins using the anchors. She tells herself, *Stay calm. Stay where you are. Edwin's in the next room. You're not in danger.* She concentrates on experiencing the floor under her feet and the slow streaming of air in and out of her lungs.

A thought flashes through her head: *The longer you stand here, the bigger a target you become. Get out now!* But Cherise doesn't. She takes a deep breath and focuses on the cool air from the now-repaired air conditioner blowing on her skin. Her stomach aches with fear, so she lets herself fully experience that, too.

Then she smiles and simply says, "Isn't Italy hot in the summer, too, Antonio?"

Antonio drops his hands. "No, *signora*. Not in Bormio, high in the Alps, where I grew up. I would ski for five months every year."

His face suddenly breaks into a huge smile. "Bormio is one of the most beautiful spots on Earth. When I retire, I will go back."

Edwin enters the room a moment later. He looks at Cherise and Antonio and experiences a sudden jolt of anger. His heart beats faster and his hands clench into fists.

But Edwin also realizes that he's back braining, so he begins using the anchors as well.

First he coughs, to get rid of some tension and to buy a couple of seconds to calm down. He also uses part of that time to scan Antonio's face. Nothing in the man's expression seems dangerous or even unusual. *Chill out,* Edwin tells himself. *He's not being weird. It's fine.*

Edwin moves his awareness to the sensations in his body—the tightness in his fists and chest, the blood pounding in his head, the tensed muscles in his legs, ready to propel him forward. He deliberately unclenches his hands and relaxes his leg muscles. Then he smiles at Cherise, walks up to her, and takes her hand.

He turns to Antonio. "Thanks for fixing the air conditioner. Need any help carrying your stuff back to your truck?"

"*Grazie*, thank you, yes," Antonio says, running one hand through his hair and picking up his toolbox. He nods in Cherise's direction and says, "Good day, *signora*." Then Edwin lets go of her hand, and the two men head out the door.

COMPASS POINTS

- In every couple, both partners' strengths, weaknesses, traumas, fears, hopes, and desires are interlocked. This interlocking is why the two people have come together.

- If you look at a couple and wonder, *Why the hell are they together?* or *What in the world do they see in each other?,* you're not seeing the things that interlock.

- The rocks in one partner's head always fit perfectly into the holes in the other's. This is no accident. It's how committed partnerships work.

- When talented therapists work with couples, they look for these metaphorical holes in each client's head. Whenever they see one, they look for the matching rock in the head of the person's partner.

12

Collaborative and Coercive Alliances

Power is the ability to influence. Control is the ability to regulate and/or shape that influence.

This may not seem like an important distinction. But it's the key to understanding the ecology of many committed partnerships.

Power people make things happen. They move. They act. They mobilize. They break through. They often break rules.

Control people make things work. They organize. They manage. They strategize. They coordinate. They devise and enforce the rules.

Properly used, power and control can each support and strengthen an intimate relationship. (Much more on this in chapter 33.) But when either one is misused, it can seriously undermine that relationship.

Every partnership is an alliance. It can either be collaborative—based on love, trust, and respect—or coercive, based on manipulation and the misuse of power or control.

Growth simply cannot happen in a coercive alliance.

The classic Rolling Stones song "Under My Thumb" perfectly describes a coercive alliance and all the dirty pain it creates. In the song, a gloating narrator explains how, after being manipulated and controlled by his partner, he has found a way to reverse the dynamic. Now she is meek, subservient, and under his thumb—and he couldn't be more proud.

This is heart eating in its purest form. The narrator loves his partner, yet at the same time he revels in his hatred and successful revenge. He could have simply chosen to leave the relationship—but, instead, he chose to stay and create more dirty pain.

When a real-life couple relates in this way, at least one of them typically ends up dead, in jail, or in the emergency room.

With such couples, the only hope for building a genuinely loving relationship is for both partners to unhook themselves from coercion and manipulation, and to build a fresh alliance based on collaboration, trust, and respect.

A committed partnership is never about giving yourself over to your partner or having them give themselves over to you. It's not about who controls the relationship or whose will triumphs. It's never about who wins and who loses. Those alliances are about power, not intimacy. In such alliances, both people ultimately lose.

BRIE AND PHIL

On Christmas Eve, when Phil gets home from work, his wife, Brie, greets him at the front door with a long, wet kiss. Then she grabs both his butt cheeks, presses her lips against his ear, and whispers, "Promise me you'll be nice to my family tonight—and that you'll only have one drink. If you're good, this dress comes off the moment we get home."

Normally there's nothing wrong with Brie flirting with her husband. But this time the flirting isn't built on sexual attraction. It's her strategy to get him to do what she wants. Instead of starting an honest discussion with him about how he sometimes angrily argues with her brothers, Brie tries to bribe him into compliance.

Because Brie has made sex into a reward, Phil begins to ask himself some questions: *Does Brie still enjoy having sex with me? When we have sex, is it because she wants to, or is it just a means to an end for her? Does she still find me sexy? Is she faking her orgasms—or her sexual pleasure in general? If so, why hasn't she talked to me about it? If she doesn't enjoy having sex with me, is she having an affair?* Suddenly Phil can't fully trust her, because Brie has sent him a vibratory message based on one of her limitations that reaches out to one of his.

In order to stand in his integrity, Phil needs to straighten his spine and ask Brie all the questions he's just asked himself.

If he does, though, it may suddenly and dramatically turn up the heat between them—but not the kind of heat that leads to fabulous sex. What began as a simple sexy (but dirty) bribe would quickly transform into a painful discussion about family, friction, sex, attraction, manipulation, and many other topics. That discussion—or argument or fight—would probably be scary as hell for both lovers. It would surely also be full of peril and possibility. But if Phil and Brie were each able to hold on to themselves, speak their truth, and move through that heat with presence and respect, it could transform their relationship for the better.

Now let's imagine that, instead, Phil wimps out. He doesn't ask Brie any of the vibratory questions that are in his head and body, because he's afraid of what her answers might be. What if she says, "I'm sorry, Phil, but you just don't turn me on anymore. I've been getting it on with your cousin the stripper"? He's suddenly very vulnerable.

So Phil ignores the ache in his belly. He takes the bait and whispers back to Brie, "It's a deal."

By choosing dirty pain, Phil hopes he will experience less fear and dread, that he will be less vulnerable, and that he and Brie will enjoy some hot sex later that night.

But of course his decision has exactly the opposite effect. Suddenly he's *more* vulnerable. He still doesn't have answers to any of his questions. Plus, if Brie doesn't keep her end of the bargain—and she might not, because in Phil's mind she's no longer entirely trustworthy—he's going to deal with more pain and disappointment.

Meanwhile, he's agreed to turn sex into a bargaining chip and their sex life into a business deal. So even if Brie *does* keep her end of the bargain, he won't know whether her passion is real or a performance—not just tonight, but from now on.

As for Brie, because Phil has agreed to her bribe, now she can't trust *him* as much, because she knows that he's more interested in his own sexual gratification than he is in shared intimacy.

Neither Phil nor Brie consciously realizes what they're doing. They're both just trying to make things work. But they're both stuck in a stream of dirty pain, by trying to replace integrity with temporary comfort.

Let's suppose that at the family gathering later that evening, Phil does as he is told. There are no arguments and the night goes smoothly.

By the time they get home, though, Brie is half-asleep, exhausted, and utterly uninterested in sex.

But Phil is eager to get it on. He pulls her close and starts removing her dress. "I'm sorry, honey," Brie says, "but I'm just not in the mood anymore. Maybe tomorrow night, okay?" Phil buries his face in her hair. "No," he whispers, "not tomorrow night. Right now. You promised me."

Now Brie has become the prisoner of her own strategy. She has to make a difficult choice:

1. She can push Phil away and try to put the blame on him. "I told you, Phil, I'm just not interested in sex right now. Leave me alone, okay? I'm not some blow-up doll you can bang whenever you're horny." This leads both spouses into confusion, distrust, and resentment.

2. She can give in and have joyless, disconnected sex with her husband. This *also* leads to confusion, distrust, and resentment.

3. She can straighten her spine, confront herself about her own actions, and say to her husband, "Phil, I'm really sorry. I shouldn't be offering sexual favors to make you and my family get along better. I'm glad things went well tonight, and I hope they'll keep going well. It's important to me that you and my family get along. I love you, and God knows there are times when I want to fuck the daylights out of you. But right now all I want to do is sleep."

In this third scenario, Brie takes herself on and admits her mistake. She also stands in her integrity and tells Phil clearly what she wants. She chooses to accept the clean pain and discomfort of becoming vulnerable to Phil.

At the same time, she speaks to Phil's fears and answers his questions—even though he never articulated them to her.

Whichever choice she makes, because Phil and Brie are interlocked, her position now blocks his. At this point, Phil has a new choice. He can pull them both back into dirty pain by trying to block her position as well: "You know what? I'm sick of your cock-teasing. You are one cold, crazy bitch." Or he can confront himself, tolerate his own disappointment, and say to himself, *Okay, so I'll go to sleep with a hard-on tonight. I can live through that.* He can also kiss his wife and say to her, "Sleep well, Brie. But listen—if there's something you want, just tell me you want it. Please don't try to get it by promising to spread your legs. I don't want to play this game anymore."

If at least one lover puts their truth on the table, Brie and Phil have a chance to move through this emotional stalemate— and to grow up.

But if neither one does, then the dirty-pain vibratory messages, manipulation, questions, distrust, and dirty pain will all continue.

Brie is not a conniving bitch. She's a loving, caring, flawed human being, just like you and me. But when Brie tried to coerce Phil into doing her bidding, she wasn't willing to look at herself and grow. She was afraid to say to Phil, "Sweetie, I want you to find a way to get along with my family. I know my brothers sometimes try to pick fights with you about politics. I've watched them get you drunk so they can get the biggest rise out of you. I wish they wouldn't do that shit, but I can't change them. Please don't let them rope you in tonight like they did on Thanksgiving."

Telling Phil what she really wanted would have made Brie vulnerable, because she had no idea how he would respond. He might have refused ("If your brothers want an argument, I'll give them an argument"), or dissed her brothers ("I'm not going to let those assholes talk trash to me again"), or dissed *her* ("Why do you always try to protect your family at my expense?"). Afraid of getting shot down by speaking her truth, Brie instead tried to get what she wanted by making Phil into her pawn.

But Brie might have been able to speak her truth if she'd used most of the anchors described in chapter 5:

1. **Soothing and resourcing herself** to quiet her mind, calm her heart, and settle her body.

2. **Pausing, and then noticing and discerning the sensations, vibrations, and emotions in her body,** instead of reacting to them.

3. **Accepting and tolerating the discomfort** instead of trying to flee from it.

4. **Staying present** and in her body as she spoke her truth and moved through the unfolding experience, with all its ambiguity and uncertainty, while responding from the best parts of herself.

Phil is not a dupe or a doofus. He doesn't just want sex from Brie. He wants a full, loving, ever-deepening partnership. But he, too, could have used the anchors to soothe himself down, notice and tolerate what he experienced in his body, straighten his spine, and speak his truth to the most important person in his life.

In a collaborative alliance, both lovers say to each other, "We have a problem. We don't know how we're going to get through it or where it will take us, but we're going to accept the pain of it, walk through it together if we can, and love and respect each other as we do it." This means that collaborative alliances include both tenderness *and* respectful self-confrontation.

In a collaborative alliance, when one partner is in pain, *both* partners recognize whose pain or problem it is and respond in the most supportive way. If it's both partners' problem, then both lean into the pain and move through it together.

But if it's one partner's problem, then the other partner *doesn't* leap in and try to fix the problem for them. They might empathize or listen, but they won't let their partner out of the responsibility of confronting themselves and growing.

Brie could have transformed her coercive alliance with Phil simply by telling him what she wanted and why. Then, together, they might have explored all the interlocking issues. They'd see that her brothers' habit of picking political fights is their own problem. Brie's desire for tranquil family gatherings is fine, but her anxiety about them is her problem. As for how Phil might best respond to her brothers, he and Brie need to talk about it. But regardless of what occurs in that discussion, when Phil has future encounters with her brothers, he needs to respond from his best self, not from what is small or weak in him.

In all of these situations, both partners need to pay attention to their bodies, because some things will show up as vibrations, without any words connected to them. Each partner needs to pause, notice what they experience in their body, and allow events to unfold.

As my longtime mentor Dr. David Schnarch often observed, in any partnership, the person who wants something less automatically controls that aspect of the relationship. A couple's home is exactly as neat as the sloppier partner wants it to be. A couple has as much sex as the lower-desire partner wants. This means that in many different aspects of every couple's relationship, one partner will usually be less than satisfied. This is entirely normal.

But the lover with the higher desire still has options. In a collaborative alliance, partners find ways to do things both together and alone, so that each person gets much of what they want or need without their partner's participation. The partner who likes things neat can have their own spotless, well-ordered office or den. The mate with the greater sex drive can masturbate occasionally.

Many couples get into trouble when they try to find ways to satisfy both partners that *only* involve doing things together. At first both partners willingly compromise. But over time, the compromises grind the lovers together relentlessly, creating conflicts—and, eventually, emotional bottlenecks.

This is when both partners have to choose. They can fall into a coercive alliance, trying to suck compliance out of each other—and creating dirty pain. Or they can straighten their spines; talk to each other honestly about what they each want; move through the clean pain and discomfort together; and create a collaborative alliance that nurtures trust, respect, and love.

A coercive alliance is one of the most familiar forms of commonplace cruelty in committed relationships. This cruelty comes in an enormous range of forms—some overt, some subtle, some covert, and some downright surreal. Physical cruelty gets 98 percent of the attention, but the other forms of cruelty are much more common.

You'll read about different varieties of commonplace cruelty in the chapters to come. You're already familiar with some of them from your own partnership. Some, such as publicly dissing your partner (e.g., wearing a sweatshirt that says, "I'm with Stupid"), are considered socially acceptable; others, such as hitting your partner, are not. A few, such as dissing your lover's family or deliberately withholding sweetness from them, fall somewhere in the messy in-between.

But they're all forms of the same basic template: eating your partner's heart.

It won't surprise you to hear that heart eating never works. Instead, it creates dirty pain for both partners.

When couples can learn to recognize commonplace cruelty as it occurs—often with the help of a therapist—they can unhook it, move through it together, and come out stronger and closer on the other side.

COMPASS POINTS

- Every partnership is an alliance. It can be collaborative—based on mutual love, trust, and respect—or coercive, based on power and manipulation.

- Growth cannot happen in a coercive alliance. What *can* happen are death, or injury, or jail time.

- A committed partnership is never about giving yourself over to your partner or having them give themselves over to you. It's not about who controls the relationship or whose will triumphs. And it's never about who wins and who loses.

- In a collaborative alliance, both lovers say to each other, "We have a problem. We're going to accept the pain of it, walk through it together, and love and respect each other as we do it."

- The person who wants something less automatically controls that aspect of the relationship. The solution to this common dilemma is not coercion or manipulation, but doing things both alone and together, so that each partner gets much of what they need without their mate's participation.

- A coercive alliance is one of the most familiar forms of commonplace cruelty in committed relationships. Commonplace cruelty takes many forms, but they all involve harming your partner as a way to deal with your own pain. This only creates dirty pain for both lovers.

- When couples can learn to recognize commonplace cruelty, they can unhook it, move through it together, and come out stronger and closer on the other side.

13

The Hook

You want something important from your partner—sex, admiration, appreciation, emotional support, fun, attention, time, money, status, approval, encouragement, cheerfulness, optimism, or creativity. Yet they can't or won't give it to you.

Meanwhile, lots of *other* people may be very willing to give it to you. They might *already* be giving it to you, especially if the "it" is appreciation or approval or encouragement.

But the person you want it from most is your partner. And no matter what you say or do, you can't get it from them.

It seems like it would be so easy for them to give it to you. They know how much you want it from them. You ask them for it, over and over. They may have routinely given it to you in the past. They may regularly give it to their siblings, parents, kids, friends, boss, coworkers, or colleagues. But, somehow, circumstances have configured themselves so that it's impossible for them to give it to you.

This isn't true about every single thing you want from your partner. But it's true about some of the things that are most important to you.

You're not alone in this. *Your partner is having the exact same experience.* Try as they might, they can't get what they want from you.

This is the central conundrum of every committed relationship.

You can pull your hair out trying to get the things you want from your partner, but this will only piss them off and leave you more frustrated (and with less hair). Eventually you realize that the only way your partner can give you what you yearn for is if they change. But you also come to understand that you can't make them change.

Meanwhile, your partner is in the exact same situation. They want you to become someone other than who you are. But you *can't* be someone other than who you are.

Your desires and frustrations interlock, and the two of you block each other in an emotional stalemate.

In every committed partnership, things are going to vibrate in exactly this way. It's unavoidable.

If you *do* try to avoid this basic conundrum by leaving the relationship and finding someone else, the same dynamic will eventually appear in the new partnership (though usually with different specifics).

If you try to lower the heat, you'll deepen the conflict and frustration, which will result in *raising* the heat. If your partner tries to lower the heat, the same thing will happen.

No matter what strategy either of you uses, you and your partner will continue to block each other, just by being who you are.

This is not the result of a defect in you or your partner or the relationship. Even if the two of you are the world's most loving and mature couple, you'll continue to experience this same dynamic, time after time.

This is the hook you and your partner are stuck on.

This is the hook *every* set of committed partners is stuck on.

All of us want to find a way to get off this hook. You probably bought this book hoping to learn strategies for wiggling off it. But there aren't any.

Most of us try to wiggle our way off by blaming our partners, or blowing our anxiety through them. Every time, these strategies embed the hook deeper.

Some of us try to avoid the hook by not having a partner, or by limiting our relationships to casual encounters. Those strategies also embed the hook deeper, because the hook isn't a result of having a committed partner. *It's a result of being alive.* With or without a partner, you're going to bump up against your own limitations and fears, over and over. (That said, intimate relationships tend to make the invisible more visible.)

But when you have a committed partnership, you'll have more opportunities to see clearly just *how* you're on the hook, because those limitations will come up faster and more often. This is because your partner matters.

What *can* you do?

For starters, stop trying to wiggle off the hook. Accept that the hook is part of your life, and part of your partnership.

Use the five anchors from chapter 5 and described in more detail in chapter 35. These will help you slow yourself down, hold on to yourself, and act from the best and strongest parts of yourself.

Choose clean pain and discomfort. Make the choice to grow up, over and over.

You and your partner will never get off the hook. But when you activate the best parts of yourselves, you can unhook the toxic aspects of the relationship, and it can become a gateway to growth and intimacy.

In committed relationships, most people do one of two things:

- **They focus on their lover.** They pressure their partner for what they want, manipulate them, argue with them, try to get them to change or give in, and perhaps blame them for difficulties in the relationship. Their partner instinctively pushes back—or gives in and becomes resentful.

- **They focus on themselves.** They try to change to please their partner, tamp down their own desires, squeeze themselves into an uncomfortable role, and perhaps blame themselves for the difficulties in the relationship.

Both of these strategies work only briefly—and both embed the hook deeper.

Many people who focus on their partners read self-help books, hoping to find the perfect strategy for getting what they want from their lover. Some turn to prayer, asking God to change their partners in just the way they'd like. Some go to therapy to learn techniques for better communication, better sex, or better self-esteem.

Many folks who focus on themselves meditate regularly to keep calm—and to avoid a sense that they're being cheated out of sweetness in their relationship. Some ask God to keep them grateful or submissive. Some go to therapy to better understand themselves, but never bring that understanding to the relationship.

Both of these approaches avoid the real work of a committed partnership. If you focus on blaming your partner, you avoid taking responsibility for your part in the relationship. If you focus only on yourself, it becomes much harder to connect with your partner. In both cases, you ignore your own internal call to grow up.

If you're going to grow up, you need to live into the partnership from *both* directions. This takes the heat and pressure off any one person and puts them where they belong: inside the relationship itself.

Even though you can't wiggle off the hook, you can transform.

Sometimes, when *you* transform, the whole relationship transforms, too. Sometimes, seemingly miraculously, so does your partner.

Sometimes, but not always.

Much depends on your intention. If you change in the hope that your partner will change too, there's no guarantee that they will. In fact, usually they won't. In committed relationships, change seldom works as a tactic.

If you change just because your partner wants you to, that won't work, either. For one thing, you'll eventually get angry and resentful; for another, the change won't stick, because you haven't really transformed. You've just agreed to do your lover's bidding.

In my office, I've watched one partner turn to the other and say, "Look, just tell me what you want and I'll do it." This usually works for only a very short time. It also usually leads to conversations like this:

"I don't want you to just follow my orders."

"Are you fucking kidding me? For the past three years you've nagged me to get your way. Now, when I finally say yes, you're pissed off. I thought you'd be happy! What the hell do you want from me?"

"Why do you have to be so goddamned cold?"

"You're dissatisfied when I say no, and now you're dissatisfied when I say yes! What the *hell* is your problem?"

In every situation, we want our partner to do the right thing—to come from the best parts of themselves and to demand the same of us.

That's what we all want, deep down. It's why we're in a relationship with them. And it's what helps to create more relationship glue.

But that's not always what we tell them. *Often we tell them exactly the opposite.* We tell them we want an open marriage, when in fact we want them to stand in their integrity, hold us accountable, and say, "You can have me or you can have someone else, but you can't have both." We yell at them to back off about our pot smoking, when we actually want them to confront us about it. We badger them to buy a new sports car when we really want them to say, "No—we already agreed not to spend more than ten thousand dollars on a car."

Deep down, our partners want exactly the same thing from us.

Here's what most of us want our partners to understand, even though we'll never say it to them:

Please do the right thing. Whatever the situation is, I want you to figure out the right thing to do and then do it.

Don't try to get me to tell you what it is, because I often won't say. Sometimes I won't even know.

Sometimes I'll tell you that I want exactly the opposite of what I really want. When I do this, please see through my bullshit, ignore it, and do the right thing anyway.

I want you always to act from the best and strongest parts of yourself.

Please help me grow up. Insist that I straighten my spine and stand up.

This is what I most want from you, no matter what I tell you, and no matter how hard I may sometimes push you in the opposite direction.

Don't try to talk to me about any of this. If you do, I'll get confused or pissed off. Just do the right thing.

If you're in a relationship that's only now becoming serious, how can you and your partner prepare yourselves for all this?

You can't.

If you read this book, or some other serious book about committed relationships, you'll better understand some of what the two of you will encounter. But none of it will perfectly prepare you for what's to come.

You can do all the premarital counseling you want. You can attend workshops and retreats for couples. Your parents can sit you down and have a talk with you. But *nothing* is going to prepare you for dealing with the things that will actually happen in your relationship in real time.

As Dr. David Schnarch liked to say, the only thing that prepares you for marriage is marriage. The only thing that makes you ready for commitment is commitment. Until you're in it, you can't fully know what it is.

It's like learning to sail a boat. You can take a sailing course, but you don't really know what sailing is until you've stepped into a boat, cast off, and started sailing.

In this book, I've presented the fullest range of examples and stories that I can. But your own partnership will throw all kinds of unexpected situations and problems at you. Things will happen that neither of you can possibly anticipate. There won't be a simple formula for handling most of these. You and your partner will have to live into each unique situation, each new problem, and each fresh solution.

If you're still trying to wiggle off the hook, now is a good time to stop.

COMPASS POINTS

- Each of us wants something important from our partner that they can't or won't give to us, no matter what we say or do. Meanwhile, our partner wants something from us that we can't or won't give to them.

- This is not the result of a defect in you or your partner or your relationship. It's the hook every set of committed partners is stuck on.

- All of us want to find a way to get off this hook. But there isn't one.

- Some of us try to avoid the hook by not having a partner, or by limiting our relationships to casual encounters. Those strategies only embed the hook deeper, because the hook isn't a result of having a committed partner. It's a result of being alive. With or without a partner, you're always going to bump up against your own limitations and fears.

- We all need to accept the hook as part of life. But when you and your partner activate the best parts of yourselves, you can unhook the toxic parts of the relationship—and your partnership can become a gateway to growth and intimacy.

- It's not enough to focus just on your lover or just on yourself. Both approaches only embed the hook deeper, because they try to avoid the real work and purpose of a committed partnership. If you're going to grow up, you need to live into the partnership from both directions.

- Sometimes, when you change, the whole relationship changes, too. Sometimes, seemingly miraculously, so does your partner. But if you change in the hope that your partner will change, they won't. If you change just because your partner wants you to, that won't work, either.

- In every situation, we want our partner to do the right thing— to come from the best parts of themselves, and to demand the same of us. That's what we all want, deep down. It's why we're in a relationship with them.

- But that's not always what we tell them. Often we tell them exactly the opposite. When we do, we want our partners to ignore our bullshit and do the right thing anyway.

- No book, workshop, retreat, or talk from your parents will prepare you for dealing with the things that will actually happen in your relationship in real time.

- Your own partnership will throw all kinds of unexpected situations and problems at you. You and your partner will have to live into each unique situation, each new problem, and each fresh solution.

14

You Are Not Each
Other's Baby

When we were infants, our lives focused on being fed, being held, and being kept warm and dry. Meanwhile, our parents focused on fulfilling these needs for us.

Soon we learned that if we cried, we'd get a nipple or a hug or something else we wanted.

As we grew older, we discovered other ways to get our needs met. We pointed; we reached out and grabbed; we said a few words; we kissed mama or daddy; we threw a tantrum. We learned ever more complex and varied ways to get what we wanted.

By the time we entered adolescence, we developed a large repertoire of techniques for getting our way: arguing, nagging, flattering, trading, promising, accusing, lying, pleasing, appeasing, threatening, fighting, and so on.

Emotionally, though, we didn't change our basic orientation. Our primary focus was still on getting what we wanted. This was all part of our normal human development.

But that development doesn't stop in early adolescence. Growing into adulthood means learning to see the world through a lens bigger than *How do I get what I want?*

Yet many people never grow beyond this question. All that changes for them are the objects of their desire. Instead of reaching for a nipple to suck on, they focus their efforts on acquiring money, or security, or sex, or love, or status, or appreciation. They may use a complex and sophisticated set of strategies, but are really just reaching for a nipple.

In some ways this is entirely understandable. The desire to have someone else take care of us, and meet our every need, is baked into our DNA as we grow in the womb.

But if we're going to be more than babies living in adult bodies, we need to do more with our lives than look for nipples to suck on.

Many physically adult people approach romance as a way to offer their nipple in exchange for someone else's. One common variation is trophy wives or husbands, who provide the nipples of youth and attractiveness in exchange for the nipples of wealth and security. It's a business deal—a socially acceptable transactional exchange in which both partners simultaneously exploit each other.

Other folks see romance as a bargain made in a Middle Eastern bazaar: they try to get as much nipple out of the other person as they can, while providing their partner with as little nipple as possible. We see this in men who get women pregnant and then disappear, and in gold diggers who marry wealthy folks and then treat them badly or divorce them.

These are all people who failed to grow up.

Sadly, much of our culture reinforces a view of romance as two infants suckling each other.

The most common theme in music—from opera to blues to Top 40—is *Make me happy by doing and being what I want.* In most of these songs, what do lovers call each other? *Baby.*[14]

But we're *not* babies. We're adults. We diminish ourselves *and* our partners by acting like infants.

Plus, acting like an infant just isn't sexy.

Part of the blame for this falls squarely on the shoulders of therapists. In therapy sessions, many therapists talk to their clients about "getting your needs met." But in a romantic relationship, it is *not* the job of either partner to meet the other's needs. That's the job of a parent with a baby.

If you view your partner as a one-stop shop for getting your needs met, eventually they're going to resent it. They'll close down on you and say, "I'm not your servant or your mama or your dildo or your sex doll. It's not my job to give you whatever you want whenever you want it."

---

14 In the early 1990s, hip-hop culture repeatedly made adults into infants. Rapper Flavor Flav wore a pacifier around his neck in a Public Enemy video; in John Singleton's *Boyz n the Hood,* seventeen-year-old Dooky (played by Dedrick Gobert) sucked on a pacifier throughout the film.

When a client in my therapy office says to me, "My partner isn't giving me what I need," I tell them, "Good. That means both of you are normal. If your partner *did* act like your surrogate mother, you'd both have a shitload of emotional work to do. It's not your partner's job to provide for you when you're hungry, or horny, or scared, or whatever you're experiencing. It's nice when they choose to do something you like, but it's not their role or obligation. Because you're an adult, you can't—and shouldn't—expect them to take care of you. Committed partnerships are about balancing the energies of autonomy and togetherness, not about people being surrogate parents to each other."

I've also had clients who bounced from one partnership to another, looking to find someone who will fulfill all their needs. They spend years—even decades—nipple shopping, with (of course) no success. They come to me thinking they need a better way to shop for the right nipple. But what they actually need is to grow up.

One common variant on this theme is when people tell me that their ex-partners abandoned them. This simply isn't true. Adults *leave* each other. They don't *abandon* each other.

You can abandon a child, because a child doesn't have the resources or abilities to fend for themselves. But when an adult leaves their partner, the ex-partner isn't going to starve to death or be at a loss about how to navigate the world.

If your partner leaves you, you'll hurt—perhaps a great deal—but you won't die or get swallowed up by the world because of it.

What we call a "fear of abandonment" is nothing more than normal fear and dread—of loss, of pain, of change, and of the unknown.

If and when your partner does leave you—or you leave your partner—this doesn't mean you're no longer an adult. So act like an adult: lick your wounds, pick yourself up, and move forward with your life.

I am not advocating that you somehow spontaneously get over your loss, or that you pick yourself up by your own bootstraps. The first is emotionally impossible; the second is physically impossible; and both are bullshit. I'm saying that each of us gets to grieve our losses—and that fully grieving makes us more human, not less. Yet we must also be mindful that we may sometimes stay stuck rather than grieve fully and move forward.

Some folks cite the Bible as a source of the message that lovers should be babies for each other. They point to Genesis 2:24, which (in the New King James Version) says, "Therefore a man shall leave his father and mother and be joined to his wife, and they shall become one flesh." They interpret this to mean that when someone gets married, it's their partner's job to take care of them—and that each partner no longer has a separate self.

But the text doesn't say anything of the sort. That one flesh is the *relationship,* with its own unique energy and life.

Being in a marriage doesn't mean you stop being a separate person. Genesis 2:24 is about commitment, not dependency.

Yes, commitment creates a new entity called *us.* But *you* and *I* never disappear. Trying to make *you* and *I* go away is a fantasy. Couples who do try to become one don't grow up; instead, they grow more and more immature together.

In any committed relationship, sooner or later your partner will let you know that they *do* have a separate self—and that they need to balance that separateness with being connected to you.

We think that emotional nourishment comes from getting our needs met. But that's not how life works. Emotional nourishment comes from growing up.

The quest for fulfilling our emotional needs can be endless. We can get stuck on a hamster wheel, chasing one form of fulfillment after another.

People who build their lives around meeting their needs tend to be anxious, fearful, and frustrated. In contrast, people who have accepted the clean pain and discomfort of growing up have a relaxed readiness and an easy confidence about them. Their focus is not on acquiring fulfillment, but on being fully present. Because of that presence, whatever happens has the potential to be emotionally nourishing.

Getting your needs met and advocating for what is important to you are two very different things. They also come from two very different places inside you.

Trying to get your needs met comes from your weakest places; you're trying to get someone else to fill those empty spots.

Advocating for what's important to you comes from your strengths. It tells the world, "This is who I am, what I stand for, and what I care about." At the same time, you don't expect or demand that anyone else give it to you—and you don't respond like a frustrated child if you don't get it.

As Dr. Schnarch often said to me, marriage is not like mother's milk—and it's not designed to be. It's not your job to make your partner happy, or fulfill their desires, or emotionally take care of them. It's not their job to make you happy, or fulfill your desires, or emotionally take care of you, either. Neither of you owes that to the other.

In a committed relationship, what you *are* each owed is the opportunity to face yourself and grow up. This is exactly what your partnership *will* supply you with.

COMPASS POINTS

- *How do I get what I want?* is an important question for an infant or a child. But if we're going to be more than babies living in adult bodies, we need to do more with our lives than chase after answers to that question.

- Many people never grow beyond this narcissistic quest—in part because that quest is often reinforced by culture, religion, and even some therapists.

- If you view your partner as a one-stop shop for getting your needs met, eventually they'll either leave you or demand something better.

- Getting your needs met and advocating for what is important to you are two very different things. Trying to get your needs met comes from your weakest places; advocating for what's important to you comes from your strengths.

- Being in a committed partnership doesn't mean you stop being a separate person. Commitment creates a new entity called *us*, but *you* and *I* never disappear.

- It's not your job to make your partner happy, or fulfill their desires, or emotionally take care of them. It's not their job to make you happy, or fulfill your desires, or emotionally take care of you, either. Neither of you owes that to the other.

- In a committed relationship, what you *are* each owed is the opportunity to face yourself and grow up. This is what your partnership *will* supply you with.

15

Monsters Operate on Vibes

We mostly experience emotions in our bodies, not only in our heads. That's why we need to pay close attention to what our bodies tell us.

During the past two decades, we've learned over and over that biology (our sensations and emotions) usually trumps biography (the stories we tell ourselves about what's happening). The more we pay attention to what we experience in our bodies, the better we understand ourselves and our relationships.

For many years, most psychologists thought that cognitive insight was the key to transformation. They told us that if we can understand the story behind something—if we can unlock its meaning—then we can unravel it, and then write a new, better story.

But this idea doesn't fully match reality.

It turns out that the key to transformation is not only cognitive insight, but also visceral experience.

When this transformation happens to someone else, we can see physical changes in their eyes and posture; we can hear the change in their voice. They straighten up. Their eyes shine with clarity. Their voice is stronger, calm, and assured.

Yet all of this usually *precedes* their cognitive understanding. That comes later—sometimes only seconds later, but often not for weeks or months.

In many cases of transformation, cognitive insight is absent entirely. People suddenly know in their bodies what they need to do, without understanding why. Or something simply seems right or wrong to them, even though they can't explain it or verbalize it.

It's essential to take this form of knowing seriously, and to not dismiss it, override it, or overrule it with questions or doubts. These bodily sensations, which are often called intuition or vibrations or vibes, are essential to understanding ourselves and each other.

If you're not sure what you think about something, consult your body. Where is there tightness or rigidity? Where is there fluidity or relaxation? Where is there pain? Where is there heat? Is it pleasant or unpleasant? Gently move your attention into that sensation, as if you're getting into a bathtub. What images and thoughts arise as you do this?

An entire branch of psychotherapy is built around awareness of the body. It's usually called somatic psychology, or body psychotherapy, or some other variation of those terms. This form of psychology doesn't dismiss thinking or cognitive awareness. It simply says, *Look to your body first.*

Our bodies are organic antennae and amplifiers, constantly broadcasting, receiving, and boosting a variety of signals. We're all familiar with the vibes we routinely broadcast to strangers: *I'm friendly. I'm busy. Come here. Leave me alone. Hurry up. I'm scared. I want you. Help me. Back off, Jack!* These vibratory messages are clear, simple, honest, and direct.

But in relationships, many of us use vibes in dishonest or contradictory ways.

The most widespread variation is sliming. We send our partner a vibe that conveys disrespect, devaluation, or dismissal, but without using nasty words or a negative tone. Our partner, who is deeply attuned to our energy, immediately picks up that vibratory message in their body. They can physically sense the dissonance between our vibe and our words. This hurts, and often they react strongly. Then we feign ignorance, pretend that we did nothing, and accuse our partner of overreacting.

This leads to crazy-making conversations like this one:

"Did you pick up the dry cleaning?"

"You bet."

"All seven pieces?"

"Of course all seven pieces! Why the hell *wouldn't* I pick up all seven pieces?"

"What's gotten into you? Why are you suddenly yelling at me? All I did was ask about the dry cleaning."

"Yeah, but I get the sense that you think I'm too dumb to be trusted with a simple errand."

"I don't know what you're talking about. If you have self-esteem issues, go see a therapist."

Sliming messages are often communicated with an ambiguous gesture or look or tone. Over time, most couples get better and better at this. Soon they can slime one another with a small movement, a slight change in posture, or a minor change in the modulation of their voice. They learn how to be cruel to each other while leaving no fingerprints.

Maybe there's a look your lover gives you just before they start hammering on you for not being as successful as their parents. After a couple of years, they don't even have to say anything. They can just give you the look—and suddenly you're shouting at them.

Meanwhile, to an outside observer, you're obviously the crazy one. Your partner didn't say a damn thing, but you're ranting and raving like they called you a monster. And, based on your behavior, the bystander wonders if maybe you are.

That's not all. Suppose the observer says to you, "What's wrong? What happened?" You might say, "What do you mean, what happened? Did you see the look my partner just gave me?" Now the bystander is *sure* you're a basket case.

When someone slimes their partner, it understandably drives the partner bananas. The partner's body knows exactly what's going on because it picks up on the micro-aggression. But they can't figure out cognitively what's happening. They just have a sense that they're being attacked. Often, the situation also seems completely out of their control. Sometimes they blame themselves, or ask themselves, *What's wrong with me?*

Sliming can be as simple as not responding when your mate calls to you from the other room. Then, a minute later, when they come in and say, "There you are. Didn't you hear me calling you?" you say, "No."

Because your partner is attuned to your energy, they know you're lying to them. They might not say anything, but now they're upset. Your small lie—that form of micro-gaslighting—hurts them and subverts the relationship.

Sliming is a classic form of commonplace cruelty in committed relationships. No direct physical harm gets inflicted, but psychological and emotional harm do.

In couples therapy, I often work each person's nervous system, as well as with the couple's collective nervous system, to help them develop resources so they can fully experience and then metabolize these constrictive energies. Not learning to metabolize and process these energies only sets the stage for further cruel and reflexive micro-aggressive actions.

Then there's the equally cruel—and equally common—combination of sliming and acquiescence. You tell your partner that you want something from them, and—often only after much argument or resistance—they give it to you. But they give it to you in a half-hearted or passive-aggressive way. Then when you say, "What's wrong?" or "What's going on?" they say, "This is what you said you wanted. But now that you're getting it, you're complaining. What the hell is wrong with you?"

In another common form of sliming, one lover does something legal and moral that the other lover is uncomfortable with. Maybe they put on edgy or unfashionable clothes, or ask for anal sex, or try to talk politics at a dinner party where it's sure to create an argument. But instead of confronting themselves about their own discomfort—or simply saying to their partner, "I'm uncomfortable with that; let's talk about it when we can"—they look their partner in the eye and say, "That's inappropriate" or "That's immature."

On the surface, this sounds like a simple observation of social limits. But the message it conveys to their lover is, *That thing you want or are doing—there's something wrong with you for wanting it or doing it. Everyone knows this—but evidently you don't, so I have to clue you in. That makes me more grown-up than you. Also, you're a pervert for doing it or saying it or wanting it, and you're a moron for not knowing that it's wrong. Shame on you.*

That's pretty serious sliming. Yet it's actually an expression of the uncomfortable partner's limits. Here's what it really means: *You've pushed me up against my own limitations, and I'm scared. So I can be comfortable again, I'm going to get you to do something, or stop doing something.*

This makes the other partner think, *Why are you so goddamn uptight? Get off my damn back!* instead of *If you're scared, either deal with it or tell me you're scared.*

When partners get slimed for being inappropriate, they often think, *I wish to God you'd stop doing this, but I'm not even sure what "this" is.* It's another way people use to get around their own issues without leaving any fingerprints.

Two other common forms of sliming are overpowering and underpowering.

Overpowering involves being so assertive or repetitive or over-communicative with your partner that they become uncomfortable. This commonly includes bullying, nagging, overexplaining, lecturing, or simply talking too loudly or slowly, as if your partner has a hearing disorder. In overpowering, you hook all sorts of extra emotional content onto what would otherwise be a simple message.

Underpowering involves giving your partner only part of what you know they want or need, especially in conversations. Through your tone or timing or level of engagement, you withhold from them something you know they want or expect. Usually this is your attention or caring.

Each of us has our own preferred ways to underpower, but here are some common variations:

- You listen to your partner briefly, then change the subject before they're finished.
- While talking with your partner, you send texts or surf the Web or check your e-mail.
- You interrupt the conversation to make or take a less-than-urgent phone call.
- You preemptively disengage: When your partner says, "Can we talk about this later?" you say "Okay" and quickly walk away or immediately disconnect the phone. Or you begin a conversation by paying close attention, then suddenly say, "I need to go," and end it.
- You pretend to pay attention, and perhaps periodically say, "Uh huh" and "Okay." But you let your partner know that you don't really give a rat's ass about the conversation—either through your bored tone or by asking them questions such as, "Who are we talking about, again?" or "Sorry, could you repeat all that?"
- You say the right words—"I'm sorry" or "That must really hurt" or "Go on, I'm listening"—but in a bored or uncommitted or uncaring tone.
- While you and your partner are having (or about to have) sex, you bring up a mundane subject—e.g., "Will you pick up Anita after school tomorrow?" or "The car is making a funny noise."

People often respond to overpowered messages with underpowered ones, and vice versa. In committed relationships, this often turns into a dance in which one partner pursues the other by overpowering, and the other flees through underpowering.

When sliming takes place in a therapy session and I call attention to it, the partner who did the sliming says, "Resmaa, I didn't do anything," and hopes their partner will acquiesce or take their side.

But what often happens instead is that the other partner calls their lover on their sliming. They straighten their spine and speak their truth. This can blow the relationship apart—or it can blow it open and create an opportunity for growth and transformation.

Two cousins to sliming are *optimistic gaslighting* and *spirit murder*. The first is an attempted dodge whose vibes can seem like a slap in the face. The second is a form of cruelty whose vibes can seem like a hard punch in the gut.

Optimistic gaslighting is a faux sense of positivity that one partner performs for the other in order to avoid a very real conflict or challenge. For example:

- "Oh, don't get upset about it; everything will work out. You'll see."
- "We're resilient. We'll be able to wait this out."
- "It's not a big deal. Hey, let's go to a movie. No, better idea—throw me on the bed and fuck me."
- "Stop worrying so much. Don't you want to live in hope rather than fear?"

These all sound like healthy responses—and if what's at stake is genuinely minor, they might be. But often one partner uses optimistic gaslighting as a form of denial. They're actually saying, *There's an important conflict in our relationship—or in some other area of our lives—that I'm too frightened to face. I don't want you to get mad at me. Or maybe I don't want to get mad at you. Or maybe both. Either way, I'm going to pretend that the conflict isn't important—or that it will go away on its own if we both deny or avoid it.*

Although this conflict is usually between the two lovers, it might come from outside the relationship. For example, imagine that sixty-year-old Adrianna loses her job in her company's recent downsizing. She knows that her chances of getting rehired at her age are very small, and she's understandably worried about her family's financial future. Although Adrianna and her husband Ben have had a long and pretty stable marriage, Adrianna's sudden unexpected job loss scares the shit out of Ben. He can't interrogate his own fear, so he waves off his wife's concerns. "Hon, you'll find a new job—maybe something much better than what you've had. Let's not wring our hands over this. You know how to land on your feet."

Those words might sound good to an outsider listening in on the conversation. But they don't to Adrianna, who picks up on Ben's vibes and energy. She can't put words to her sense of apprehension, but her body recognizes that his optimism is a performance.

Ben needs to confront his own fear, experience it as clean pain, and move through it. He probably also needs to say to Adrianna, "Holy crap. I'm scared half to death that we'll end up living in a studio apartment for the rest of our lives." Until he does, his optimistic gaslighting will likely continue—and Adrianna will continue to distrust each repeated performance.

Spirit murder, the most toxic of all of these moves, is a vibratory challenge to someone's value or existence, often expressed (or accompanied) by words of contempt. The energetic message of spirit murder is: *You're worthless or subhuman. You don't belong. You don't deserve to belong.*

The verbal message paired with these vibes is usually less direct. For example:

- "You do know how to tell time, don't you?"
- "I'm calling the twelve-year-old next door. Maybe he can teach you something about maturity. You're certainly refusing to learn anything about it from me."
- "Congratulations! You're now officially the most pathetic man I've ever met."
- "This is why I tell my family that you were raised by wolves."

If you want to see a classic example of spirit murder, go online, find videos of the 2022 confirmation hearings of Supreme Court Justice Ketanji Brown Jackson, and watch her being questioned by Lindsay Graham, Tom Cotton, and Marsha Blackburn. Their marginally veiled attacks and attempts to dominate her straddled the line of overt sadism.

If both members of a couple get stuck in mutual spirit murder, the relationship is probably over. But if both can grow up enough to directly acknowledge, express, and metabolize their own pain, then their relationship has an opportunity to grow out of a negative feedback loop into a positive one.

COMPASS POINTS

- We mostly experience emotions in our bodies, not our heads. That's why we need to pay close attention to what our bodies tell us.
- Biology (our sensations and emotions) usually trumps biography (the stories we tell ourselves about what is happening).
- The key to transformation is not only cognitive insight, but also visceral experience.
- When this transformation happens to someone else, we can see physical changes in them. Cognitive understanding usually comes later.
- Sometimes there's no cognitive understanding at all. Someone suddenly knows in their body what they need to do, without understanding why. Or something simply seems right or wrong.
- Lovers often hurt each other through vibratory messages— especially through sliming, in which one partner sends a vibe that conveys contempt, disrespect, or dismissal, but without using overt cues. Then they deny the sliming.
- *Optimistic gaslighting* is a form of faux positivity that one partner performs for the other in order to avoid addressing a conflict or challenge. This performance may look good to an outsider, but the person's partner may experience it as a slap in the face.
- *Spirit murder,* the most toxic of all of these moves, is a vibratory challenge to someone's value or existence, often expressed or accompanied by words of contempt. The energetic message of spirit murder is: *You're worthless or subhuman. You don't belong.* The target usually experiences spirit murder as a punch in the gut.
- When someone calls their lover on their sliming, or gaslighting, or spirit murder, it can blow the relationship apart—or blow it open and create growth and transformation.

16

The Communication Trap

Most couples think they don't communicate clearly. They come to therapy hoping to learn to communicate better.

Wanting to be helpful, therapists give them a bagful of communication tools. *Use "I" statements. Take turns speaking and listening, without interrupting. Say, "Here's what I heard," and then paraphrase what your partner said.*

These can be helpful, but they're only technical fixes. When a couple is stuck in an emotional bottleneck, these tools become ineffectual. They're like throwing a drowning person an oar.

Most couples already communicate extremely well. As Dr. Schnarch taught me, the real issue is that neither partner likes the messages they get from the other.

People often say they wish their partner understood them better. What they really mean, though, is, "I wish my partner would agree with me more" or "I wish my partner would do—or think, or experience—what I want them to."

In my office, clients often say to me, "Resmaa, I keep telling and telling my partner, 'I want this,' or 'I don't like that,' or 'You'd make me so happy if you'd just do X, Y, and Z.' And after all these years, they still don't hear me."

I tell them, "Your partner hears you loud and clear. They're just not willing or able to do or be what you want.

"You keep telling them the same thing over and over, expecting them to have an epiphany and suddenly become a different person. But that's not going to happen. If it were possible, it would have happened already.

"This doesn't mean you shouldn't advocate strongly for what you want. But it does mean you need to come from the best parts of yourself, not the weak and whiny parts.

"The two of you have to keep grinding on this. Your relationship will only get better if you work through it. You have to stand up for who you are and what's important to you—and then, somehow, the two of you have to move through it together. It might happen tomorrow, or it might take years. But there's no other clean way."

In the old comic strip *Peanuts,* when Lucy promises Charlie Brown that she's not going to pull the football away when he runs up to kick it, he knows perfectly well what's going to happen. She's going to do exactly what she's done before: pull the ball away from him. Even though she says, "I promise not to do it this time," both of them know exactly what that means: *Of course I'm going to do it this time, just like the hundred times before.*

The only way this pattern is going to change is if Charlie raises his game. He needs to do something different, such as run up to her, stop, put his hands on his hips, and stare at her, instead of kicking the ball. But he needs to do it because it's what he wants, not as a way to try to change Lucy.

The real question each of us needs to ask ourselves is never *How can I communicate better with my partner?* or *How can I get my partner to give me different messages?* It's *How can I learn to tolerate the messages my partner gives me that I don't like?* The five anchors can help us do this.

When you do receive a painful message from your partner—that they don't give a rat's ass about your long commute, or your mandolin trio, or your huge erection (or aching clitoris)—you need to use the five anchors to soothe yourself down and try to stay loving and connected.

Recently I've been working with Sara and Uma, a young couple who have been married for five years. In our first session, Uma laid out what she believed was the problem.

SARA AND UMA

"Sara doesn't listen to me. She blows off everything I say—if she pays attention at all."

Sara responded immediately. "That's not true at all. I do listen and I do pay attention."

"You sure don't act like you do," Uma said. She looked at me. "I tell her, 'If you're not going to listen to me, then you ain't gettin' none.'"

"Jesus, not again," Sara said. "Resmaa, she's been doing this for the past five years. She's always held sex over my head. It pisses me off."

Uma sighed and said to me, "We keep going round and round like this. I'm really tired of it. We need to learn how to communicate better."

I said to Uma, "I don't care if you have sex with your wife or not. But you just told me that you think Sara doesn't hear you. So help me understand something. If you think that the way to get her to hear you is to tell her she can't hump you, how has that made her hear you better over the past five years?"

Uma said angrily, "I don't have to hump her if I don't want to."

I looked at both of them and said, "You two actually have great communication. Uma, you've made it very clear to Sara that if she doesn't do what you say, she's not getting any. She's heard that. She just said so a minute ago. You've told her exactly what you want and what the consequences are. She's just not interested in doing what you want.

"It sounds to me like your idea of communication is her obeying you. But she's communicated perfectly well that she's not going to do whatever you want her to do, whether you have sex with her or not.

"You two are here because you've been communicating really well, and neither one of you likes what you're hearing."

I turned to Sara. "Have you been hearing what she's been telling you these past five years?"

Sara laughed and said, "Yes, sir. Loud and clear."

Most of us wish our partners would think the way we do and agree with us about everything, or at least everything important. But that's not how committed relationships work. Your partner will *never* agree with you about everything, or even most things. Sometimes they won't even agree with you on what's important and what isn't. *That's why they're your partner.*

This is a plus, not a minus. If the two of you agreed on almost everything, you would have some serious issues to work through. You'd also get bored with each other—so bored that you'd likely break up, or withdraw from each other, or want to have affairs with other people.

When you first got together, it might have *seemed* like you agreed on almost everything. But that was an illusion. If you both enjoyed kayaking (or seeing plays, or visiting the zoo) together, what you mostly enjoyed was being with each other. If you both liked many of the same movies, you also probably didn't talk about the ones you had differing opinions on. Even when the two of you were enjoying red hot sex, you were doing different things: you were having sex with your lover, and they were having sex with you.

Throughout all of these activities, the two of you communicated very clearly. Without even talking about it, you agreed that being with each other was more important than being a fan of kayaking or plays or zoos or whatever you were doing. You also had an unspoken agreement to not talk about the things that might call out any conflicts between you.

But once a commitment was made, those conflicts—as well as your likes, dislikes, preferences, and opinions—naturally started bubbling to the surface.

The longer you're with your partner, the better you get at "communicating." We saw earlier how a tiny gesture or a momentary glance can communicate messages such as *You're not important to me right now* or *I'm sick of your bullshit* or *Come and take me, NOW.*

Sometimes these messages are cognitive, but more often we sense them wordlessly, in our bodies. And there's a potentially confusing flip side to both of these aspects.

On the cognitive side, we can grow so attuned to every signal our partner gives us that we may sometimes take personally what isn't personal at all.

When Allie gets home, her lover, Joel, kisses her and asks her how her day went. She gives him a disgusted sigh. Joel pulls away and asks angrily, "What did I do?" Allie drops her handbag on the sofa and says, "You didn't do anything, honey. You asked me about my day, and my day sucked, so I sighed."

In the middle of the night, Tina touches her wife Amy's shoulder. Suddenly Amy gets out of bed and hurries away. When she returns a few minutes later, Tina says sadly, "You used to like it when I pulled you close in the middle of the night." Amy says, "And I still do. I suddenly realized we forgot to let the cat in."

We can make a similar mistake with our body's signals. If your stomach tightens just as your partner drives up, you might think, *Uh oh. Trouble ahead. I can sense it.* But people's stomachs naturally constrict and expand all the time. Because the two events—your partner driving up and your stomach tightening—coincided, you might have imagined meaning where none existed.

In this situation, it's important to shelve the assumed meaning for a brief time and get more information. This can be as simple as reminding yourself that your partner matters to you—and then reminding them of the same thing by touching their arm and saying, "Hey, hon. How are you doing?"

When you first fall in love with your partner, it's easy to overlook or ignore signs of potential conflict. After a few years, though, it becomes even easier to do the opposite: imagine conflicts or problems that don't exist. This is yet another reason why committed partnerships are not for the faint of heart.

COMPASS POINTS

- Most couples think they don't communicate clearly, so they go to therapy to learn communication tools. But when a couple is stuck in an emotional stalemate, those tools are ineffectual.
- Most couples already communicate extremely well. The real issue is that neither partner likes the messages they get from the other.
- The question each of us needs to ask ourselves is *How can I learn to tolerate the messages my partner gives me that I don't like?* The five anchors can help us do this.
- Your partner will never agree with you about everything, or even most things. That's why they're your partner.
- When you and your partner first got together, it might have seemed like you agreed on almost everything. But without even talking about it, you agreed that you wouldn't talk about those things that might call out any conflicts between you.
- Once you and your partner committed to each other, those conflicts—as well as your likes, dislikes, preferences, and opinions—naturally started bubbling to the surface.
- The longer you're with your partner, the better you naturally get at communicating. But sometimes we can grow so attuned to our partner's signals—and to signals from our own bodies—that we imagine conflicts that don't exist.

17

Both/And

In life, many of our choices appear to be *either/or*—stay together or break up, exercise or let my body go, keep my job or stay home to raise the kids.

But many of these apparent dualities are actually *both/and*. Both options are true or valid or valuable, though not necessarily at the same time.

This is particularly the case with couples, who experience all sorts of apparent dualities: my way vs. her way, my family vs. his family, what I want vs. what you want.

Every *either/or* conundrum naturally makes both partners uncomfortable. Each conundrum also naturally pushes couples toward emotional bottlenecks—and toward growth.

Part of your job as a loving partner is to *not* try to block, avoid, or flee from this discomfort. It also means not trying to coax, debate, argue, bully, threaten, trick, bribe, or bullshit your partner into letting you get your way. It *also* means not giving in to your partner's attempts to use any of these same dirty-pain strategies.

Instead, both of you need to live into the *either/or* conundrum until it transforms into *both/and*. You may also need to encourage your lover to follow your lead.

Each situation has both limitations and possibilities. Most of us tend to focus reflexively on the limitations, but when we shift to focusing on the possibilities, a different dynamic can unfold.

In its simplest form, *both/and* can mean clean compromise or creative solutions. *Do we stay together or break up?* Maybe you and your spouse stay married, but each of you maintains and pays for your own apartment. *Do I exercise or let my body go?* Perhaps you and your lover can take long walks or bike rides together—mostly enjoying each other's company, but moving your bodies at the same time. *Do I keep my job or stay home to raise the kids?* Maybe you arrange to cut back to three days a week and work from home on two of those days.

Those examples are almost too easy. Most *both/and* situations involve something that's deeply important to both partners, so there won't often be such a simple, cognitive, or tactical solution. Usually you and your partner will need to keep grinding against each other, while staying as loving and present as you can, until an alchemical transformation occurs.

When this happens, you'll know it. And the result will never be *I win and my partner loses,* or vice versa. It will be some form of *both/and.*

HECTOR, IRINA, AND BRIAN

Hector and Irina have been married for almost twenty years. Hector is Black; Irina is white. They live in Cincinnati, a few miles from Irina's dad, Brian. Irina has two sisters, one in Seattle, the other in Baltimore.

Brian is a bigot. He's not a hood-wearing, hate-mongering sort of bigot, but he never approved of Irina's marriage to a Black man. When she and Hector first announced their engagement, Brian said to Hector, "I don't understand why you couldn't find yourself a nice Black woman. There's plenty of them around."

Over the past twenty years, relations between Hector and Brian have remained stiff and tense. At family gatherings, Brian is polite to his son-in-law but treats him like an outsider. Meanwhile, he hugs and banters with the white husbands of Irina's sisters.

Irina loves her father, who in most respects has been a good dad to her. But she hates his racism. She's challenged him about it on many occasions, but he just says, "Sweetie, it's how I was raised. People shouldn't marry animals. Men shouldn't marry men. And white people shouldn't marry Black people. I don't hate Hector. He seems like a decent man. I just don't think he should be married to you."

One day Irina got a call from her father. "Sweetie, I need your help. You know those back problems I've been having all these years? Today the doctor told me I'm going to need spine surgery. That means eight weeks of recovery in bed. I'm hoping you can help."

As Irina soon discovered, "help" meant one of three things: staying with her dad in his home for eight weeks; letting him recover in her and Hector's den for those weeks; or hiring a live-in aide to care for Brian for almost two months.

The aide was out of the question: Irina and Hector didn't have the money for one, and Brian didn't either. Irina spoke to both her sisters, but neither could leave her job and family for more than a few days.

Irina faced a huge dilemma. She didn't want to leave her husband and home for eight weeks. But she also didn't want Hector to have to endure Brian for that long.

Irina and Hector talked about the issue over and over, but they kept going in circles. They both sensed that they were stuck in a huge double bind. There seemed to be only two choices, and both sucked.

The same questions kept coming up for Irina: *How do we deal with the fact that I love my husband and my father? How can I help my dad without making things difficult or impossible for Hector?* Both spouses managed to avoid blaming or sliming each other—but both seemed stuck in an emotional bottleneck.

Whenever they discussed the situation, each partner was careful to use the five anchors to soothe themselves down, stay present, and not blame the other. On several occasions, one mate reminded the other, "Whatever we do or don't do, it's going to be difficult and painful. Let's go for the clean pain and discomfort."

They ground together on this issue for almost three weeks. Meanwhile, Brian's surgery date drew closer and closer.

With surgery only a few days away, Irina and Hector finally reached critical mass. As they discussed their options over breakfast for the umpteenth time, Irina suddenly burst into tears, stood up, and shouted, "I *KNOW* MY DADDY IS A DICK SOMETIMES! I HATE THAT PART OF HIM! I WISH I COULD UNDICKIFY HIM! BUT I CAN'T! AND I CAN'T MAKE HIM NOT BE MY DADDY!"

Hector kissed his wife on the back of her neck and said, "Ri, I wish we could undickify the whole world."

For reasons neither spouse could explain, they had popped out of the bottleneck.

"We take him in," Hector said. "But we refuse to take in his dickishness. He has to leave that outside our door. And I need to be the one to tell him."

Irina wiped her eyes and nodded. "That's right. You do."

That afternoon, Hector called Brian and offered to let him stay in their home during his recovery. But Hector also laid down clear ground rules: "This is our home, which means *we* make the rules, and everyone in our home has to follow them. You'll be our guest, and we promise to treat you with care and respect. We expect the same from you, just as we would from any guest. If you break a household rule, or disrespect anyone in our home, you'll have to go somewhere else. None of this is negotiable. Is all of this clear to you, Brian?"

For a few seconds there was silence on the other end of the line. Then Brian said softly, "Thank you for your kindness, Hector. I accept your offer."

Irina and Hector were able to create a *both/and* solution once they understood that it would have to be on *their* terms as a couple. Not Irina's terms. Not Hector's. Not Brian's. Their decision had to be based on the integrity of their relationship—and on being willing to allow new things to emerge.

They couldn't have gotten to that solution if they hadn't willingly and respectfully let themselves grind together on the dilemma for weeks, accepting the clean pain and discomfort involved. They also needed to use the five anchors to hold on to themselves, so they wouldn't lose their minds and start blaming each other.

This process didn't just create a workable solution for Hector and Irina; it helped both spouses build capacity in their relationship. They came out of critical mass stronger, more flexible, more resilient, and better able to handle future conflicts.

Our very bodies are *both/and* organisms. If you regularly observe what your body experiences over a week or two, you'll notice it going through a cycle of rigidness and fluidity, like a long-term in-breath and out-breath. You may be relaxed and open—naturally in alignment with the world—for a day or a week or a month. Then, for no reason you can discern, for a time you may become tight and constricted, or awkward and out of alignment with everything.

Your relationship with your lover follows a similar, natural cycle of fluidity and rigidness. There will be times when things seem to flow naturally and effortlessly between you, when there is a natural sense of alignment. Your life together becomes a spontaneous dance. You anticipate each other's needs. You can sense what your partner is experiencing or thinking.

Then, one day, something shifts, and nothing seems to happen easily. Everything seems like it's in a rigid state. Simple communication becomes almost impossible. "Are you wearing your watch?" "If you want to know the time, look at the clock." "I don't want to know the time. I want to know if you're wearing your watch." "Why else would you want to know that?" "Because I see what looks like your watch lying on the driveway." "Why didn't you say that in the first place?" "PLEASE TELL ME IF YOU'RE WEARING YOUR FUCKING WATCH." "Stop yelling to me from the other room! What's wrong with you this morning?"

You know what I'm about to say: when this happens, nothing is going wrong. It's part of the natural cycle of being human and in a committed relationship. It doesn't need to be analyzed or fixed. Just hold on to yourself, without blaming yourself or your partner, until the two of you have made it through the rapids and the currents have naturally settled down.

In committed relationships, there will also be periods of comfortable stasis and periods of painful growth. For weeks or months, you and your partner may face no major challenges. Then, in the same week—*boom!*—your teenage daughter gets arrested for shoplifting, your car dies, and your partner admits to regularly spending time and money on a porn site. If you're wondering *What the hell happened?*, the answer is that life happened.

Serenity and difficulty both naturally ebb and flow in any committed partnership. Use the five anchors to hold on to yourself, and keep sailing forward together.

Both/and is baked into the nature of committed relationships. If you break your arm, or wreck your car, or get in a fight with your sister, it's your problem in many ways. But in other ways it's also a problem that you and your partner share. If your arm is broken, the two of you have to renegotiate how your infant daughter's diaper gets changed and how the snow gets shoveled. If your car is in the shop, the two of you have to figure out how both of you will get to work. If you and your sister aren't speaking to each other, your lover may get worried e-mails from your mother.

Both/and is even baked into abusive relationships. When one partner becomes an abuser and the other a victim, there is often a hidden, secondary aspect of the relationship in which those roles are reversed. When one person is primarily concerned with power and the other with control, there may also be an undercurrent in which the opposite occurs simultaneously. I'll say much more about this aspect of committed partnerships in later chapters.

Both/and is who you and your partner *are*. Any committed partnership is always a combination of three entities: you, me, and the two of us together.

COMPASS POINTS

- In life, many of our choices appear to be *either/or*. But many of these apparent dualities are actually *both/and*. Both options are true or valid or valuable.

- Every *either/or* conundrum naturally pushes couples toward emotional bottlenecks—and toward growth.

- Both partners need to live into the *either/or* conundrum—grinding against each other as much as necessary, while staying as loving and present as they can—until an alchemical transformation occurs.

- Our bodies are *both/and* organisms, naturally going through cycles of rigidness and fluidity.

- Committed relationships follow a similar, natural cycle, alternating between times of flow and times of brittleness or constriction, as well as between periods of comfortable stasis and periods of painful growth.

- *Both/and* is baked into the very nature of committed relationships. Any committed partnership is always a combination of three entities: you, me, and the two of us together.

18

The Big Four

Therapists often say that the four biggest sources of conflict in any committed partnership are money, sex, kids, and in-laws.

Although this is true, the deeper issue is that most couples—and most therapists—approach these conflicts as problems to be solved. But most of these dilemmas cannot be solved tactically, strategically, or according to a blueprint.

They are the four big things you and your lover can't easily compromise around. They are also the biggest ongoing sources of pressure in couples' faces, day after day. As a result, they create some of the biggest and most frequent opportunities for growth.

This is true even when the conflicts originate outside the relationship.

CHEN, BROCK, AND DAIYU

Chen and Brock are concerned about Chen's ninety-three-year-old mother, Daiyu, who lives on her own in an apartment. For years, Chen and her husband have implored Daiyu to move to an assisted-living apartment, but Daiyu always refuses.

Daiyu smokes two packs of cigarettes a day and often smokes in bed, even though Chen and Brock have repeatedly urged her not to.

One night, Daiyu falls asleep with a cigarette in her hand; when the smoke alarm wakes her a few minutes later, the edge of her blanket is smoldering. She rolls up the blanket, throws it in the shower stall, and turns on the water.

The only immediate damage is to the blanket, but Chen and Brock are deeply worried. They agree that Daiyu could easily start a dangerous fire. They also agree that Daiyu's living situation is no longer safe for her—or other tenants. Nevertheless, they suddenly find themselves in serious conflict—and each person's position is tied deeply to their integrity.

"We have to move her," Chen insists. "She'll burn the building down. We need to put down a deposit in an assisted-living facility and tell her she has to move."

"I wish it were that easy," Brock says. "But you can't force anyone into assisted living."

"Then let's put her in a nursing home."

"We can't do that, either. She doesn't need that kind of care."

Chen says, "So we should just let her burn the goddamn building down?"

"I'm saying she's a very stubborn woman and a nicotine addict, and there's no law against smoking or stubbornness. We're not going to change your mom. We've been trying for twenty years and we've gotten nowhere. Like the Serenity Prayer says: *Give me the serenity to accept the things I cannot change, the courage to change the things I can, and the wisdom to know the difference.*"

"You want to abandon my mother?"

"No," Brock says. "I want us to abandon the illusion that we can get her to move. And I don't want to get caught up in her addictive system."

Chen puts her face up close to her husband's. "When you married me, you joined my family. You're *already* caught up in it. If you bail, you're bailing on *me*. Brock, I need you with me on this. I don't need you backing off and spouting sanctimonious bullshit."

Both spouses agree on what the problem is. Both agree on what the solution should be. But they're 180 degrees apart on what they can do about it. Furthermore, each partner's position is tied deeply to their own integrity, so they both find it that much harder to compromise.

How will Chen and Brock resolve this seemingly intractable conflict? They will have to keep grinding on the problem together, with each of them using the five anchors to hold on to themselves, until a transformation occurs.

If Chen and Brock both stay with it, accept and tolerate the clean pain and discomfort involved, and stick by each other, they will both grow in the process, and eventually a course of action may emerge.

I don't know what the specific resolution will be. The couple might decide to give Daiyu the gift of an e-cigarette, then remove all the Kools from Daiyu's apartment. When Daiyu objects, they might both say, "Mom, you have a phone. Dial 911 if you believe that's the right thing to do." Or they might make a deal with Daiyu that one of them will check in with her by phone or Skype every night at ten and push her to agree not to smoke from then until the following morning.

Suppose that, instead, Brock had responded to Chen's comment about sanctimonious bullshit by saying, "You know what you are? You're an enabler. You're part of a fucked-up addictive system, and now you're demanding that I be part of it. I'm not going there. If your codependent relationship with your mother is more important than your relationship with me, then say so, and I'll start packing up tonight." Now it's up to Chen to decide how to respond. If, like Brock, she chooses to blow her anxiety and frustration through her partner, then both lovers will plunge into a lagoon of dirty pain.

Couples sometimes think they can solve problems in these four areas one at a time, like fixing four different problems with a car. While this can work for small, practical concerns (e.g., who manages the checkbook and who drives the couple's daughter to soccer practice), it doesn't usually work for foundational conflicts.

This is because the big four don't exist separately; they're inherently linked together. Some examples:

- Kris and Heidi have much less sex than Heidi wants, but Kris is often too tired from working long hours in order to pay Grandpa's rent and their son Drew's school tuition.

- Rosa often gives her ten-year-old son, Arturo, small amounts of money to buy things he wants. But Arturo sometimes doesn't do his chores or his homework. Kelly, Arturo's stepdad, urges Rosa not to give Arturo money when he doesn't do what he's supposed to. Rosa tells Kelly, "I wasn't raised in a mean, stingy household like you were, and I don't want my son raised that way, either."

- Brock and Chen's disagreement over Daiyu causes them to pull away from each other emotionally and sexually. As they grind together around Daiyu, they also start to argue about money and kids. "Maybe Mom will move if we agree to pay for her assisted-living unit." "Why should we do that when she has plenty of money?" "So we can get her out of the freaking apartment, that's why." "I am not plundering our daughter's college fund to bail out your goddamn mother."

When faced with these kinds of problems, many partners try to lower the heat so that they don't get pushed into emotional stalemates. But this never works for long, because the things that are important to both lovers—the things tied to their integrity—will keep coming up, over and over. Even when they try to avoid such situations, events will always force them to face them.

These situations require ongoing attention, energy, compassion, courage, and mindfulness from both partners. Together, they have to walk into and through each issue, not knowing what will happen. Meanwhile, each partner needs to hold on to themselves using the five anchors, while demanding the best from their partner and themselves.

Negotiation and compromise are essential to any loving relationship. But with the things that really matter, negotiation and compromise will not keep people out of emotional bottlenecks. Eventually, people simply have to raise their game and grow up.

COMPASS POINTS

- The four biggest sources of conflict in any committed partnership are money, sex, kids, and in-laws.
- None of these dilemmas can be resolved tactically, strategically, or according to a blueprint. In fact, using those approaches usually makes the situation much worse.
- These conflicts are not problems to be solved. They are the four building blocks of stalemate—the four things couples can't easily compromise on. They also create some of the biggest and most frequent opportunities for growth.
- Couples can't usually resolve problems in these areas one at a time, because the four building blocks of stalemate don't exist separately; they naturally interlock.
- Instead, these situations require ongoing attention, energy, compassion, courage, and mindfulness from both partners. Together they have to walk into and through each issue, not knowing what will happen.
- With the things that really matter, negotiation and compromise will not keep people out of emotional bottlenecks. Eventually, people have to raise their games and grow up.

19

The Maps in Our Heads— and How They Can Mislead Us

In our heads, we each have a mental map of the world, which we use to help us navigate life.

Your own world map includes a smaller map of your partner's brain terrain—or, at least, what you believe your lover's brain terrain to be. It's a working simulation of their brain inside your brain.

The longer you're with your partner, the more nuanced, detailed, and accurate you believe your map of their brain is. Nevertheless, this map *always* has both accurate and inaccurate information, because it's based on many different things: your experience with your partner, your own life history, your tolerance for ambiguity and uncertainty, the degree to which you can adapt and be flexible, and your ability to stay solid, centered, and committed.

Because of this map, you are often (but not always) able to predict what your partner will say or do in certain situations. When Freda gives her husband, Louis, a certain look, he knows that the next words out of her mouth are likely to be, "Sugar, that dog won't hunt." When Corinne is reading at the kitchen table and suddenly senses Bobbi's fingertips lightly touching the base of her spine, she knows this is an invitation to head into the bedroom—or to make love there in the kitchen. When Ariella says, "I have a favor to ask you," Harvey knows that she's about to ask him to change one of his habits.

This mind-mapping[15] helps us recognize when something isn't right, such as when our partner is deceiving us, or being inauthentic,

---

15 *Mind-mapping* is another widely used term coined by my mentor Dr. David Schnarch.

or in serious emotional trouble. We can sense that something is wrong because what they say or do doesn't match the map in our head.

However, past conflicts or trauma can get in the way of our ability to build an accurate mind-map of our partner. When something activates a traumatic memory in our body, we may overlay that trauma on top of our mental map and respond to that trauma.

And when reality and our mental map don't match, we have to make a choice: go with reality; go with our (possibly inaccurate) map; gather more information; or accept the uncertainty and ambiguity for now, and revisit the discrepancy later.

If we respond from a place of trauma and immediately go with the map, we can make both ourselves and our partner crazy.

One notable aspect of every mental map is that it can never be as dynamic and emergent as a flesh-and-blood human being. Simply because it's a map, it encourages us to expect (or even demand) relational consistency from our partner. But simple consistency is the stuff of robots and computer programs. It's inadequate for human relationships.

To create more room for growth in ourselves—and in our relationship with our partner—we need *persistence* more than *consistency*. When we persist in holding onto ourselves when the heat gets turned up under us; when we persist in living out of the strongest and most life-affirming parts of ourselves; and when we accept and lean into clean pain and discomfort, over and over, then growth and new possibilities can emerge.

MADISON AND HENRY

When Madison's partner, Henry, doesn't call her after he lands in Chicago, as they'd agreed, she reflexively thinks, *He's having an affair* or *He's been in an accident* or *He doesn't love me anymore*. Madison then has an impulse to punish or confront Henry, instead of calling him to get more information.

Madison starts back braining. She texts Henry, RU ALL RIGHT. Henry doesn't respond for the next hour. Just as Madison starts to text U BASTARD, WHY DID I EVER TRUST U, her phone rings. It's Henry, breathing hard. "Hi, hon. A tornado blew through Schaumburg and they had to reroute us to Milwaukee. I had to run to catch the last train to Chicago. Just made it."

When something about our partner catches us by surprise—or when we encounter something entirely new to us—it can overwhelm us, and we can respond reflexively from a place of trauma or stuckness. This is what happened when villagers first looked at Dr. Frankenstein's monster. Even though he was mostly just wandering around, everyone freaked out. "Oh my God, run! We're not safe around this hideous creature! He's going to do terrible things!"

It's also easy to forget that people change. This is the central paradox of committed relationships. We want our partners to stay the same in the ways we appreciate, but we also want them to change those attributes that bother us.

Over time, some of the things we like about our partner will stay the same, but others will naturally change. And some of the things we dislike about them will improve; some will get worse; and some won't change at all.

But even though our partner—or our situation—has changed, we may refuse to change our mental map. This is a recipe for problems, because reality always trumps our ideas about it.

Every one of us with a partner needs to regularly amend our mental map of them as we go through life. We need to let go of any inaccurate elements—including our fears, hopes, and dreams—and deal with our partner as they actually are.

Sometimes we're slow to do this, especially when our partner changes in a way that we don't care for. Suddenly our partner doesn't match our map. That scares the bejeezus out of us.

When a couple reaches an emotional stalemate, both partners can sometimes have trouble distinguishing their mental maps from what is actually happening. They may respond to the pressure and grinding by coming from the past rather than the present—or from trauma rather than from trust.

In these situations, each lover can use the five anchors to move into and through the conflict:

1. **Soothe and resource themselves** to quiet their mind, calm their heart, and settle their body.

2. **Pause, and notice the sensations, vibrations, and emotions in their bodies,** instead of reacting to them.

3. **Accept and tolerate the discomfort** instead of trying to flee from it.

4. **Stay present and in their bodies** as they move through the unfolding experience, with all its ambiguity and uncertainty, and respond from the best parts of themselves.

5. **Metabolize any energy** that remains.

Because we use our mind-maps all the time, it's easy to forget that they're maps. But reality will help keep us honest. As soon as the map in our head stops reflecting how things are, we'll know it, because we'll be surprised, shocked, or confused.

The mental map we have about our partner needs to be solid enough so we don't have to reinvent our relationship with them every morning. But it also needs to be flexible enough to adapt to a changing reality. Our mental map of our partner needs to be like a healthy spine: solid, yet flexible. It also needs to be updated frequently with new information, as that information emerges.

COMPASS POINTS

- In your head, you have a mental map of the world. This includes a smaller map of your partner's brain. This map contains both accurate and inaccurate information.

- Because of this map, you are often (but not always) able to predict what your partner will say or do in certain situations. It also helps you recognize when something isn't right—if your partner is deceiving you, or being inauthentic, or in serious emotional trouble.

- Past conflicts or trauma can get in the way of your ability to build an accurate mind-map of your partner.

- When reality and your mental map don't match, you have to make a choice: go with reality; go with your (possibly inaccurate) map; gather more information; or accept the uncertainty and ambiguity for now, and revisit the discrepancy later.

- If you respond from a place of trauma and immediately go with the map, you can make yourself and your partner crazy.

- You need to regularly amend your mental map of your partner as you go through life, so you can deal with your partner as they actually are.

- When a couple reaches an emotional stalemate, both partners can sometimes have trouble distinguishing their mental maps from what is actually happening. That's when they need to use the five anchors to move into and through the conflict.
- Reality will help keep you honest. As soon as the map in your head stops reflecting how things are, you'll know it, because you'll be surprised, shocked, or confused.
- The mental map you have about your partner needs to be solid enough so you don't have to reinvent your relationship with them every morning, but flexible enough to adapt to a changing reality.
- Our mental map may encourage us to expect (or even demand) relational consistency from our partner. But we need persistence more than consistency. When we persist in holding onto ourselves when the heat gets turned up under us; when we persist in living out of the strongest and most life-affirming parts of ourselves; and when we accept and lean into clean pain, over and over, then growth and new possibilities can emerge.

20

People Can Tolerate Being Used, but They Hate Being Discarded or Discounted

In my thirty-plus years as a therapist, I've learned that most people can tolerate being taken advantage of, so long as the relationship meets some need or serves some purpose for them.

This is why so many people have affairs with married folks. Most of these people understand on some level that their married lovers will *never* leave their spouses. Usually they know it in their bodies as aches or urgings, but not in their cognitive brains. Yet they appreciate the attention, gratitude, sex, excitement, fun, prestige, gifts, or money that their lovers provide. It's temporary gratification, but at least it's gratification.

Most affairs with married people follow a single predictable trajectory. Sooner or later, the person being cheated on wakes up, straightens their spine, and takes a stand. They tell their partner, "I can't stop you from having an affair. But if you keep having it, don't expect me to stick around." Sometimes, realizing that the game is up, their partner may dump their lover-on-the-side hard and fast.

For the jilted lover, this hurts like hell. The message they hear is, *You're not important to me. In fact, you never were.* And they're right.

Something similar happens with our partner when we steal their choice. When we have an affair and don't tell our partner that they are now in a three-person relationship whether they like it or not, we become a choice thief. When we use some of the family savings to buy cocaine and don't tell our partner, we become a choice thief. In each case, we ignore our partner in favor of a person, object, or habit. Through our actions, we tell them, *My Ashley Madison hookup or coke habit matters to me, but what you want or need doesn't.*

People can't stand being ignored or discounted—or, worse, cast aside, crumpled up, and kicked to the curb. Yet that's exactly how affairs with married people typically end.

No one wants our partner (or ex-partner) to hate us or be mad at us. But we'd rather have their hate or anger than their indifference. We'll start a fight or make a scene so we don't have to accept the fact that we don't matter to them.

Sometimes we'll smash their window, or paint graffiti on their door, so that we force them to care about us in some way. It's not the way we want them to care about us—but at least we're back on their radar screen.

In a committed relationship, the thing we want most is to be important to our partner. We also want them to communicate to us just how important we are to them, and we know how much they want the same thing from us. This gives both lovers the ability to slime each other big-time.

One of the most common—and most painful—forms of commonplace cruelty is the small, dismissive motion or gesture or facial expression that conveys this message: *You don't matter. You're not important to me.* When our partner does this to us, suddenly we experience fury, or shame, or terror—yet without understanding why.

A similar form of sliming occurs when we try to engage with our partner, and they respond in an angry monotone, "I don't care" or "It doesn't matter" or (slimiest of all) "It's fine." Meanwhile, the vibe they send to us screams, *I care and it does matter—a lot. But right now I'm pissed as hell, so I'm going to pretend I don't care and refuse to engage with you. You won't be able to do anything about my anger or my sliming, so you'll sense that you don't matter.* This is a classic form of underpowering, which I described in chapter 15. We sense that something is missing, that our partner has emotionally dropped away. We also get caught in their double message.

In either of these situations, the ability to stay anchored and soothe yourself is crucial. The lizard brain in the back of your skull will almost certainly get activated. *You think I don't matter?* your Godzilla brain may shout. *Fuck you. I'll matter to all the people on the fishing boats I'm about to destroy.*

But you're not a lizard. You don't have to mindlessly follow the messages from the back of your brain. And you have the power to stop yourself before you destroy anything. Recall and practice the five anchors from chapters 5 and 35.

As kids, most of us were taught how to handle bullying and insults. But few of us were taught how to handle the pain of other people's indifference, especially when that indifference comes from someone we care about. As adults, we need to build our skills for staying centered and calm in the face of indifference, so that we don't fight, flee, freeze, fawn, or annihilate.

There's a flip side to this. Just as there are hundreds of ways in which we can subtly diss or dismiss our partners, there are innumerable simple, subtle ways in which we can show that they matter to us.

We're all familiar with the obvious demonstrations: bringing them flowers; walking up behind them and kissing them on their neck; or saying, "I love you. Let's go out for dinner tonight."

There are also personal rememberings. These are things you do for your partner that acknowledge something they care deeply about—even if you don't give a damn about it yourself. Maybe your mate really likes having a clean and orderly car, because it makes life seem less chaotic to them. So, while they're at the gym, you get the car washed and waxed, as a small surprise. Or maybe they're excited about going to their upcoming high school reunion. So, a few days before the reunion, you make and send them a video montage of photos of them when they were a teenager. These rememberings can do a great deal to hold relationships together.

All of these are great, but there's one other category of rememberings: the small, intimate things you and your partner can do that are natural, almost matter-of-fact affirmations of your connection and couplehood. Some examples:

- You and your partner are sitting on the sofa watching a movie. Your partner stretches out their legs and puts their feet on your lap. You respond by gently resting your hand on their shin.
- Your partner calls you at work. You answer not with, "Yo. What?" but with, "Hey, darling. How's your morning been?"
- You offer to refill your partner's empty coffee cup. As you pour the coffee, they lightly touch your shoulder.

All of these gestures, and a thousand others like them, communicate the same simple but deeply important message: *You matter to me.*

These gestures, which I call *cueings*, are invitations for intimacy and connection. They're not come-ons for sex (though if the energy in the moment happens to lead to sex, that's fine) or performances of noble intent.

Most couples naturally offer each other these cueings. This is why, if our partner suddenly stops offering them to us, our body goes on alert. Cognitively, we may not realize—or be able to articulate— what the problem is. But we can sense in our body that something is missing. We might even ask our lover, "What's wrong?"

Typically, when couples reach gridlock, they stop providing these small cueings to each other. Or, sometimes, only one partner will stop providing them—and the other will become unsettled by it. In response, they might stop their own cueing, thereby turning up the heat on both partners. Or they might *increase* their own cueing, hoping to get their partner to resume their typical cueing in response. This usually turns up the heat, too.

When a lack of cueing by one or both partners becomes the new norm, it usually means that critical mass—and an opportunity for both partners to up their games—is near at hand.

COMPASS POINTS

- Most people don't mind being taken advantage of, so long as the relationship meets some need or serves some purpose for them.
- But people can't stand being ignored or discounted—or, worse, cast aside.
- We'd rather have our partner's (or ex-partner's) hate or anger than their indifference, even if we have to start a fight or make a scene in order to get back on their radar screen.
- One small motion or gesture or facial expression can convey the message, *You don't matter* or *You're not important to me.* So can phrases such as "I don't care" or "It doesn't matter" or "It's fine," uttered in an angry monotone. These are forms of serious sliming.

- Most of us were taught as children how to handle bullying and insults. But few of us were taught how to handle the pain of other people's indifference, especially when it comes from someone we care about.
- As adults, we all need to build our skills for staying centered and calm in the face of indifference, so that we don't fight, flee, freeze, fawn, or annihilate.
- Just as there are hundreds of ways in which we can subtly diss or dismiss our partners, there are innumerable ways in which we can show that they matter to us.
- These include rememberings: things you do for your partner that acknowledge something they care deeply about—even if you don't give a damn about it yourself.
- They also include cueings: small, intimate things you and your partner can do that are natural, almost matter-of-fact affirmations of your connection and couplehood.
- Typically, when couples reach gridlock, they stop providing these small cueings to each other. When a lack of cueing by one or both partners becomes the new norm, it usually means that critical mass—and an opportunity for both partners to up their games—is near at hand.

21

Getting on Your Back to Get Your Partner Off Your Back

People often use sex to keep their partner at bay or to pacify them.

When a conflict arises, or when one partner senses that a conflict is nearing an emotional stalemate, they may be unwilling to rock the boat or stand in their own integrity. Instead of moving through clean pain and discomfort with their partner, they try to distract or win over the partner by having extra sex—or their partner's favorite kind of sex.

But this isn't about the kind or amount of sex the lovers have. It's about whether both people are acting from their strengths or their limitations.

This dynamic can lower the heat in the relationship by bribing the other lover into compliance or passivity. It also keeps both partners from growing up. It's the equivalent of popping a nipple in a crying baby's mouth.

A breast full of milk is exactly the right thing to pacify a crying, hungry baby. But trying to pacify an adult partner with a breast—or a vagina, penis, or mouth—makes one partner into a wet nurse and the other into an infant.

On the surface, this seems to work for both lovers: one gets lots of their favorite sex, and the other gets relief from some of the natural pressures in the relationship. Except that, after a while, the sex isn't that great, because it's become a business deal. *You back off about my pot smoking, and I'll do you just the way you like.*

This relief is an illusion. The tension may temporarily subside, but the conflict doesn't go away. In fact, because sex has devolved into a subtle form of exchange, a new source of friction gets created astride the old one.

Sometimes people reverse this approach. Indirectly, they ask their partners for sexual favors in exchange for not confronting them about a conflict or issue. In essence, they say to their partner, *Give me the sex I want, and I'll leave you alone about the difficult parts of our relationship.*

Using sex to lower the heat in a relationship may work for a while, but it never succeeds in the long term, because it does nothing to resolve the unavoidable conflict. This conflict is not about the particular relationship or the specific people in it. It's baked into the dynamics of having someone else matter.

Both lovers still keep grinding up against each other. Furthermore, when one partner realizes that their lover is trying to appease or distract them through sex, they begin to lose respect for them.

I often hear stories of such realization from my therapy clients. Someone is on their back, looking up at their partner, and suddenly they understand the dirty-pain game they've been playing. Something shifts inside them, and a moment later they push their partner away and say, "You need to get off me!"

It's a harsh moment, but an honest one. It means the bullshit is over. Now both partners have to deal with what they shoved under the bed when they banged each other into dirty passivity on top of it.

A common variant on this theme is the uninspired sex that one lover has with another out of duty, or charity, or even pity. It's the sex one partner gives the other before they go out of town for a week, or the blow job one partner asks for from the other when they've had a tough day at work.

This sex has the same effect as pacifier sex: it undermines both people's respect for each other. The partner who gives it loses respect for the recipient, because the recipient settles for sex that doesn't require both partners' full presence. The recipient loses respect for the giver, because the giver fails to either say no to sex or to be fully present and intimate within it.

Over time, when one partner settles for uninspired and obligatory sex, the other partner usually stops wanting to have sex with them. The giver knows that they're serving up sexual fast food, yet their partner is acting like it's prime rib.

People want to be wanted, sexually and otherwise. When sex becomes just a physical release, or a bribe, or a biscuit for good behavior, or an act of charity or obligation, sooner or later the relationship will reach an emotional bottleneck.

In bed, like everywhere else, there's no healthy or honest alternative to growing up.

COMPASS POINTS

- When a conflict arises, or when one partner senses that a conflict is nearing an emotional stalemate, they may try to distract or win over their partner by having extra sex—or their partner's favorite kind of sex.

- Sometimes people reverse this approach by indirectly asking their partner for sexual favors in exchange for not confronting them about a conflict or issue.

- Using sex to lower the heat in a relationship may work temporarily, but it never succeeds in the long term, because it does nothing to resolve the unavoidable conflict.

- A common variant on this theme is mercy sex: uninspired sex that one lover has with another out of duty, or charity, or even pity.

- Pacifier sex and mercy sex have the same effect: they undermine both partners' respect for each other.

- When sex becomes just a physical release, or a bribe, or a biscuit for good behavior, or an act of charity or obligation, sooner or later the relationship will reach an emotional bottleneck.

- In bed, like everywhere else, there's no healthy or honest alternative to growing up.

22

Why Most Couples Stop
Having Sex

I've observed that most couples stop having sex for at least five to seven years during the course of a long-term partnership. Sometimes all at one time, and sometimes on and off.

In any partnership, both people need to show up for themselves and for each other. When that doesn't happen, sex loses its imperative—or goes away entirely.

If a couple isn't having sex, we think it's pathological, that something is wrong. But in the great majority of couples it's exactly the opposite.

When a couple isn't having sex, it's for a reason. If they can move into that reason and confront it, they can sometimes unhook it. Somebody—maybe both lovers—need to raise their game.

But that's not what usually happens. Instead, without talking about it, they make an agreement: *I go out with my friends, you go out with your friends, we pay the bills, we take care of the kids. Don't mess with me about what I do to blow off steam, and I won't mess with you about no sex.* They back off from each other and go to their separate corners.

They need to do just the opposite: grind against each other in multiple ways until they reach an emotional bottleneck. This is a place where one or both partners can't go on anymore in the same way. Your position and your partner's positions can always block each other. You're in an interlocking conundrum where something *has* to change, either in one partner or in both.

Emotional bottlenecks are scary, because they're places of peril and possibility. They're also where we do much of our most important emotional work with our partners.

FELICIA AND ANDRÉ

I worked with a married couple, Felicia and André. Felicia is Black; André is white. They hadn't had sex for many months. In fact, Felicia had moved out of the bedroom, so they didn't even sleep in the same bed.

They'd been married for twenty-three years, and it turned out that for twenty of those years, André had called the shots and always gotten his way. Not just with sex, but in general. Without ever discussing it, that was the deal they had made.

Felicia was tiny—barely five feet tall—and André was tall and broad, with a booming voice. When he got anxious, he would raise his voice and lean forward, creating a presence that some people found threatening.

After grinding against each other in this way for two decades, Felicia couldn't do it anymore. She didn't say anything to André; she just started sleeping on the living room couch.

André had no idea what the problem was. He kept trying to get her to talk with him about it, but she wouldn't. He also tried to get her to go back to sleeping in the bedroom. She wouldn't do that, either.

André finally confronted her. As she lay on the couch, he stood over her and said angrily, "Tell me something. Are you ever going to sleep in our bed again?"

"I don't know. Leave me alone."

"Are you going to tell me what the hell is wrong?"

"It doesn't matter," Felicia said, rolling to face away from him.

"It matters to me. I'm your husband. You won't have sex with me, you won't sleep in the same bed with me, and now you won't talk to me."

"Good night," Felicia said.

André pulled the pillow out from under her head. "No. Talk to me."

She turned back to face him. "Keep your damn hands to yourself. And give me my fucking pillow back."

He tossed the pillow in her face. "Why the hell are you being so bitchy?"

"If I talk, you won't listen. You'll just argue with me and tell me why I'm wrong. You haven't listened to me for twenty years."

"That's crap," André said. "Of course I listen to you."

"There, you just did it again," Felicia said. "You argued with me and told me I was wrong."

"Okay," André said. "I'll shut up and just listen. Talk to me. Tell me what's going on."

She sat up. "I don't mean listen as in nod your head and not talk. I mean listen as in actually give a flying fuck about me or what I'm saying."

"A fuck, flying or otherwise, would be pretty good right now. Or have you forgotten how?"

"Goddamn, André. I'm tired of your wanting me to take care of your every need. That's what most of the men in this fucked-up world expect from their women. And it's what white folks have demanded from Black folks for centuries. Maybe once in a while you could ask me what *I* want or need."

"That's how I began this conversation," André said, "and you said to me, 'It doesn't matter.'"

"You're right, it doesn't," Felicia said, getting up. "I'm going to my sister's. Maybe there I can get some sleep."

As she left the room, she turned and glared at André. "Look at you, standing there like some goddamned statue, clenching your fists. Do you think I like having you throw things in my face? I swear, André, if you ever try to hit me, I'll put your sorry ass in jail for the rest of your fucking life."

"Why in hell would I want to hit you?" André shouted. "You're my wife!"

But Felicia was already out of sight.

When Felicia and André first came to me, they both told me they had communication problems. But they were actually communicating very well. Through his actions, André kept saying, *Do what I want*, and through *her* actions, Felicia kept responding, *Not anymore*.

This dynamic first showed up in my office when they discussed sex. André was upset that Felicia wouldn't have sex with him. "I want you," he said. "I hate sleeping alone. I hate not having sex."

I asked André to rate the sex he'd had with his wife over the years. He said, "Eh. Okay."

"That's all?" I asked. "If the sex is mediocre, why do you keep trying to screw her?"

"Well, she's my wife. I mean, we're married."

"So you want to screw her because she's your wife. At what point did you stop wanting to screw her because you wanted *her*?"

Sexually, neither spouse was choosing the other. Is it any wonder they'd stopped having sex?

Then I asked Felicia, "When you were younger, did you ever walk into a room and see somebody attractive, and you noticed them and they noticed you? And even though you didn't say anything, you picked up his vibe, and you sent him back a vibe that you were open to some type of interaction?"

She said, "Yeah, sure."

"When was the last time you did that with your husband?"

"Umm . . . a long time ago."

"Why?" I asked. "Did he lose his appeal?"

"No. He's still a good-looking man. But he doesn't help me have good vibes about myself."

I said to Felicia, "That's not his job. Having good vibes about yourself is *your* job. Anyway, if it *was* his job, it doesn't sound like he'd be very good at it. The issue is this: can you bring yourself forward and be connected to André without simply giving yourself over to him?"

At first Felicia was silent. Then she said softly, "That will be hard."

I said to André, "I want to ask you the same question I asked Felicia. When was the last time you sent her a *You're awesome, step into my arms* vibe?"

André frowned. "Maybe ten years ago. She'd always act funny about it. I'd tell her how gorgeous she looked, and she'd snort and say, 'Yeah, right. Me and my big fat ass.' I finally stopped trying after I did just what you said—I lowered my voice into my best Barry White imitation and started singing, 'I'm Qualified to Satisfy You.' She laughed, just like I thought she would. But then she said, 'Give me a damn break. You think a white man can channel Barry?'"

I said to Felicia and André, "There's nothing wrong with either of you. If you stopped communicating those types of vibratory messages ten years ago, why would you want to have sex with each other now? And how good would the sex be when you actually had it?"

At our next session, I asked André, "Who would you say has the stronger sexual desire, you or Felicia?"

"Definitely me. I've always wanted sex way more often than she does—at least three or four times a week."

"Felicia," I said, "Would you agree with that?"

"Absolutely. For years he's always been after me for sex—and if he doesn't get it, he gets all upset. He acts like a dick or like a pouty child. At first it bothered me, but now I mostly ignore it."

I asked her, "Is this just true for sex? Or do you experience him pressuring you for other things?"

She leaned forward. "He pressures me about everything. He wants me to do the things and go to the places *he* likes. He wants his friends to be my friends. Whenever he wants something, he turns to me to fulfill it, like I'm his goddamned employee. He stands over me and gets this half-weepy, half-demanding look on his face."

Felicia's eyes grew brighter. She turned to her husband. "You want to know why I've been sleeping on the sofa? It's because I can't be your goddamned servant and mommy anymore. I'm not going to do whatever you want just because you want it. If I'm ever going to have sex with you again, it's going to be because I *want* to, not because it's in the fucking marriage contract."

Listening to Felicia and André, most people think, *Man, what a mess.* But it's not a mess at all. Something is going very right. After twenty years, Felicia and André are starting to deal with their lack of relationship glue, and with what's actually happening between them. They and their relationship are poised for growth and transformation.

One of the fallacies about male sexuality is that a man has to have some type of physical release in order to keep the pressure in his body down. Implicitly or explicitly, he tells his partner, "It's your job to make it so I don't have blue balls." He comes home from work and says, "Darling, it's been such a tough day. I gotta have a blow job."

When sex for you or your partner is more about physical release than about wanting the other person, eventually your relationship will reach an emotional stalemate. No one wants to be just a flesh machine that gives their partner pleasant sensations, a convenient way for their partner to come. You want your partner to be present. You want them to want *you.*

Something is going very right when a lover says, "I'm done having sex with you just so you can come; I want you to be there. I want to be wanted for who I am. If we're going to do this relationship, we're going to do it differently from now on."

A variation on this theme is when one partner dissociates and goes away emotionally during sex. Eventually the other partner needs to say, "You're just not there when we make love, and I hate it. I'd rather not do it at all than have sex with a robot. When you disappear like that, what's happening for you? Where do you go, and why to do you go there?"

Two sessions later I said to André, "You told me you want to have sex three or four times a week. But you never once said that you want Felicia. You just said that she's your wife and that husbands and wives should have sex. Tell me about that."

André looked surprised. "People are supposed to have sex with their spouses. That's part of what marriage is, right? Or am I wrong about that, too?"

I said, "In all our meetings, you haven't said a word about what attracts you to Felicia. But you both said that there was a real attraction early on. Something happened in between. That makes me wonder: When did you stop trusting Felicia?"

André drew in a sharp breath. Felicia looked shocked.

I waited.

After five or six seconds, André sighed. He said softly, "Twenty years ago."

"So you stopped treating her like the woman you loved and started treating her as a one-stop shop for meeting your own needs. What happened that made you stop trusting her?"

It wasn't until the following session that André was willing to answer that question. He turned to Felicia and said, "I stopped trusting you when I realized you were never going to stand up to your mother. You let your mom boss you around. You do whatever she wants, whatever she says. You let her manipulate you and guilt-trip you. You always put her first. Before me. Before yourself."

Felicia leaned forward and half-shouted, *"What?"*

"You've never said to her, 'Mom, this is *my* life, and in my life I'm important. You not only won't let *me* into the center of your life, you won't let *yourself* into the center of your life."

Felicia sat in shocked silence.

André said to her, "Remember how we used to argue about this when we first got married? You'd yell at me for an hour for insulting your family, but you'd almost never say no to them, no matter what they demanded of you. I finally realized that no matter what I said, you and your family would keep acting exactly the same way. So I stopped arguing."

The game was beginning to change. Now both André and Felicia had a chance to grow up.

RENEE AND MARIANA

Renee came to me with a very different problem involving sex. She and her wife had been together for eighteen years. Like any couple, they'd had to learn—separately and together—how to stay anchored when big waves arose and their boats rocked. They'd weathered many storms together and remained committed to each other. But now they were both sixty, and their sex life had largely evaporated.

"It's not that we're not interested," Renee explained. "It's that our bodies won't always cooperate. We'll be making out on the sofa and caressing each other. When we were forty, or fifty, or even fifty-five, a biochemical rush would kick in. Each of us would get turned on, and we'd both ride that train. We'd take off each other's clothes and go at it.

"But now, when we get to the point where the rush would kick in, *nothing happens.* So we feel each other up some more, but that urgency, that rush of *gotta have more, gotta have it now* just doesn't show up. Neither of us gets that wet, and most of the time we wind up just cuddling.

"I love Mariana. I'm not going to rush off to a bar to pick up some forty-year-old divorcee looking for a thrill.

"But, Resmaa, here's the thing. If I did pick up a younger woman, I don't think I'd have any trouble getting seriously turned on.

"I'm not sure what I think about this. I'm not even sure what I'm *supposed* to think. Part of me wants to blame myself for not being turned on by the woman I love. Another part wants to blame Mariana for not turning me on the way she used to. A third part says, *See a sex therapist.* Help me out here."

I started to speak. "Renee, nothing is—"

"Yeah, yeah, nothing is going wrong. Wait a second, because there's more. If I look at porn, at some twenty-year-old spreading her legs, *that* can get me wet and excited. But the woman I'm married to and love with all my heart doesn't anymore."

I said, "You and Mariana definitely have a problem. It's this: *You're getting older.* Just like everybody else."

Renee and Mariana have a *problem,* but they don't have an *issue*—unless one of them decides to create one. They haven't stopped loving each other, or physically expressing their affection for each other. Their bodies have changed because they've aged. Renee spoke in terms of biological urgings, but that's only one of many ways that age changes our bodies. As Renee and Mariana have grown older together, their aging bodies have changed, and so have some aspects of sex for them.

I said earlier that simply by being who you are, you will often block your partner, and just by being who they are, they will block you. *This is a normal and unavoidable part of any committed relationship.* No matter how much Renee and Mariana love, care for, and understand each other, as they get older they are going to block each other in this way.

I said to Renee, "Don't make this into something that it isn't. If you blame yourself, or your wife, then you make a problem into an issue. In that case, the *real* issue is your inability to anchor yourself when a problem appears. What's important is that you and Mariana figure out how to deal with this together. If the two of you decide, *We're getting older, so let's just accept the change and work on deepening what we have rather than wishing we had what we used to,* then that's cool. If either or both of you decide to get hormone injections to effect some biochemistry around sex, that's fine, too, provided it's something you both want and decide on together. What's important isn't *what* you decide. What's important is how the two of you go through this together.

"Meanwhile, each of you is still responsible for soothing yourself down and not blowing your anxiety through the other partner. You never know exactly what's going to happen, or what your partner will do—so keep using the five anchors to keep as steady as possible.

"The two of you are fortunate. You've both worked hard to grow up for many years. If you hadn't, the whole nature of the problem could be different. You might be pursuing things outside of your commitment to each other. Mariana could be making appointments for liposuction and a facelift, or you could be visiting some lesbian swingers' club. But you don't have to deal with any of that type of dirty pain—just the clean pain of aging and growing older together.

"Renee, you need to take yourself on here. The changes in your sex life scare you. Now you have to decide how you'll respond to that. You can blame yourself. You can blame Mariana. You can blame God. Or you can say to Mariana, 'I love you more than anything. But our bodies are changing, and the changes scare me. Let's talk about what to do.'"

Renee frowned. "What about my getting turned on by photos of women I've never met and never will?"

I said, "Listen. It's easy to get turned on by a stranger. If you've never met someone, all you know about them is they've got a great-looking body. You've never heard them fart or say something stupid or curse at their neighbor. You've never argued with them or made money decisions with them or had to deal with their crazy family.

"Every night, when you get in bed with Mariana, you've gone through another day of seeing her warts and limitations, and she's gone through another day of seeing yours. You've negotiated things and made difficult decisions together and solved problems together. None of that is particularly sexy. How many couples do you think get turned on by figuring out a schedule for sharing the car? Not many.

"Compare that with someone who's never argued with you, never had to work through anything with you, and never blocked you. Plus, she's got a nice body, whatever that means for you. *Of course* she's a bigger turn-on."

Renee laughed. "Are you giving me permission to not have any guilt over this?"

"No. I'm telling you that you don't *need* my permission; you need your own. You and Mariana have gotten where you are through hard work and integrity. You can let go of the guilt and stand in your integrity instead. You already know how to do this."

When you get good sex in a long-term committed relationship, that's great. But the process of standing up and trying to get good sex is much more important. There's no guarantee that you'll get it. But it means you're dealing honestly with your partner. That's when transformation becomes possible.

When you straighten your spine and take a stand, your sex life may improve. The very way you think about and handle sex may transform as well. Or the two of you may come out the other side separately, and the better sex will be with a different partner.

What's for certain, though, is that the two of you will go through peril and possibility together. If you grow up and become closer and stronger, this will make for better sex, and possibly expand its meaning and texture for you. It also might make everything else between you better.

But "better" doesn't necessarily mean "with bodies that are as responsive as they were years ago." As we age, almost everything about sex and intimacy changes for us—including what we want, what gives us pleasure, what's important to us, and what we're capable of.

As we age, our technical biological prowess may diminish.[16] The older we get, the more we get forced up against new biological limits. If we don't have a process for soothing ourselves down and accepting the clean pain and discomfort of those limits, we're going to go crazy.

But those very limits also offer the potential for growth. As we bump up against them, and metabolize our emotions around them, our approach to intimacy can evolve. Once again, what looks like a limit turns out to be fuel for transformation.

Life is never-ending emergence. This is true for a fetus in the womb, an infant learning to use their hands, an elder dealing with their aging body, and someone on their deathbed. Each moment unfolds into the next, emerging from a timeless and spaceless darkness into an ever-changing, ever-present *now*. For each of us, every breath, every moment, every experience, and every limitation is an opportunity to grow and transform.[17]

COMPASS POINTS

- People stop having sex when sex with their mates isn't worth having.
- Most couples stop having sex for five to seven years during their partnerships—not all at once, but on and off.
- When a couple isn't having sex, it's for a reason. If they can move into that reason and confront it, they can unhook it. Usually, one or both of the lovers needs to raise their game.
- Many couples stop having sex because they stopped sending each other sexual vibrations like they did when they dated. Instead, they treat sex as an ordinary activity, like drinking water.
- One common fallacy about male sexuality is that a man has to have some kind of sexual release to keep the pressure in his body down. When a man treats sex as simply a form of

---

16 Some people do have medical issues related to sex—erectile dysfunction, poor lubrication, etc.—that have nothing to do with aging. If you think this might be the case for you or your partner, check with an MD in order to rule out a medical problem.

17 Zenju Earthlyn Manuel has written wisely and beautifully about this process in her book *Opening to Darkness*.

physical release, eventually his partner will refuse to have sex with him.

- When someone disappears emotionally during sex, their partner, too, will eventually stop having sex with them.

- When you get good sex in a long-term relationship, that's great. But the process of standing up and trying to get good sex is more important. That's when transformation becomes possible.

23

Little Traumas Can
Cause Big Problems

Many of us carry some traumatic responses in our bodies. When we're put in a situation that reminds our body of an original trauma, it can cause us to fight, flee, freeze, fawn, or annihilate. Like Dr. Frankenstein's monster, we watch our own body respond in ways we don't understand and can't easily control.

I want to be clear here. Not all individuals and couples struggle with trauma. In many cases, people simply need to begin growing up. But some couples do stay stuck in a cruel or painful pattern because of past trauma. My work with high-conflict couples has shown me how trauma can cause otherwise rational people to have overblown reactions to seemingly minor situations.

When people have such reactions, most therapists—and most lovers—don't know how to address them. Therapists typically rush to use cognitive processes such as anger management. But anger management doesn't work on our Godzilla brains any more than it would work on Godzilla. Godzilla is not reasonable.

With trauma, anger isn't the issue. Instead, it could be that the body is trying to complete the action that occurred when it created the trauma, so it can release the energy stored inside the trauma.

Trauma is personal, but, it is not *only* personal. More about this shortly.

Sometimes partners drive themselves and their partners crazy because of unresolved trauma. But if they can complete the action around that trauma, they can metabolize the energy and move through it.

You are not responsible for healing your partner's trauma, nor are they responsible for healing yours. Each of you needs to grow up and learn to deal with life on its own terms. A good therapist can provide guidance and support, but they can't heal your trauma for you.

Still, some therapists can be more helpful than others. Certain therapists are trauma specialists: they have experience, education, and training in helping folks work through trauma. If you know or suspect that you need to do trauma work, consult with a therapist who has such a background. If you're already seeing a therapist, ask them about their own experience and training in trauma work; if necessary, ask them for a referral to a trauma specialist.

In general, the deeper the trauma, the more important it is to consult with a therapist who specializes in trauma work.

Traumatic, reflexive responses aren't logical or cognitive. They happen in the body, which is hardwired to protect itself and to recognize danger, whether it's emotional or physical, perceived or real.

From a survival standpoint, this is a crucial ability. If you're walking through the woods and suddenly a bear appears, your logical, thinking mind won't operate fast enough to process the danger. Instead, your body will respond automatically. Suddenly you're running away, even while your thinking brain is going, *Huh? Why the hell am I running away?* And then a second later it realizes, *Oh shit, that was a bear.*

Because the body is fast but not logical, it may decide that something is dangerous even when it isn't. Your body may make no distinction between a gunshot and a firecracker, or between falling from a skyscraper and falling off a four-foot wall—especially if it experienced an earlier fall as perilous. At times, your body may also make no distinction between dangerous closeness (e.g., someone who stands directly in front of you, shouting insults) and unexpected but safe closeness (e.g., while you're filling out a form online, your partner sneaks up behind you and whispers in your ear).

Whenever your body perceives that an event is dangerous, no matter how minor—usually because it's too much or too soon or too fast or too loud or too painful—it can store that event as trauma. This trauma then gets stuck in your body.

Events themselves don't create trauma. But the body can develop traumatic responses to events—and these events can be either real or perceived.

Traumatic responses are particular to each person. Culture, life experience, and self-image may all impact how, and if, traumatic responses appear. One person's *no big deal* experience is another's *oh shit* experience.

Biology usually trumps biography. Your body's reflexive responses can't be reasoned with. Whatever story you tell it, it will hold on to the trauma until you release the energy behind it. Even though your cognitive brain might tell you, *It's okay; I only fell four feet and I landed on grass,* if your body responded to the fall by creating a trauma response, that trauma can stay stuck in your body until you find a way to complete the action and metabolize the constricting energy.

No one, including you, can predict how your body will respond to any particular event. One person can go through war or disaster or abuse and come out the other side basically intact. Someone else can fall off a bicycle and get stuck in a traumatic response for decades. A third person can be frightened by something as simple as a loud, unexpected noise. They immediately look around, orient themselves, see that there's no danger, and forget about it. A fourth person can hear the same noise, but their body remembers it for years.

CAMILLA

Imagine ten-year-old Camilla, who wakes up one morning with a pain in her belly. Her parents take her to the doctor, who tells them that Camilla has a hernia and that it can be repaired through routine surgery.

Camilla's parents explain to her that something has torn inside her and that they will need to bring her to the hospital to get it fixed. They assure her that this isn't her fault and that she will be fine once the hernia is fixed. Camilla accepts the explanation without fear or anxiety.

The next morning everything goes well. A nurse has Camilla take off her clothes, put on a hospital gown, and lie down on a gurney. But when the nurse straps her in to keep her in place, her body rebels. She starts to scream and struggle. The anesthesiologist hurries over, holds her down, and forces a mask over her face to quickly put her under.

Pause for a moment, please. Notice what you're experiencing in your body right now. As you read the previous paragraph, what parts of your body tightened? Did you have an urge to move or act? Did a memory or other image arise?

Whatever occurred in your body in those few moments, imagine all of those experiences being stuck in your body for years—and not knowing how to free yourself from them. That is a glimpse of trauma and how it operates.

The operation is successful, and soon Camilla goes home. Her parents explain to her what happened in pre-op, including why the people in the hospital strapped her in and put a mask over her face. She nods and says, "Okay." Everyone, including Camilla, soon forgets about those few painful moments in pre-op.

But her body, which can't think or reason, doesn't forget. To her body, those moments before the operation were dangerous and terrifying.

A few weeks after the operation, Camilla's parents notice that she's acting a little differently, though they can't put their finger on it. Then, one day at school, a boy stands too close to her and she punches him in the face. Two days later, when a friend playfully sticks a straw in her ear, Camilla decks her, too.

Nobody, including Camilla, connects this to what happened in pre-op. But from then on, when someone gets physically close to her without her permission, her body gets activated. To her Godzilla brain, someone is strapping her down and smothering her again.

Two years later, Camilla goes on her first camping trip with her family. When she crawls into a sleeping bag that first night, her body gets activated. She lunges out and cries panicked tears until her bewildered parents pack up and drive thirty miles to a motel.

Flash forward twenty years. Camilla and her partner, Lynn, are in my office. Lynn complains to Camilla, "Every time we start to get closer, you push me away." Camilla half-shouts, "Of course I push you away! You're always on me for something. It's like you don't know how to back off."

Every time Camilla physically pushes Lynn away, or emotionally drops away, even Camilla has no idea why. This is because what's happening isn't cognitive. *The back of her brain is reacting to the pre-op incident as if it is happening in real time, and it's responding by trying to complete the action.* And all of this is happening to her without context, because the human body isn't wired to understand context. It just wants to be safe.

So Camilla internalizes these trauma responses as character flaws or emotional dysfunctions. She thinks, *Something must be wrong with me,* rather than *Something happened to me.*

> At age twenty-seven, Camilla barely remembers the pre-op incident. But the trauma is still stored deep in her body. Her seemingly overblown reactions are her body's attempt to protect her.

Camilla's trauma was caused by a single, specific incident. But our bodies can also experience trauma in a less specific, more cumulative way. If you grow up in a neighborhood that's full of violence—in a tough neighborhood in Chicago; or in Ashkelon, an Israeli city that often gets shelled by Hamas; or in Gaza, which often gets pounded by the Israeli army—your body may slowly absorb the danger, day by day. You may not personally experience any particular traumatic event, but your body may nevertheless respond to the ongoing danger and the ambient violence in traumatized ways.

Imagine that you're walking down the midway at the state fair, carrying your baby girl, who's holding a balloon on a string. The balloon hits a metal awning and pops. Next thing you know, you're running with your daughter in your arms, then rolling to the ground, protecting her with your body.

A pedestrian stops and tugs at your arm to help you up, and you belt her in the stomach and scream, *"Don't touch my daughter!"* Before you know it, your daughter is screaming her head off, the Good Samaritan is calling you a douche bag, and a policeman is booking you for assault. Meanwhile, your brain is going, *What the fuck just happened?*

What happened is that the back of your brain overcoupled a sequence of items with the sound of the small explosion. That overcoupling might have saved your life in south Chicago or Gaza or Ashkelon. But at the Maryland State Fair, it overwhelmed your cognitive processes, causing you to flip into fight-or-flight mode.

Let's go back through this incident again, but this time we'll slow it way down and look at what might have taken place inside your head.

Before the sound of the small explosion even reached your conscious awareness, your brain was focused on a variety of physical sensations: the smell from the nearby bumper cars, your sweaty shirt sticking to your chest, a warm breeze blowing against the back of your neck.

Then the loud *pop* registered in your consciousness. This sound let loose a flood of memories and images in your brain: a balled-up fist, a wall being blown down, a car smashing into a telephone pole, a brick falling and landing on a sidewalk.

A fraction of a second later, concepts and mental chatter related to your surroundings flashed into your brain: *It's so noisy and crowded. Why did I think Babette would like it here? It's a goddamn sea of nameless faces. This would be a perfect place for a homegrown terrorist to set off a bomb.*

In less than a second after that, you instinctively pulled your daughter closer, then started running. You looked around for possible sources of danger, but all you saw were crowds of people. Any of them could have a gun or an explosive device. You rolled to the ground to get below any gunfire and tucked your daughter's small body under your chest to protect her.

Breathing hard, you lay splayed out on the midway, surrounded by people—frightened, vulnerable, alone, and full of dread.

Then a passerby pulled at your arm, and you went ballistic.

Overcoupling can occur with almost anything that's potentially painful or dangerous. Let's suppose that you and your lover often fight about money, and there's a certain look they always give you just before the shouting begins. After a year or two, all they have to do is give you that look and your back brain gets activated. They don't even have to say anything—but suddenly you're angry, frightened, and shaking, and you don't even know why.

The activation doesn't even have to be a look. Your partner might say to you at the dinner table, "I need to talk with you about our finances," and the next thing you know, you're standing up, clenching the table tightly, and ready to fight or run.

Your brain has overcoupled money discussions with fighting, frustration, anger, accusations, shame about past financial decisions, and fear of poverty—and created a trauma response.

When you experience trauma, your body releases a surge of survival energy. Once the danger has passed, you may need to metabolize that energy through actions such as pausing and breathing deeply; shaking or crying; stopping, looking around, and orienting yourself; taking a walk or a run; or consciously grounding yourself in your body, and in the here and now.

But if those surges of trauma energy don't get metabolized, over time they can build up and get trapped inside your nervous system. These can lead to headaches, fears, stomachaches, nightmares, or persistent muscle tension, especially when they combine with other stressors.

Unfortunately, most people, including most therapists, approach trauma only cognitively. They look for past events that are mentally frightening or horrifying or disgusting. Then they try to cognitively work through those events using talk therapy. This process takes a very long time, if it works at all. Sometimes it simply repeats and deepens the trauma, because it speeds up the brain instead of slowing down the body and its processing. *Because the trauma is stored in the body, it needs to be metabolized and released by the body.*

Cognitively, we can say to our partner, or to ourselves, "Look, it wasn't a big deal. Drop it. Get over it." And mentally we can try to override the sensations and urges. But sometimes our body simply can't.

When couples try to work through trauma in a purely cognitive way, the body usually remains unaffected. Over time, people can learn to cognitively *manage* trauma through meditation, deep breathing, and other focusing exercises. This keeps people out of each other's faces and can reduce their reactivity with each other. But it doesn't complete the action or release the trauma energy. The cognitive work becomes a Band-Aid that protects the trauma wound but doesn't heal it.

Similarly, yoga and meditation don't usually heal trauma. When properly practiced, each can encourage mindfulness, relaxation, and spiritual insight. But neither one works with the body's energy in a way that enables it to move through and resolve trauma.

Furthermore, many folks misuse meditation or yoga. Instead of using them to become more present, they use it as a way to dissociate or move into a trance state. They avoid the body's trapped energy rather than encourage it to emerge, so that they can metabolize it. This dodge, commonly called *spiritual bypassing*, only pulls the body *away* from what it needs to do to heal trauma.

This is why, in therapy, my client and I may not even look for or talk about the incident at the core of their trauma. Instead, I ask questions about what they sense in their body. *When you think about your partner smothering you, what do you experience in your body? Where do you experience it? Does it come and go or stay steady? Does it ever move? What makes it worse or better?* I may ask them to focus on that particular body sensation; then I say, *What images pop into your head as you experience this?* This helps people begin to become familiar with the sensation, so they can learn to slow the process down and, eventually, metabolize the pent-up trauma.

When (or immediately after) we experience an overwhelming event, we need to let our bodies metabolize the energy, without thinking that we're doing something weird or out of control or socially unacceptable. We need to allow our partners to do this, too, without dissing them for it or freaking out over it. When people don't metabolize the energy in this way, it stays inside them and can create more problems.

This is why, when we reach an emotional bottleneck with our partner, our body can sometimes respond as if we are in a fight, flee, or freeze situation. We may suddenly lash out at our partner, or start an argument, or run out of the room, or go ballistic. Meanwhile, our own brain is asking, *What the hell am I doing? Why am I so upset?*

Because our reaction makes little or no cognitive sense, we may start to think we're crazy or messed up. But we're not. We're experiencing a normal trauma response that makes sense to our body.

In some situations, if you observe carefully, the body will show you what it needs to do. It may keep trying to repeat a series of movements. Or it may try to recreate the situation related to the trauma, until the action is completed and the energy is released.

This is biological, not cognitive. The key to healing is not finding some *aha!* moment, but retraining your body, just as the key to building muscle is not reading and thinking about bodybuilding, but going to the gym and working out.

With couples, it's quite common for *both partners* to have traumatic responses to each other. You'll recall from chapter 11 that in partnerships, the rocks in one lover's head fit perfectly into the holes in the other's. This is often true of trauma as well. Through their relationship, each partner tries to complete the action behind their own trauma. But what happens instead is that their partner's response only reinforces the same trauma. *In an attempt to complete the actions and heal, the two people keep wounding each other.*[18] The relationship is bringing these things forward, so that each partner can address their own trauma and limitations head on.

In the heat of an emotional bottleneck, if the lovers can reach critical mass, raise their games, and metabolize the energy behind

---

18 In extreme cases, couples stuck in this dynamic may form what is called a *trauma bond.* This typically occurs when an abusive partner alternately punishes and rewards their lover—or when both partners do this to each other. The person in the victim role then stays stuck in the relationship, hoping for the next reward—and/or an end to the recurring punishment—from the partner in the perpetrator role.

their trauma, they create the opportunity to move from *fight, flee, or freeze* to *love and let themselves be loved and known.*

We tend to think of trauma as personal—and often it is. Danielle freezes up around large dogs because she was chased and bitten by a Doberman when she was seven. Cosimo hates being in crowded, noisy outdoor gatherings because he was at the Route 91 Harvest Music Festival in 2017 when gunman Stephen Paddock opened fire on the crowd. Marya can't bring herself to eat spinach because, four years ago, a slice of spanakopita gave her serious food poisoning.

But some trauma isn't personal at all. Trauma can also be *historical, intergenerational,* or *persistent and institutional.*

Remember the gallows and noose that were displayed outside the US Capitol by rioters during the January 2021 insurrection? If you have a white body, you were probably disgusted and horrified when you saw it. But if you have an African American body, you might have looked at it and had a trauma response—a sudden urge to run, or scream, or tear the gallows to pieces.

That's classic *historical trauma*. Although you personally may not have been threatened with lynching, many Black Americans from previous generations were chased down, captured, and hung—and your body may hold that historical information as trauma.

Intergenerational trauma is trauma that gets passed down from parents to children—and, often, to grandchildren, great-grandchildren, and beyond. This transmission partly occurs through what people teach their kids and how they raise them. But it can be transmitted genetically as well. When a parent experiences trauma in response to a particular event, that trauma may be passed down to their children through the expression of their DNA[19], along with an inherited aversion to similar events. (This is another reason why, in therapy, my client and I may not look for, or try to talk about, the specific incident behind their trauma.)

If your mother nearly drowned on two occasions in the year before you were born, you might have inherited a decontextualized lifelong uneasiness about swimming in the ocean—an uneasiness that can't be explained by the events of your own life. While your cognitive

---

19 In 2015, Rachel Yehuda published the first study to clearly show that stress can cause inheritable gene defects in humans ("Holocaust Exposure Induced Intergenerational Effects in FKBP5 Methylation," *Biological Psychiatry* 80, 372-80). This process of passing down trauma through our genes is called *epigenetics*. For a more interesting and accessible read, I recommend Olga Khazan's article from *The Atlantic,* "Inherited Trauma Shapes Your Health," at https://www.theatlantic.com/health/archive/2018/10/trauma-inherited-generations/573055/.

mind may not make a connection between the sea and danger, your DNA expression does.

Persistent and institutional trauma is trauma resulting from the repeated actions (or inaction) of a socially sanctioned institution—or, in some cases, by a culture or sub-culture. Think of the many immigrant children who were forcibly separated from their parents at the US border by US Immigration and Customs Enforcement officers, and then kept separated for months in detention centers. Many of these kids—and many of their parents—now suffer this type of trauma. The separations were done impersonally, on a large group of people, but the trauma is experienced very personally, by many hundreds of individual human bodies.

Any of these forms of trauma can create conflicts in a committed relationship, just as personal trauma can. But when historical or intergenerational trauma is involved, the situation can be quite confusing, because a partner's responses can't be directly connected to their own lived experience. Nevertheless, the trauma is real, and either or both lovers may need to interrogate the trauma with a trusted healer, therapist, or counselor in order to move through it.

This is not mere systems theory or a purely cognitive awareness. I'm talking about actual energy flows in and between flesh-and-blood human bodies. When trauma is involved, you and your partner may not need to investigate the *history* behind the trauma—but you do need to acknowledge and work with the traumatic *energy* stuck inside your bodies.

COMPASS POINTS

- Sometimes partners make each other crazy because of unresolved trauma. If they can complete the action around the trauma, they can move through it and heal.
- Trauma isn't logical because it takes place not only in cognitive functions, but primarily in the body.
- Events don't create trauma. The body creates trauma in response to specific events. A loud noise, a bicycle accident, or an unexpected loss can all cause trauma.
- Most of us carry trauma in our bodies. When we encounter a situation that reminds our body of the original trauma, it can cause us to fight, flee, or freeze.

- Couples often activate each other's trauma energy. Suddenly they're fighting, fleeing, freezing, or going emotionally blank, without understanding why.
- When we experience trauma, our body releases a surge of survival energy. Once the real or perceived danger has passed, we need to metabolize that energy—either in the moment or later on.
- If you and your lover can metabolize the energy behind your traumas, you create an opportunity to move from *fight, flee, or freeze* to *love and accept love.*
- Not all trauma is personal. Trauma can also be historical, intergenerational, or persistent and institutional.
- When trauma is involved, you and your partner may not need to investigate the history behind the trauma—but you do need to acknowledge and work with the traumatic energy stuck inside your bodies.

24

What We Come into This World With

Many different experiences and elements make us what we are: our life history, our biology, our psychology, our culture, our family of origin, and dozens of other influences.

Most of us assume that these forces start to mold us as soon as we're born. But that's not true. They begin much earlier.

We therapists often ask our clients about the circumstances in which they grew up. But we often make the mistake of starting our inquiry with birth.

When a pregnant woman drinks enough alcohol to damage her fetus, the child may grow up with fetal alcohol syndrome, which creates a range of emotional, mental, and physical problems. Certain medicinal and recreational drugs can also cause lifelong damage to a developing fetus. But these aren't the only chemicals that can have long-lasting effects on a child in a womb.

IMOGENE, KARYN, AND RAYMOND

Picture Imogene, a nineteen-year-old single mom-to-be who lives in a rough part of Las Vegas. She's healthy, takes good care of herself, and eats reasonably well. She doesn't smoke, and during her pregnancy she doesn't touch alcohol or drugs. But she lives on a dangerous block, surrounded by violence, street crime, and ongoing chaos. Her baby's father has skipped town. She lives with her older sister, whose boyfriend is sometimes abusive. It's a difficult and stressful environment.

In response, Imogene's body regularly produces lots of stress hormones, such as cortisol and epinephrine. Those hormones travel into her fetus's bloodstream, and they affect her daughter's developing central nervous system. As a result, from the time that baby girl is born, she may have certain sensitivities—or oversensitivities—to her environment.

When Imogene's daughter, Karyn, is two months old, she and her mother move to a much safer, quieter neighborhood. Nevertheless, Karyn grows up a very distressed child who takes great care to protect herself. Whenever she goes someplace new, she immediately looks around for escape routes and places she can hide, if she needs to.

Now let's flash forward twenty-five years. Karyn is living in suburban Atlanta with her fiancé, Raymond. They mostly get along well, but whenever Raymond gets upset, even slightly, Karyn withdraws, leaving the house to be by herself for a few hours. When he asks her what's wrong, she usually says, "Nothing. Leave me alone." For the next day or two, she won't touch Raymond or let him touch her.

At Raymond's insistence, he and Karyn start seeing a therapist. The therapist asks Karyn to talk about her years growing up. Karyn describes a childhood that includes a loving mother, a caring stepfather who came into her life when she was seven, and a safe, middle-class neighborhood.

Everything Karyn reports is accurate. But she's missing one deeply important piece: what life was like for her in the womb.

Even before she was born, Karyn learned how to swim away from threats to keep herself safe. Years before she had any cognitive awareness of what danger was, her body was flooded with hormones that responded to potential threats.

A few weeks into therapy, she admits, "Whenever Raymond starts to grumble about something, I want to run and hide. It just doesn't seem safe around him."

"Has Raymond ever physically harmed you or threatened to harm you?" the therapist asks.

"Hell, no," Karyn says. "If he tried even once, I'd be out of there for good in five seconds."

"So why do you think it sometimes doesn't seem safe around him?"

"I don't know," Karyn says.

Karyn was formed in a womb filled with stress soup. As a result, she came into this world with certain biological inclinations. She tends to respond to the world—and, especially, to potential danger, whether real or imagined—with a focus on self-protection.

Fortunately, this is only a tendency, not a psychological prison or her inevitable fate. In therapy, Karyn can investigate this tendency, unhook it, heal, and grow up out of it.

To do this, though, it will help if she—and her fiancé and therapist—understand the circumstances under which she began life in her mom's belly.

When a client like Karyn—or anyone who might be described as high-strung or tightly wired—shows up in my office, I've learned to ask this simple question: *When you were in your mother's womb, what was going on in your family and your neighborhood?*

COMPASS POINTS

- Many forces make us who we are, including our life history, our biology, our psychology, our culture, and our family of origin. We typically think that these forces start to mold us as soon as we're born—but the process actually begins in the womb.

- It's common knowledge that alcohol and drugs can harm a fetus's development. But when a pregnant woman is under a great deal of stress, her stress hormones, such as cortisol and epinephrine, can also have long-lasting effects on her fetus's nervous system.

- Typically, these effects are tendencies, not immutable characteristics. In therapy, a client with one of these tendencies can learn to investigate it, unhook it, heal, and grow up out of it.

- Most therapists will ask a client about their family of origin and their upbringing. But the wisest ones also know to ask, "When you were in your mother's womb, what was going on in your family?"

25

Trying to Get Milk from
a Coke Machine: A Dialogue
with James Maddock

The late Dr. James Maddock, one of my mentors, knew more than almost anyone about the realities of committed relationships. He often expressed these realities in pithy and memorable ways. ("The rocks in your head fit perfectly into the holes in your partner's" is one example.)

He also had his share of eccentricities. He had a thing about wizards: his office was full of wizard pictures and figurines, and whenever we'd meet, he'd be holding a mug of tea with a wizard painted on it.

Doc, as I called him, was privileged to have had the famous psychiatrist Dr. Milton Erickson as his mentor. Dr. Erickson was truly a wizard of therapy, and Doc's way of remembering and honoring him was through his wizard collection.

Dr. Maddock himself looked nothing like a wizard. He looked like musician John Denver, with sandy brown hair and a white beard.

In Doc's coaching sessions with me, I always knew we were onto something important when he'd slump in his chair, look down at his mug, and slowly unwrap the string of the tea bag from the handle. Then he'd look up and say something that would perfectly nail what was going on.

Often, when I'd begin to get an insight, he'd look at me and gently say, "Come on." Then he'd beckon me with his hand, like a parking lot attendant guiding a car forward. He saw where I was heading and would coach me to go the rest of the way.

Dr. Maddock died in 2009. I miss him enormously. Sometimes in my therapy office, when I find myself at a loss about how to help a couple stuck in dirty pain, I ask myself, *What would Doc say?*

The interview that follows is an imaginary dialogue between Dr. Maddock and me, based on some of his key concepts. Dr. Maddock's widow, Dr. Noel Larson—herself an experienced and highly respected psychotherapist—has read and approved this dialogue.

RM: Doc, I titled this chapter after something you said to me. Can you explain to my readers what you meant?

JM: Imagine you want some cold milk, so you walk up to a vending machine, put money into it, and push a button. A few seconds later, it gives you a Coke. At first you're upset and disappointed and confused. But then you look, and you realize it's a Coke machine.

RM: It's going to give you Coke, no matter how much you want milk.

JM: Yes. You can marshal every argument in the world for why you should get milk instead of Coke. You can plead with it. You can give it an ultimatum. You can threaten it. You can get angry and shake it. But every time, it's going to give you Coke. If you keep putting money into that Coke machine and pushing that button, hoping to get milk, you're going to be disappointed every time. You can't coerce a Coke machine into dispensing milk, no matter how loud you shout or what arguments you muster.

RM: But if you keep putting money in, pushing that button, and hoping for milk, you're not paying attention.

JM: True. But it's exactly what people do with their partners. If you want something from them that they're not giving to you, you can't make them provide it. And they're not likely to spontaneously start providing it. Say you want your partner to tell you how much they appreciate all the repairs you do around the house. Maybe your last two partners did that regularly. But the person you've been married to for the past seven years doesn't give a damn. They'll come up to you and say, "The front doorknob's broken," and expect you to fix it, and never thank you. So maybe you're thinking, *I've been doing this for seven years. I must have repaired a hundred things. Eventually my partner is going to be grateful.* But you'd be completely wrong.

RM: Your partner is going to keep doing exactly what they've been doing for the past seven years.

JM: Yes. We need to be as realistic about our partners as we'd be with a vending machine. After you put money into a machine a couple of times and get Coke instead of milk each time, you're not going to say to the machine, "What's your problem? Why can't you give me a carton of milk?" But with our partners, we say to them for years, "Why won't you be who I want you to be instead of who you are?"

RM: It's a combination of yearning, denial, and magical thinking.

JM: And a failure to grow up. When most of us fail to get what we want from our partners, we try again and again and again, usually in the same way. Our strategy is endless repetition. Each time we fail—and then we blame our partners, or think they don't understand us, or accuse them of holding back. But they understand us perfectly well. They know *exactly* what we want. They just have no interest in giving it to us. Or no ability to. Or they are content with who they are, and they're not interested in modifying or amputating any aspects of a self they're familiar and comfortable with. And in some cases, not giving us what we want may be the healthiest thing to do—for them *and* for us.

RM: Meanwhile, *we* don't do anything differently.

JM: That's not very sensible, is it?

RM: That's one of the essential conundrums of committed relationships: each lover asks the other to be something other than what they are at that time.

JM: Eventually both people have to grow up and realize what they're doing. Unfortunately, most people don't. They revert to coercion or manipulation or nagging or arguing or deal-making—*if you do this for me, I'll do that for you.*

RM: Those are all forms of dirty pain.

JM: But it's where a lot of couples go.

RM: If someone keeps nagging their partner—*Come on, baby, it's my birthday, do it for me, just this once*—they might get what they want, but there's not going to be any sweetness to it. It'll be dutiful and perfunctory, and it will leave both people less close and less happy with each other. And they'll both miss the honey and the relationship glue that they could have experienced.

JM: So let's talk a little about why this happens. Sometimes people in committed relationships believe that they're owed something from their partner. "Look, sugar. I committed to you. I'm not running around with anyone else. I'm not raising kids with anyone else. I'm not paying bills with anyone else. I make a good living. I treat you the way I want to be treated. *Now* can I have what I want, when I want it?"

RM: That's not how relationships work. We're not trained dogs. We don't say to each other, "I'm sitting up and begging, just the way you asked. Now where's my biscuit?" That's not a marriage. It's barely a business transaction.

JM: Do you see how all this is just a variation of the Coke machine? "I put my money in; I pushed the button; now give me milk, damn it."

RM: But if you actually hold on to yourself and do something different, then the whole dynamic has a chance to change.

JM: Not always. If there's nothing but Cokes in the machine, you still can't get milk from it.

RM: But maybe you can change how you look at the situation. You know, *Hey, I'm thirsty. Milk's my number one choice, but Coke will do.* Or, instead of wishing the Coke machine would give you milk, look for milk somewhere else. I don't mean have an affair or an open marriage. I mean that if you want your partner to appreciate your repair skills, and they haven't appreciated them for the past seven years, stop expecting them to. Hire yourself out to neighbors to do small repairs. Then use the extra money to take your partner out to a nice restaurant. Suddenly they may start saying, "Hey, those repair skills of yours are pretty cool."

JM: Or they may not.

RM: But, either way, you're growing yourself up, bit by bit. When you stop trying to get validation for fixing things, it forces you to begin asking questions like, *Why do I want or need to be validated for this in order to believe that I'm a good partner or a worthy human being?* That's an important question to ask.

JM: This doesn't mean you should give up on ever getting milk. It also doesn't mean that wanting milk is wrong. You might even keep advocating for milk—but not in that simple, repetitive, nagging way. You won't be trying to coerce your partner or bargain with them. You're simply saying, "This is who I am and what's important to me." Over time, that can create some important pressure that supports the evolution of the relationship. Or that pressure can cause the relationship to end. Either way, that pressure is necessary.

RM: Occasionally I get a client who is either a nag or a bully. They're convinced they can eventually get milk from a Coke machine, if only they keep pressing long enough or hard enough.

JM: What do you tell them?

RM: If the person is a nag, I say, "So the right way to get along with your lover is to nag them until they give in. If that's the case and everything's cool, then what the hell are the two of you doing in my office?" Then I look at their partner and say, "When your lover nags you over and over, does that get you hot? Do you lean over and whisper in their ear, 'Oh God, please, nag me harder'?"

JM: And if they're a bully?

RM: I lean forward and say loudly—with a smile, to let them know that I'm partly kidding—"YOU'RE A FUCKING BULLY, YOU KNOW THAT? EXPLAIN TO ME HOW BELLIGERENCE AND AGGRESSION ARE FORMS OF INTIMACY."

JM: You've just brought up another common dynamic in committed relationships. It goes like this: *I'm going to feed you bullshit, or treat you like shit, or both. Call me on my bullshit. Confront me so I can grow up. That's what I really want. But when you do confront me, I'll fight you every step of the way. Now, deal with it.*

RM: It's part of what I call commonplace cruelty.

JM: We all do this with our partners. That's why we're with them in the first place. We want them to help us grow up. Then we resist and tell them, "*Make* me grow up," with a hint of pubescent angst. Then we fight them, hard.

RM: It's crazy making. And as common as milk or Coke. But ideally, throughout all this, we learn to confront ourselves and soothe ourselves down enough to grow up without being cruel to the person we love.

JM: The two things people want most in committed relationships are to grow up and to not grow up.

RM: The pressure in the relationship is going to force you to choose, over and over—grow up or don't grow up. That's why these relationships are so painful.

JM: And so important.

RM: Thank you, Doc. Rest in peace. I'll take it from here.

COMPASS POINTS

- When most of us fail to get what we want from our partners, we try again and again, usually in the same way. Then we blame our partners, or think they don't understand us, or accuse them of holding back.

- But our partners understand us perfectly well. They know *exactly* what we want. They just have no interest in giving it to us. Or no ability to.

- One of the essential conundrums of committed relationships is that each lover asks the other to be something other than what they are at that time.

- Eventually both people have to grow up and realize what they're doing.

- If you actually hold on to yourself and do something different, then the whole dynamic has a chance to change.

- Another common dynamic in committed relationships goes like this: *Call me on my bullshit. Confront me so I can grow up. But when you do confront me, I'll fight you every step of the way. Now, deal with it.*

- These pressures are going to force both partners to choose, over and over—grow up or don't grow up.

26

Virtues and Limitations

In committed partnerships, almost all of us resist changing.

When we look at our partner's resistance, we think we see stubbornness or thoughtlessness. When they look at us, they think they see the same things. But we're both usually wrong.

People in committed relationships usually resist change because of their integrity. *Whatever our partner wants us to change, we resist because we see it as a virtue.*

CLAUDIA AND HASSAN

Claudia wants her husband, Hassan, to dress more stylishly, especially when they go to parties and events. She's sometimes embarrassed by how careless—and outright dorky—his outfits are. She often talks to him about this, but he shrugs and says, "Darling, what can I say? I just don't care about fashion. There are more important things in this world to worry about."

Meanwhile, Hassan wishes Claudia would put gas in the car when the tank is almost empty. Often when he gets in the car in the morning, he has to fill it up in order to get to work. He mentions this repeatedly to Claudia, who tells him, "You try running errands with a fussy two-year-old. When I have Anna with me, I need to get home as soon as possible, before she has a meltdown."

To Claudia, Hassan's lack of fashion sense is a limitation. But to Hassan, it's a virtue. He's a program officer for an organization that serves Middle Eastern refugees. He tells his wife, "I spend my day thinking about how to keep families from dying or falling apart. I just can't make myself worry about whether my pants and shoes match."

To Hassan, Claudia's habit of leaving him with an empty gas tank is a limitation. But to Claudia, it's a virtue. She tells her husband, "I'm just trying to be a good mother and a good neighbor. I want to get through the day without having to deal with a tantrum in the middle of the produce aisle. Remember when Anna flung that eggplant at the produce manager's head?"

There is (of course) nothing wrong with Claudia or Hassan. Each is acting out of their own integrity—out of what is important to them. But in doing so, each can't help but frustrate the other.

This is because *Hassan's and Claudia's virtues are also their limitations.* Hassan's deep concern for refugee families is wrapped into his lack of concern about his appearance. Claudia's care for their daughter's well-being, the peace of mind of their neighbors, and her own sanity is wrapped into her lack of care about gassing up the car.

If you look closely, you'll discover that *everyone's* virtues are also their limitations. Our strengths are also our weaknesses.

LeBron prides himself on never being late, but he can get obsessive about watching the clock. Susanna believes in being calm and thoughtful, but at times she seems cold and slow to respond. Bette loves kids, but she never says no when her self-absorbed adult children expect her to be their free, private daycare provider. I'm an assertive guy, and my assertiveness has made a huge positive difference in my life, but my wife tells me that sometimes I can be a bully.

This same dynamic occurs in the way couples interact with the world. Hal and Chris regularly volunteer for many good causes, but sometimes they're so busy with those causes that they neglect their teenage sons. Margie and Erik throw fantastic dinner parties for their friends; this ticks off their parents and siblings, who only get invited on Thanksgiving and Christmas. Rachel and Leah routinely find homes for stray dogs; right now they have five of them, and the dogs' barking keeps most of the block awake at night.

Virtue and limitation are two sides of one coin. Whenever one begins to vibrate, the other naturally vibrates as well.

Most of us are good at recognizing and living according to our virtues. But we have a much harder time recognizing, admitting to, and letting go of our limitations—precisely because they are our virtues' flip side.

No relationship highlights this paradox more clearly than an intimate partnership.

It may seem like no big deal for Hassan to pay a little more attention to how he dresses and for Claudia to fill up the car with gas now and then. So why are they grinding together over such small, simple things?

Because to them it's not about clothing or the car. It's about their integrity, about who they are. Hassan hears Claudia's complaint as *I want you to care more about looking fashionable than about displaced families.* Claudia hears Hassan's complaint as *I want you to care more about our car than about our child, our neighbors, and your sanity.* Each thinks they hear the other say, *I want you to stop living according to one of your virtues.*

But that's not what Hassan and Claudia are actually saying. Each is asking the other to look at one of their limitations.

Most of us naturally—and vigorously—resist any call to dump one of our virtues, because our virtues are tied so closely to who we are and what we stand for. But if we were asked, "Would you be okay with getting rid of your biggest limitations?" not many of us would answer, "Hell, no! I cherish my limitations."

One of the hallmarks of an emotional bottleneck is when one or both partners rebuff repair attempts under the guise of maintaining a virtue, or standing on principle, or establishing and holding a healthy boundary. But when something is *genuinely* about virtue, we would welcome any repair attempt rather than try to avoid it, thwart it, or shut it down.

For Claudia and Hassan to begin working through their emotional bottleneck, each partner needs to recognize their limitation and grow beyond it, *while still finding a way to maintain its related virtue.* Alternatively, they can let go of that virtue and replace it with a bigger or more important one.

To get there, though, the couple may need to grind together further. Each spouse may also need to confront themselves about some important things. For example:

- Claudia thinks that Hassan doesn't appreciate all she does as a mom. But because it was her idea to be a stay-at-home mom during Anna's first three years, she believes that she can't raise the issue with her husband. She's afraid he'll just spread his hands and say, "But this is what you wanted!"

- Hassan genuinely doesn't care about fashion, or getting the house repainted, or cleaning the living room before guests come to visit. But their neighbors do, and one of them recently reported their house to the city as an eyesore. Hassan doesn't want to deal with any of this, so he uses his job—and the large-scale acts of service it involves—as an excuse to avoid these conflicts. This forces Claudia to handle them.

- Both partners haven't yet figured out how to be parents together. Until just before Anna was born, they both held high-powered jobs that ate up their time from Monday morning through Friday evening. They balanced this out with weekends full of fun, sex, and relaxation together. But as soon as Anna was born, everything changed. Even though they anticipated most of the changes, after two years they're still frustrated and shell-shocked. Yet each is afraid to bring up the issue, because they're worried that their partner will say, "But this is *exactly* the life we planned together."

Claudia and Hassan's friends and coworkers think of them as great people, because they regularly get to see their virtues. But their limitations—the flip side of those virtues—mostly show up at home.

In fact, someone's biggest public virtue—the thing they're most known and rewarded for—is often what most pisses off their partner.

If you're a famous negotiator, your partner may refuse to negotiate with you about who mows the lawn. If you're known as a philanthropist, your partner may say, "You give away too much money." If you're a highly skilled pediatrician, your partner may insist on taking your kids to another pediatrician whenever they get sick.

No matter what we think of ourselves, our partner will *always* see the limitations beneath each of our virtues—and point them out to us. This will hurt. But it can be a clean form of pain if we honestly look at those limitations, own them, and work to grow beyond them. When we do, this investigation can help us to condition and temper our relationship with our partner.

Most of us address our limitations only when we absolutely have to—when we're up against ourselves. This typically happens when we've already tried all the other strategies with our partner, and they've all failed.

This is when we need to remind ourselves that the only clean way to get through is to grow up.

COMPASS POINTS

- When our partner wants us to change, we usually resist, because the thing they want to change is something we see as a virtue—something related to our integrity.
- But our virtues are also our limitations; our strengths are also our weaknesses. Virtue and limitation are two sides of the same coin. Whenever one begins to vibrate, the other naturally vibrates as well.
- No relationship highlights this paradox more clearly than an intimate partnership.
- Most of us are good at recognizing and living according to our virtues. But we have a much harder time recognizing, admitting to, and letting go of our limitations.
- Our virtues tend to be very public, while our limitations mostly show up at home.
- Often our biggest public virtue—the thing we're most known and rewarded for—is what most pisses off our partner.
- No matter what we think of ourselves, our partner will *always* see the limitations beneath each of our virtues—and point them out to us.
- This will hurt. But it can be a clean form of pain if we honestly look at our limitations, own them, and work to grow beyond them.

27

When Something
Is Missing

In my work with couples, I often hear one partner say, "Resmaa, I've always sensed that something's missing in our relationship."

As the client and I explore this sensation, we almost always discover that it's visceral, not merely cognitive. The client experiences the absence in their body.

Often what's missing is a full commitment from the other partner. This can result in one lover regularly asking for more and the other reflexively withdrawing. The relationship becomes a dance of constant flight and pursuit. One common version of this is the overpowering and underpowering I described in chapter 15.

When one person senses that something in their partnership is missing, it also usually means that at least one of the partners didn't really choose the other. They chose security or hotness or money or circumstances or connections, but they didn't choose the other person.

The cliché of the billionaire and the trophy partner perfectly fits this template. After a few months or years of living the high life, the trophy partner starts to sense that something is missing. The billionaire responds by buying their partner a new house, or an extravagant vacation, or some magnificent new bling. This settles things down for a short time, but eventually the same problem returns, because the trophy partner is beginning to stand in their integrity.

In other situations where one lover senses that something is missing, it's because they let someone else—their parents, their partner, or their spiritual leader—make the choice for them. Or they may have gotten involved with their partner not because they wanted to be with that unique human being, but because the person had the right set of characteristics. Perhaps they made a lot of money, or they had the right family connections, or they were prominent in a certain profession, or they offered a quick ticket out of town, or they pleased mom and dad, or they pissed the hell out of mom and dad.

Or maybe, years ago, they were simply afraid to say no. They didn't want to hurt their suitor, or they worried that no one better would come along, or they feared losing a passable (or familiar) long-term relationship.

People rarely talk about this topic, even to their partners. But I've learned that everyone always knows whether they chose their partner or not. All you have to do is ask them. And in my office, I routinely do.

Sometimes people don't choose their partners because they're afraid to choose. Choosing makes people vulnerable. It opens them to the possibility of making a bad choice, of losing, of being rejected, or of ending up with nothing. It may seem safer to let someone else choose for them. So they choose not to choose, thinking that then they can't lose or be disappointed.

But that's not how things play out. They eventually *do* end up disappointed. Choosing not to choose actually makes them *more* vulnerable, even though they think it will have the opposite effect.

Eventually they sense that something is missing. And something is: their own commitment. They end up in a therapist's office, hoping to unsnarl their tangle of wants and fears and disappointments.

Choosing to commit to other human beings is frightening. We have no idea what the future will bring, or how our partner will change, or how *we* will change, or what alternative future might play out if we don't commit.

But guess what? If you *don't* commit to someone, or something, or some purpose, you'll *still* have no idea what the future will bring, or how you will change, or what would have happened if you had committed. It's the same conundrum experienced from the other side.

One common variation of being afraid to choose is being afraid to *want,* because wanting makes you even more vulnerable to loss, failure, frustration, and disappointment. By refusing to choose their partner—by instead acquiescing and simply allowing themselves to be chosen—the person denies their own desires, hoping this will somehow protect them. But it never does.

Instead, not wanting eventually creates all kinds of relationship problems. Often it sets up a negative feedback loop like this one: *I'm afraid to want my husband, because wanting makes me vulnerable to rejection and loss, and those hurt like hell. If I do choose him and later he leaves me or dies, I won't be able to take the pain. So I won't choose him; instead, I'll let him choose me. I'll say yes. But I'm not choosing him—and too damn bad for him.*

This line of thought may then take a pernicious turn: *But why the hell does my partner want me if I don't want them? And how can I respect them if they don't confront me about this? There must be something wrong with them. So I'm going to treat them badly. They must deserve it, to stay in a relationship with someone like me.*

Meanwhile, the other partner's thoughts often go something like this: *I don't know why, but I don't fully trust my partner. They haven't cheated on me or mistreated the kids or misspent our money, but something seems untrustworthy or inauthentic about them. I can't put my finger on it, though.*

That's the best-case scenario. If the person is being mistreated, they might also think, *Why the hell does my partner treat me so shitty? It's like they're mad at me just for being with them. But they don't seem to want to leave, either. The whole thing makes no sense. It's starting to make me crazy—and angry.*

This dynamic naturally leads to an emotional bottleneck. Eventually, the partner who has avoided choosing or wanting has to confront themselves. They also have to make a choice: either make a genuine commitment to their partner—and to their own integrity—or leave the relationship.

If they continue to refuse to choose, then their partner has to make a choice of their own: leave the relationship in order to maintain their integrity, or accept the ongoing dirty pain of avoiding the call to grow up.

This other partner also needs to confront themselves with some important questions: *Why did I settle for so little for so long? What do I actually want from this partnership? In what ways will I advocate for what I want? And if my partner refuses to change, am I going to leave or stay in a constricted and unsatisfying relationship?*

Here's the thing: Even if one partner didn't choose the other in the past, that doesn't mean the relationship is doomed. Both people in the relationship still have the chance to choose each other *now*.

The bright line of choosing and wanting always appears right now. If both partners can lean into their suffering's edge and stay with that clean pain and discomfort; if they can both allow their bodies to stir and quake with what needs to emerge; and if they can both accept the unfolding peril and possibility, they both have the opportunity to grow up, grow closer, and become a loving couple.

Many relationships have gone from stalemate to resolution, and from distrust to trust, when the non-choosing partner straightens their spine and says, "Honey, I'm sorry for holding back for such a long time. But now I'm ready. I want to be your partner. I'm willing to be vulnerable to you. I want to take the risk of moving through life together with you."

In practice, this usually happens only after the other partner straightens their own spine and says, "It's now or never. Either choose me, with all my warts and all the risks of being in an adult relationship, or I'm getting the hell out."

In life, with or without a committed relationship, there's no way of avoiding peril and possibility.

COMPASS POINTS

- When one partner senses that something is missing in their relationship, it usually means one of the partners didn't really choose the other. They chose security or hotness or money or circumstances or connections, but not the other person.

- Everyone always knows whether they chose their partner or not. All you have to do is ask them.

- Sometimes people don't choose their partners because they're afraid to choose. They know that choosing makes them vulnerable. But choosing not to choose only makes them more vulnerable—and disappointed.

- Choosing to commit to another human being is frightening. If you commit, you have no idea what the future will bring. But if you don't commit, you *still* have no idea what the future will bring. It's the same conundrum experienced from the other side.

- One common variation of being afraid to choose is being afraid to *want*, because wanting makes you even more vulnerable to loss, failure, frustration, and disappointment.

But not wanting eventually creates all kinds of relationship problems—and, eventually, an emotional bottleneck.

- Sooner or later, the partner who has avoided choosing or wanting has to confront themselves. They have to either make a genuine commitment to their partner or leave the relationship. If they continue to refuse to choose, the relationship will probably end, because the other partner will need to leave in order to maintain their integrity.

- Even if one partner didn't choose the other in the past, that doesn't mean the relationship is doomed. Both partners still have the chance to choose each other *now*.

- In practice, this usually happens only after the other partner straightens their spine and says, "It's now or never. Either jump in all the way or I'm getting out."

28

The Dance of Protection and Growth

When a couple has been together for years, each member automatically develops an internal narrative about their partner and their relationship—including its strengths and benefits, its weaknesses and limitations, what is possible, and what is not.

This narrative isn't something that each partner thinks about that much, except in moments of strong conflict. It mostly gets carried in their body. Typically, each of these narratives includes a bodily recollection of something painful that the person's partner did in the past.

These painful memories usually cause the person to develop a protective stance—or a set of protective behaviors—to try to avoid being hurt again in the same way. They're like scabs on wounds.

These stances and behaviors usually provide some genuine protection—but they can also keep people stuck. In many couples, over time these two protective scabs grind against each other, over and over. This can create pain, further conflict, and eventual gridlock.

MEG AND JEAN-PIERRE

Nine years ago, while washing the dinner dishes, Jean-Pierre accidentally shattered his wife Meg's favorite tea mug, which she'd recently received as a birthday gift from her best friend. Since then, Meg has kept her mugs separate from all their other dishes, and she insists that Jean-Pierre never touch any of them.

Since that day nine years earlier, Jean-Pierre has been deliberately over-careful when he handles any of Meg's other favorite possessions. This annoys her almost as much as when he shattered her mug.

A few months after the broken-mug incident, Meg and Jean-Pierre went to his parents' home for Thanksgiving dinner. As Jean-Pierre's father served them, Meg saw that his toupee was starting to slide down one side of his head. She quickly said, as gently as she could, "Bryce, your hairpiece is slipping. It might fall into the gravy." Bryce turned bright red, slammed the serving plate on the table, stormed out of the room, and didn't reappear for over an hour. The rest of the evening was tense and unpleasant for everyone.

Since then, Meg is very quiet whenever she and Jean-Pierre spend time with his parents. She speaks only when she is asked a question, and then gives the briefest, simplest answer she can.

This drives Jean-Pierre half crazy. He knows that his father seriously overreacted during that dinner. But he also believes that Meg is seriously overreacting, too.

Whenever they try to talk about either issue, Jean-Pierre and Meg rub their scabs together until they become raw and painful. The spouses always end up going in circles, getting angry at each other, and raising their voices.

"The hairpiece incident happened nine years ago. Why can't you just let it go?"

"It's not about the hairpiece. It's never been about the hairpiece. It's about your father's fragile ego and his nasty temper. I don't want him ever getting angry at me again."

"I don't want him getting angry at you again, either. But I can't control him. He's not my puppet."

"Why are you taking his side?"

"I'm not taking his fucking side! I agree with you—he was harsh and rude."

"That's exactly why I keep my mouth shut around him."

"But that's rude, too, Meg. It makes every family gathering difficult."

"So you're saying it's actually my fault?"

"No. I'm saying you should just be your usual self when we visit my parents."

"So, tell me—are *you* being your usual self or not when you get all OCD with some of my stuff?"

"I don't want to ruin another one of your favorite things."

"You broke the damn mug nine years ago. Why can't you let it go? I certainly did—a long time ago."

"You were so upset at losing that mug. I don't want to upset you like that again."

"What's so goddamn wrong with my being upset when my favorite mug gets broken? If I'm upset, just let me be upset!"

"So, let me get this straight. You're not okay with my father being upset—but *I* should be okay with *you* getting upset!"

"*I* got upset because you broke something I cared about! Your father got upset because he's a self-absorbed prick."

"You don't sound to me like you've let go of my breaking the mug at all."

You're probably shaking your head at these two. But you also know exactly what I'm about to say: nothing is going wrong.

Everything that Meg and Jean-Pierre are arguing about actually happened. Jean-Pierre *did* break her favorite mug. Jean-Pierre's father *did* get deeply embarrassed and angry at Meg. Together, these two narratives have created gridlock for the couple. Meg and Jean-Pierre have been grinding together on these issues for years—and they have gotten nowhere. Meanwhile, both of them are hurting like hell.

Together, both spouses need to ask themselves, *Now what? What different course can we chart together?* And they need to do this *without* forgetting or dismissing the past.

For couples in gridlock, this is always difficult, and sometimes it can be impossible. That's why couples sometimes need to bring in a therapist. A talented therapist can notice where the rocks and holes are in each partner's personality, and recognize how these create gridlock in the relationship. With some coaching or questioning from the therapist, both partners can then begin to unhook things. This can allow healing to begin.

You'll recall from chapter 23 that the body's natural response to trauma is to attempt to complete the original action that was thwarted, so that the traumatic energy that has gotten stuck in the body can be metabolized. The original situation that created the trauma—or variations of it—will get reenacted, over and over, until the body is able to complete the original action.

The same thing is happening with Jean-Pierre and Meg. They will keep returning to the same issues, and the same two precipitating incidents, until they can move through and out of their stuckness together.

I can't know in advance what this might look like. Neither can Meg or Jean-Pierre. Remember, it's never possible to see what's on the other side of the leap that both partners need to make.

This leap may or may not involve Jean-Pierre's father. It might or might not involve tea mugs. (I hope it's clear by now that if Jean-Pierre buys Meg a gorgeous new tea mug, this won't make a damn bit of difference. It might even create more dirty pain.) It might involve an argument about her possessions vs. his possessions vs. their possessions. It might involve Meg's anger at *her own* parents for being egotistical and controlling. It might involve Jean-Pierre's anger at Meg, because he thinks she passively accepts character flaws in her own parents that she can't accept in his.

Whatever engenders such a leap, if and when both partners do take it together, they will both know it in their bodies.

COMPASS POINTS

- When a couple has been together for years, each member automatically develops an internal narrative about their partner and their relationship. Typically, each of these narratives includes a bodily recollection of something painful that the person's partner did in the past.

- These painful memories usually cause the person to develop a protective stance—or a set of protective behaviors—to try to avoid being hurt again in the same way.

- These stances and behaviors can keep couples stuck, creating pain, further conflict, and eventual gridlock.

- In the midst of this gridlock, both spouses need to ask themselves, *Now what? What different course can we chart together?* And they need to do this without forgetting or dismissing the past.

- This is difficult—and sometimes impossible. That's why couples sometimes need to bring in a therapist, who can notice where the rocks and holes are in each partner's personality, and recognize how these create gridlock in the relationship. With some coaching or questioning from the therapist, both partners can then begin to unhook things.

29

Resistance and Ambivalence

All of us want to change for the better. At the same time, we don't want to change at all.

Sometimes, as you make a move toward growth, your partner will support you. Sometimes they'll resist you. Sometimes they'll do both at once.

Sometimes when they do support you, you'll resist that support.

Sometimes, when your partner makes their own move toward growth, the same dynamic will occur with the roles reversed.

When your partner sees this ambivalence and resistance in you, it drives them half crazy. Meanwhile, you see the same resistance and ambivalence in them, and it drives *you* half crazy.

Yet—as you now know—nothing is going wrong. Resistance and ambivalence are normal in committed relationships. In fact, they're extremely beneficial, because they help us make important decisions about who we want to be and how we want to live.

Ambivalence isn't problematic or painful when little is at stake. If you and your lover can't decide which romantic comedy to see, or which tree to have a picnic under, you're probably ambivalent because the choices aren't that different. You could choose by flipping a coin. Either result would probably work out fine.

But when we struggle with something important or difficult, we're ambivalent because there's *so much* at stake. The wrong choice can create a deep wave of pain.

Usually when we're ambivalent, our first inclination is to make a quick choice in order to lower the heat on ourselves.

I see this all the time in my office. When couples reach emotional stalemates, they often say to me, "Resmaa, we're stuck. We just can't decide. Tell us what you recommend or what we should do."

I tell them, "Hell, no. You're sitting in uncertainty and it's turning the heat way up on you. That's exactly what needs to happen. Now you're telling me that you want to lower that heat by making a premature decision. But if you do that, something important won't have a chance to cook, and you'll deprive yourselves of an opportunity to transform.

"Instead of looking for a quick and dirty way to resolve your ambivalence, the two of you need to lean into it. Each of you needs to hold on to yourself, soothe yourself down, and stay anchored in the uncertainty you're facing and the ambivalence you experience. Don't try to run from them. Stay put and let them simmer.

"I don't know where this is going to take you any more than you do. But I do know that there's no way to run around what you're facing. Together, you're going to have to live into and through it. That's your only clean option."

Resistance is inherently neither good nor bad, right nor wrong. What's important is where it comes from and what its purpose is. When it comes from a strong part of you—for example, when you resist your lover's desire to overspend—it supports your partnership and your commitment to each other. It may also lead to an important emotional bottleneck.

But when it comes from a weak part of you—if you're so afraid of being poor that you resist your lover's plans for an affordable getaway with you—then it can create unnecessary conflict and dirty pain. This may *also* lead to an important emotional bottleneck.

Any time you have the impulse and opportunity to grow, you're going to face an equal amount of resistance. Some of it may come from inside you. Some may come from your family, friends, neighbors, coworkers, culture, or religion. Some of it may come from your partner. The more potential for growth that a situation offers, or the more important that growth will be, the greater the resistance that will arise.

NICK AND SANDY

After twenty years as a floor nurse, Nick takes a job as a hospital administrator. For the first time in his career, he now sits at a desk most of the day. Within a few weeks, he begins to sense the inactivity in his body. His back often bothers him, and by the end of the day his knees ache. He knows he needs to do something to address the pain and discomfort.

Nick begins exercising regularly at the gym. After a few weeks, his back and knees stop bothering him. He also begins losing weight—about half a pound a week.

After a year of twice-a-week workouts, Nick is in the best physical shape of his life. He's not especially muscular, but he's definitely stronger, and he's lost the few extra pounds that he'd carried around for the past few years.

To Nick's surprise, his improved health and physical condition don't impress his husband Sandy. In fact, sometimes Sandy gets testy when Nick leaves for the gym. "Enjoy your hot date with the kettlebell," he often says without looking up from his phone.

At family gatherings, Nick's parents are also unsupportive of his exercise regimen. His father sometimes refers to him as "Nick LaLanne," and on two occasions his mother tells him, "You make us seem old and out of shape." Nick just smiles and shrugs, not knowing what else to say or do.

Nick is bewildered by these reactions. He's not trying to hurt anyone or send a message of any kind; he's just working out for a couple of hours every few days—something that lots of people do. But as the months pass, and the snide comments from his husband and parents continue, his bewilderment turns into simmering anger.

Then, during Christmas dinner at his parents' home, his father suddenly blurts out, "Tell me, Mr. Universe, what exactly are you trying to prove? That you're better than the rest of us?" Nick loses his cool. He grabs a popover and beans his father on the forehead with it.

Because it's only a popover, his father just makes a disgusted face. But everyone else at the table, including Sandy, turns and stares disapprovingly at him. Now Nick is both angry and ashamed. He wants to scream and run out of the house.

When Nick wants to scream, run away, and beat himself up for having all these emotions, nothing is going wrong.

Everything that's arising for Nick—anger, shame, bewilderment, frustration, a desire to scream and run—is exactly what is supposed to come up. The resistance brings it all to the surface, so he can begin to address it.

Resistance is often a good sign—a sign that real growth is happening, or at least possible. Our job is to embrace it, work with it, and metabolize it, rather than try to banish it or keep it at bay.

Sometimes—especially when we make unwise choices or decisions—resistance can be enormously beneficial, even lifesaving. Suppose Nick went on an unhealthy crash diet, or began sticking his fingers down his throat after supper. Sandy might naturally resist his efforts out of love and concern.

Without resistance, there would be no growth. A crucial alchemical process goes on inside us *because* of resistance, not in spite of it.

But to metabolize resistance, you have to be willing to experience pain, slow down the process of metabolizing it, and work through it.

When resistance arises, there are three common ways in which we will be tempted to create dirty pain. All three distract us from the important task of metabolizing the resistance, moving through it, and growing up. Each one is sanctioned—and even encouraged—by some parts of our culture.

1. *We focus on our partner's resistance and fight with them about it.* This is probably not the only—or even the primary—source of resistance we encounter. But by focusing on that one stream of resistance, and pouring our energy into overcoming it, we try to blow all our fear and anger— and our own internal resistance—through our partner.

2. *We externalize the resistance as Satan, or society, or The Man.* Instead of doing the necessary work of moving toward our best self, we devote ourselves to Jesus, or political organizing, or the struggle for social justice.[20]

3. *We internalize the resistance as our ego or our dysfunction or our negative thoughts.* Under the guise of confronting ourselves, we break ourselves into parts and pit one part against the other. Instead of metabolizing and moving through our resistance, we battle with ourselves.

---

20 I'm not dissing Jesus or political organizing or social justice. I strongly support all three. But I don't support using any of them as a form of bypassing, or as a substitute for growing up. Religion, political organizing, and social justice are all 100 percent compatible with growth and transformation.

But the resistance you experience when you move toward something important would be there even if you didn't have a partner. It would be there even if you didn't believe in God, or political action, or social justice. It would be there even if your brain was full of self-esteem and positive thoughts.

Each of these three responses is just a form of noise. If you let yourself be distracted by the noise, and start pushing to overcome it or shut it down, you're not doing the real work of growing up.

The key to metabolizing resistance, pausing, confronting yourself, and working through ambivalence is always the same: your own integrity and your willingness to grow into your best self.

This integrity appears in two forms. First, you choose to accept clean pain and discomfort in order to grow. Second, you become willing to climb over whatever needs to be climbed over—in yourself, in your partner, in the world—in order to stand in that integrity.

Climbing over resistance doesn't mean fighting a battle. It means being willing to focus, tolerate pain, and grow.

Ambivalence and resistance are essential to our personal evolution. We need to work through them, accepting the uncertainty and the unknown, in order to become loving, grown-up human beings.

COMPASS POINTS

- Resistance and ambivalence are not only normal in committed relationships, but extremely beneficial, because they help us make important decisions about who we want to be and how we want to live.
- Ambivalence isn't problematic or painful when little is at stake. But when we struggle with something important or difficult, we're ambivalent because *so much* is at stake.
- Usually when we're ambivalent, our first inclination is to make a quick choice, in order to lower the heat on ourselves. We need to do the opposite: lean into it, stay put, and let the conflict cook.
- Any time you have the impulse and opportunity to grow, you're going to face an equal amount of resistance. The greater or more important the potential growth, the greater the resistance.

- Resistance is actually a good sign—a sign that real growth is happening, or at least possible. Our job is to embrace it, work with it, and metabolize it, rather than try to banish it or keep it at bay.

- Without resistance, there would be no growth. A crucial alchemical process goes on inside us *because* of resistance, not in spite of it.

- To metabolize resistance, you have to be willing to experience clean pain and discomfort, and work through it.

- When resistance arises, we will be tempted to create dirty pain in three ways: we can focus on our partner's resistance and fight with them about it; we can externalize the resistance as Satan, or society, or The Man; or we can internalize the resistance as our ego or our dysfunction or our negative thoughts.

- The key to metabolizing resistance and working through ambivalence is always your own integrity, your willingness to grow into your best self.

30

Changing without Growing

There is a fundamental difference between changing for the better and growing up.

I see this all the time in my therapy practice. I have clients who have stopped beating on their partners, or drinking, or drugging, or prowling the bars for late-night hookups. I acknowledge all of these positive behavioral changes. But that doesn't mean the people who made them have grown up.

The dry drunk is a classic case. They've stopped drinking, but they haven't changed their way of being in the world. They still live according to an addict's mentality. Often they get addicted to recovery, obnoxiously preaching the gospel of the Twelve Steps to everyone they meet.

Also common is the formerly violent partner who has learned to pound a punching bag, or a pillow, or a keyboard instead of their partner. While they may no longer be a physical threat, they may not have grown up much at all.

In both these cases, and countless others, people improve their behavior, but their fundamental way of being in the world remains the same. They make healthier choices, but they don't choose to take themselves on and grow up.

We often settle for these behavioral changes from our partners because things become so much better than how they used to be.

But these changes are not enough. You don't have to settle for them in your partner. And you don't have to settle for them in yourself, either. Demand nothing less than continued growth from both of you. That's why the two of you are together in the first place.

Most of us want our partner to grow up, but we don't want to grow up ourselves. Instead, we make some changes for the better and hope we can squeak by. But if our partner is alert and maintains their integrity, they won't let us do it; they'll continue to demand the best from us.

If you stand in your own integrity, you won't let your partner squeak by, either.

If the two of you do come to an unspoken agreement that you'll both settle for improved behavior but no transformation, watch out. Many of your earlier issues will magically reappear. Before you know it, the two of you will be back in an emotional bottleneck.

When you find yourself there, all the sobriety and physical safety in the world won't get you through it. There's no healthy alternative to sailing into the uncertain waters of clean pain and discomfort.

What it takes to actually grow up and transform is very different from what it takes to simply change for the better. The two of you have to face continued heat and pressure until you reach critical mass. Then and only then do you go through a fundamental, alchemical transformation.

This is why holding on to yourself by using the five anchors is so important. They keep you from blowing apart, or folding up, or running away when the pressure and heat reach their peak. (Or, if you do blow apart, fold up, or run away, they can help you the next time a high-pressure situation unfolds.)

Each time you and your partner make it through an emotional bottleneck, there's a sense of relief. For a time, the energy between you may more strongly align. You may think, *Whew. I'm glad that's over.*

Yes, the particular conflict may be over. But the two of you will soon face a new difficulty or conflict or conundrum. (When this happens, nothing is going wrong.)

That's why you need to make an ongoing commitment to growth and change—and to encouraging growth and change in your partner.

In practice, this means being willing do so something you *really* don't want to do, time after time, in one new situation after another.

If you're just changing to appease or soothe your partner, or make them happy, or get them off your back, you won't be able to maintain this commitment over the long haul, because the energies of performance and conciliation are weak and short-lived.

In contrast, when you genuinely commit to growing up, the energy behind your commitment is strong, vibrant, emergent, and naturally renewing. It's bigger than just you and your partner. It's a resource you tap into rather than one you dredge up from inside yourself.

Each time you and your partner make it through a new emotional bottleneck—each time you take a leap together—you make a little more room for further growth in your bodies and in your relationship. Each time, you temper and condition your bodies for making another leap, whenever one becomes necessary. And each time, taking that next leap may become a little bit easier.

COMPASS POINTS

- There is a fundamental difference between changing for the better and growing up.
- Often people improve their behavior, but their fundamental way of being in the world remains the same. They don't take themselves on and grow up.
- We may settle for these behavioral changes from our partners because things become so much better than they used to be. But they're not enough.
- Demand nothing less than continued growth from both of you. That's why the two of you are together in the first place.
- If the two of you come to an unspoken agreement that you'll both settle for improved behavior but no transformation, many of your earlier issues will reappear, and the two of you will be back in an emotional bottleneck.
- What it takes to actually grow up and transform is very different from what it takes to simply change for the better. The two of you have to face continued heat and pressure until you reach critical mass.
- This is why holding on to yourself by using the five anchors is so important.
- Because you and your partner will face one new difficulty or conflict or conundrum after another, you need to make an ongoing commitment to growth and change—and to encouraging growth and change in your partner.

- In practice, this means being willing do so something you *really* don't want to do, time after time, in one new situation after another.
- If you're just changing to appease your partner, or make them happy, or get them off your back, you won't be able to maintain this commitment over the long haul, because the energies of performance and conciliation are weak and short-lived.
- In contrast, when you genuinely commit to growing up, the energy behind your commitment is strong, vibrant, emergent, and naturally renewing.
- Each time you and your partner make it through a new emotional bottleneck—each time you take a leap together—you make a little more room for further growth in your bodies and in your relationship.

31

The Twin Terrors of
Togetherness and Autonomy

You can't have a healthy partnership without both togetherness and autonomy. Without togetherness, the relationship is a business deal in which both partners use each other for their own ends. Without autonomy, both partners eventually suffocate each other.

We each need to build our capacity to experience both togetherness *and* autonomy, and to switch between them as the situation warrants.

We've already seen how our Godzilla brain is terrified of togetherness and intimacy. That part of our brain hates our partner because our love for them makes us vulnerable to them. The more committed we are, and the more vulnerable we become, the more frightened our lizard brain can get.

Yet at the same time, a different part of our brain—the part that thinks like bees—is equally terrified of autonomy. Our bee brain doesn't want us to grow up and think for ourselves. Instead, it wants our partner to belong to us, and for us to belong to our partner. This is the part of your brain that wants you and your lover to be each other's baby.[21]

Whenever your partner wants more intimacy than you do, your lizard brain can get activated, and you may experience fear or anxiety.

---

21 I'm being metaphorical here. The physical design of the human brain is nothing like that of a bee brain. (But I'm not being metaphorical about our lizard brain. We do share certain structures of our brain with lizards.) I'm also being metaphorical about how bees act and process information. We now know that bees do behave and make decisions as individuals. In fact, recent experiments suggest that the "hive mentality" may be more illusory than real.

But whenever your partner wants more autonomy than you do, your bee brain can get activated—and you may experience just as much fear or anxiety.

All of this is baked into our DNA. It's not wrong or dysfunctional. It's how normal, healthy humans are wired. None of it is a mistake or something to overcome. It's a call—in two different voices—to grow up.

Our job isn't to get rid of the messages from our lizard and bee brains. We need them for our happiness and survival—and our maturity. Without your lizard brain, you could end up as a member of a mind-control cult, doing the bidding of Holy Herbert. Without your bee brain, you might be living alone in an Idaho cave, stockpiling weapons and posting "Keep Out" signs.

Our job is to metabolize the messages from both our bee and lizard brains, using the five anchors and the opportunities for reps that life presents us with. Over time, practicing these reps regularly will help us become the people we most want to be.

Any of us can shift from our lizard brain to our bee brain—and back again—in an instant. We can even experience both at the same time.

For example:

RAYNELLE AND QUINTON

Raynelle: We haven't gone out together in weeks. It seems like you're ignoring me.
Quinton: Let's go to a movie! I'm totally up for it.
Raynelle: When?
Quinton: Now.
Raynelle: Now it seems like you're pressuring me.

When Raynelle says to Quinton, "It seems like you're ignoring me," she's speaking from her bee brain, which fears autonomy. A few seconds later, when she says, "Now it seems like you're pressuring me," she's speaking from her lizard brain, which recoils from togetherness. Those words in turn briefly activate Quinton's own bee brain, which tells him, *She's pushing you away! Sting her!* In the heat of this situation, he might also think, *Huh? What the hell is wrong with you? You just said a few seconds ago that you want us to do something fun together.*

But he doesn't have to speak that thought or react from his bee brain. He can do better. He can hold on to himself and take a mental step back. This gives him the chance to ask himself, *What is Raynelle really asking me for?*

The answer is not *a fun date right now,* or she would have said, "Great! Let's see what's playing."

The answer is not *an immediate solution,* or his response wouldn't seem like pressure to her.

The answer is not *something other than a movie,* or she wouldn't have asked, "When?"

Because Quinton is able to hold on to himself and slow himself down, he shifts from one part of his brain to another. He responds from a strong, grown-up place rather than a confused, frustrated, primitive place.

He kisses Raynelle on the forehead and says, "I've missed going out with you, too, and I'm sorry it's been so long. Let's plan on a couple of evenings out soon. What times are best for you? Or would you rather figure that out later?"

Quinton's response is not merely an expression of love and caring; it's also a call for Raynelle to make a similar shift and grow up.

If she heeds that call and shifts to a grown-up part of her brain, she might say, "Thanks, hon; let's talk about it tonight," or "Let me check." But if she continues to respond from her lizard brain—if, for example, she says, "You're just saying that because you know your ass is guilty"—then Quinton needs to repeat his internal process a second time. Once again, he needs to choose between responding from a weak or a strong part of himself. If he goes with the strong, adult part of his brain, then he'll challenge Raynelle to grow up with him once more: "I'm guilty of loving you with all my heart. Guilty as hell but not a bit ashamed. Let's go out soon, whenever you're ready. My first choice is Saturday night, but suggest another time if you like."

This situation presented Raynelle and Quinton with a life rep—and, as you can see, Quinton used the five anchors to transform the situation from one of conflict to one of connection and caring.

COMPASS POINTS

- You can't have a healthy partnership without both intimacy and autonomy.
- We each need to build our capacity to experience both intimacy *and* autonomy, and to switch between them as the situation warrants.

- A part of your brain—the part that thinks like bees—is terrified of autonomy. It wants your partner to belong to you and for you to belong to your partner.
- When your partner wants more intimacy than you do, it may scare your lizard brain. But whenever your partner wants more autonomy than you do, it may frighten your bee brain.
- Any of us can shift from our lizard brain to our bee brain—and back again—in an instant. Both parts can even get activated at once.
- It's possible to shift just as quickly from our bee or lizard brain to a strong, grown-up part of our brain.
- Our job isn't to get rid of the messages from our lizard and bee brains. Our job is to metabolize the messages from both parts of our brain and to use them to help us grow up.

PART 2

Commitment, Power, and Control

32

When Commonplace Cruelty
Turns Physical

Each of us is cruel to our partner sometimes. We slime them. We eat their heart. We forge a coercive alliance. We treat them like shit. Emotionally or spiritually, we punch them in the gut. But we usually keep any impulses to physically harm them in check.

We're cruel to our partners because—for a short time—it works. It briefly satisfies us to blow our own pain and anxiety through them. It gives us a sense that we have some power. It creates a truckload of dirty pain, but until that truck pulls up and unloads, we have some brief, welcome relief.

All of this cruelty is 100 percent socially acceptable. No one goes to jail for it.

Unless the cruelty gets physical. Once there's physical cruelty of any kind—however brief or limited—everything flips. *That* form of cruelty is considered 100 percent unacceptable.

And it should be.

But in our culture, we don't say, "Physical cruelty is wrong. It needs to stop, and the people involved need to heal and grow up." Instead, we shout, "ANYONE WHO IS PHYSICALLY CRUEL TO THEIR PARTNER IS A MONSTER!"

And that's completely true.

But in the great majority of cases, the person is an ordinary human monster, just like you or me.

They simply got caught practicing the one and only form of commonplace cruelty that our culture forbids.

Welcome Home, Monsters

In most relationships where there has been physical cruelty, the two lovers think they're uniquely shameful or screwed up—that they're fundamentally different from other, normal couples. They're not.

I've worked with hundreds of such couples, both in my private therapy practice and as the clinical director for the Tubman Family Alliance, a domestic violence treatment center in Minneapolis. I've also worked with hundreds of individuals who have been physically cruel to their partners and hundreds of individual folks who have been on the receiving end of that cruelty. Here are some of the first things I tell most of these people:

"You're not special at all. You're just like everybody else. You experience the same things, and you have the same urges.[22] As an impulse, cruelty comes naturally to human beings, like compassion, empathy, generosity, and kindness.

"You're not even that unusual in terms of there being physical cruelty in your relationship. In a study of over 14,000 young adults, there was physical cruelty in 24 percent of all partnerships.

"When someone is cruel to their partner—physically or otherwise—it's not because they're a hopelessly violent asshole. It's almost always because they can't tolerate the heat of the situation they and their partner are in.[23]

"Cruelty of any kind can act as a release valve for that heat. You lost your shit because you were caught in an emotional bottleneck with your partner. Instead of connecting to your integrity, and addressing what needed to be addressed in yourself and your relationship, you tried to blow all your pain through your partner. You got overwhelmed, and you didn't have the internal skills or resources to deal with it. Now it's your responsibility to get off your ass and build them.

"This was fundamentally an act of avoidance. Instead of each of you confronting yourselves, at least one of you was physically cruel to your partner. Which is why, in therapy, we'll focus on what it means to confront yourself. We won't just focus on the physical cruelty.

---

22 The exceptions involve people who have serious personality disorders. I'll discuss these in the section that follows.

23 Cruelty of course does not occur in a cultural vacuum. In the United States, where I live, there is a long streak of historical cruelty that runs through our culture and our bodies. It was brought to the Americas by conquerors, colonizers, and missionaries; over the past 400 years, it has widely manifested itself through genocide, land theft, white-body supremacy, plantation ethics, mass shootings, rape culture, and myriad other forms. (Please note that this is about culture, not skin pigmentation. These cultural currents flow through the bodies of Americans of all skin tones. If you imagine that the purpose of this footnote is to simply diss white-bodied people, you've missed its point.)

"Each of you taking yourself on is the only way you'll be able grow up, learn to stand in your integrity, and stop being so cruel to your partner.

"The solution for you is the same as for everyone: learn to tolerate the inevitable heat and friction of being in an intimate partnership. Practice the five anchors to soothe yourself, slow yourself down, and stay present when the heat gets turned up under you. Act from the strongest parts of yourself, not the weakest. And accept the pain of growing up.

"You're here to begin to learn how to do all of these things."

Two Notable Exceptions

More than 90 percent of physical cruelty in committed relationships is the result of ordinary human monsters being unable to tolerate the inevitable heat and friction in their partnerships. When they're overwhelmed, they respond from the weakest parts of themselves and inflict physical harm on their partners. The use of alcohol or drugs often worsens their response.

That's the kind of cruelty this chapter focuses on. But for the next five paragraphs, I need to talk about the exceptions.

There are two small groups of people who don't fit the profile of ordinary human monsters: people with *antisocial personality disorder* (usually called *sociopaths* or *psychopaths*) and folks with the grandiose form of *narcissistic personality disorder* (usually called *grandiose narcissists*[24]). These people genuinely *are* wired differently— and dangerously.

The sociopath enjoys manipulating and inflicting harm on others and does so purely for sport. The grandiose narcissist is so reflexively self-involved that no one else matters to them. People in both groups have no conscience and no capacity for empathy. Both types of folks have a total disregard for other people's needs, desires, and concerns. Unlike ordinary human monsters, they are often *regularly* abusive or violent. They also have one other shared trait: they *never* heal, transform, or grow up.

---

24 There is also a second subgroup of people with narcissistic personality disorder, called *vulnerable narcissists*. These people have a milder form of narcissism and typically do have the ability to empathize, heal, transform, and grow up. And there is a third group, called *malignant narcissists,* who are both sociopaths and grandiose narcissists. People in this last group are particularly dangerous, often cruel, and sometimes violent.

About four to five percent of all people fit one of these two profiles. (Estimates vary, and no one has yet done an accurate head count, but that percentage is probably in the ballpark.)

A good therapist can smell a sociopath or grandiose narcissist—sometimes immediately, and almost always over time. Here are the scents these people give off:

1. No matter how much therapy, guidance, or training they receive, they're exactly the same in the fifth and tenth therapy sessions as they were in the first.

2. They never really understand that the cruel things they do are wrong.

3. Their partners almost never say, "I love my mate" or "I want my family healthy and whole" or "I want a better relationship"; instead, they're *terrified* and worried about their safety and survival.

If you believe your partner is a sociopath or grandiose narcissist, take your situation *very* seriously, and consult with a therapist as soon as you safely can. If necessary, call the police.

Where We Draw the Line

It's essential that we draw a bright line between ordinary human monsters who become briefly physically cruel and people with serious personality disorders. But that's not where the line currently gets drawn.

Instead, our culture—including the vast majority of mental health professionals—draws a single bright line between all people who have been physically cruel and all those who have not. The person who slaps or pushes or grabs their partner in the heat of an argument, even once, usually gets dumped into the same category as the sociopath. Someone can be as emotionally and spiritually cruel as they please, and they're often considered decent and normal. But anyone who is in any way physically cruel is suddenly an unredeemable villain and a beast. In this common view, the only thing separating you and me from the Boston Strangler and Jack the Ripper is a grab or a shake.

Of course, anyone who becomes violent needs to be held fully accountable for their actions—and needs to face serious negative consequences. My point here is not that violence is sometimes justified, but that we don't yet have a cultural mechanism for discerning the many different trajectories that can lead to violence.

It gets worse. Many incidents of physical cruelty in couples never get reported to the police. As a result, the person who regularly punches out their partner but never gets busted for it is considered an upstanding citizen, while the woman who slaps her unfaithful lover once, but has a neighbor who calls the police, may be seen as a violent nutcase.

When there is physical cruelty in a partnership, the person who is cruel is often branded a batterer, a perpetrator, or a maniac. The person on the receiving end of the physical cruelty is typically branded a victim. But only rarely do those designations tell the whole story. I'll say much more about this in chapters 33 and 34.

Three Bad Ideas

The term *domestic violence* originally meant *violence in the home* or *violence in committed couples*—but over the years it has morphed to mean *women getting the shit beat out of them by their asshole male partners.* That's an accurate description of *some* of the physical cruelty that occurs in committed relationships. But not most of it. Reality is usually much more complex.

In fact, our culture now suffers from three huge, interlocked misconceptions:

1. *When physical cruelty occurs in couples, almost 100 percent of it involves men hurting women.* Sexism, sexual harassment, and an unexamined tolerance for sexual abuse and assault all play significant roles in our culture. Nevertheless, it's important to note that women are not the sole sufferers of physical cruelty. Overall, in cases of physical cruelty in couples, about three-quarters of it is inflicted by men, and about three-quarters is inflicted on women. According to a 2010 report from the Centers for Disease Control and Prevention,[25] about 24 percent of all women have been on the receiving end of physical cruelty from their partners. (This percentage is confirmed by many other surveys.) But so have about 14 percent of all men. Furthermore, multiple studies show that physical cruelty occurs in gay and lesbian couples at roughly the same rates as it does in hetero couples.

   Gender doesn't necessarily change the basic dynamics of a committed partnership; neither does sexual orientation.

---

25 *National Intimate Partner and Sexual Violence Survey, 2010 Summary Report, Executive Summary,* www.cdc.gov/violenceprevention/pdf/nisvs_executive_summary-a.pdf.

That said, when it comes to sheer carnage, men are much more responsible. Eighty percent of the people who kill their partners are male.

2. *Couples are either nonviolent (and decent) or violent (and screwed up).* This is like saying couples are either thirsty or not thirsty, either law-abiding or criminal, or either beautiful or ugly.

   Among us ordinary monsters, physical cruelty is mostly situational. The great majority of people in committed relationships share the same basic motivations and emotions, and follow the same basic arc as they grind against each other. The only differences are in how much heat they are able to tolerate, how able they are to slow themselves down and soothe themselves, and what they do when the heat becomes intolerable.

3. *Once a perp, always a perp.* Once someone is physically cruel to their partner—in any way, in any context, and for any reason—we tend to lump them in with sociopaths. We think, *They're not a member of our tribe. They're incapable of changing, healing, or growing up. They're debris. We need to sweep them up and throw them away in prison. If we don't, they'll only beat on someone else.*

   This just isn't so. Given the right guidance and treatment, and a willingness to confront themselves and grow up, many people do heal and stop being physically cruel to their partners. I've watched innumerable individuals and couples heal, time after time after time. The right treatment works.

   But it's also true that the wrong treatment—or no treatment at all—doesn't work, for the same reason that an antibiotic, or doing nothing, won't heal a broken wrist.

   What if, instead of merely removing and disposing of human debris, we helped individuals and couples actually grow up?

Treating People Right

Sometimes people who are physically cruel to their partners need to go to jail. The criminal justice system holds a place in helping our society deal with people who cause serious physical harm.

But legal interventions alone never solve the problem of human monsters not knowing how to navigate committed relationships.

The reality is that once people pay for their crimes and get released, many of them repeat exactly the same patterns. We see this as evidence that they're unchangeable, irredeemable, violent assholes.

Occasionally that's exactly what they are. But much more often, they're ordinary monsters who haven't been asked to grow up and who haven't been given any serious training in how to do it.

When these folks get out of jail, one of two things typically happens:

- Their old partner has waited for them. Now that they're back together, the heat gets turned up under them in exactly the same ways as before. The same two people find themselves dealing with the same old emotional stalemates. The ecology of the relationship hasn't changed. In one common variation on this theme, the person who gets out of jail *has* changed, but not really for the better. They've learned to stop being physically cruel to their partner—but they've also learned how to be *more* emotionally and spiritually cruel. Instead of hitting their partner, they twist an emotional knife into their partner's heart, over and over. But because there's no physical harm, they don't have to go back to jail for it.

- The person who gets out of jail no longer has the same partner. But because they haven't grown up, they find a new partner whose rocks fit perfectly into the holes in their head in the same way that their previous partner's rocks did. Soon the same pattern of interrelating reemerges, with similar dynamics and similar emotional bottlenecks. The heat gets turned up in the same way. Unless someone in the relationship begins to confront themselves, there will likely be physical cruelty in this new partnership.

This is why punishment—though often necessary—is never enough. People have to learn to work with the actual dynamics of a committed relationship.

But in many cases they have no idea how to manage such a relationship. They may be equally clueless about how to take themselves on, accept their own pain, and grow up. Their commonplace cruelty may be so tied in with who they are, how they interact with one another, and how they navigate the world that they need help from outside the relationship.

This is exactly what a talented therapist can offer. They can help a couple look at the entire ecology of their relationship and understand its dynamics. They can help each lover learn to use the five anchors to tolerate the unavoidable heat, friction, pain, and uncertainty of being in a committed relationship. Most of all, they can help each partner straighten their spine, look the other person in the eye, and say, "I choose *you*. And because I choose you, I'm going to accept the pain of being in emotional bottlenecks with you. When I'm hurting, I won't hurt you to try to reduce my own pain. It's my job to deal with my emotional pain, not yours. Right now I'm scared half to death, but I'm making a commitment. Not just to you, but to myself—a commitment to grow up.

"Now it's your turn. Will you take yourself on? And will you choose *me*? And no matter what happens, no more being violent."

COMPASS POINTS

- Each of us is emotionally and spiritually cruel to our partner sometimes, but we usually keep any impulses to physically harm them in check.
- Most of the cruel things we do to our partner are 100 percent socially acceptable. But physical cruelty—however brief or limited—is 100 percent unacceptable.
- And it should be. But instead of helping couples heal, we focus on punishing the person who was physically cruel.
- In most relationships where there has been physical cruelty, both partners have the same emotions and impulses as other couples. One or both lovers simply couldn't tolerate the heat and emotional stalemates of the intimate partnership.
- Physical cruelty is fundamentally an act of avoidance. Instead of confronting themselves, one lover tries to blow their pain and anxiety through the other.
- In couples in which there has been physical cruelty, the solution is the same as for everyone: learn to tolerate the inevitable heat and friction of being in an intimate partnership; practice the five anchors; stay present when the

heat gets turned up; act from strengths, not weaknesses; and accept the pain of growing up.

- There are two small groups of people who don't fit this normal profile: people with *antisocial personality disorder* (usually called *sociopaths* or *psychopaths*) and folks with the grandiose form of *narcissistic personality disorder* (usually called *grandiose narcissists*). These people genuinely *are* wired differently—and dangerously. They *never* heal, transform, or grow up.

- It's essential that we draw a bright line between ordinary human monsters who become briefly physically cruel and people with serious personality disorders. But instead we draw the line between people who have been physically cruel and those who have not. The person who slaps or pushes or grabs their partner in the heat of an argument, even once, gets dumped into the same category as the sociopath.

- Our culture suffers from three huge, interlocked misconceptions about physical cruelty in couples:

  * *Almost all physical cruelty involves men hurting women.* In fact, 24 percent of women and 14 percent of men have been on the receiving end of physical cruelty from their partners, and physical cruelty occurs in gay and lesbian couples at roughly the same rates as it does in hetero couples.

  * *Couples are either nonviolent (and decent) or violent (and screwed up).* Among us ordinary monsters, physical cruelty is mostly situational, not baked in.

  * *Once a perp, always a perp.* This just isn't so. Given the right guidance and treatment, and a willingness to confront themselves and grow up, many people do heal and stop being physically cruel to their partners. The right treatment works.

- Legal interventions alone never solve the problem of human monsters not knowing how to navigate committed relationships. They may need help. This is exactly what a talented therapist can offer.

33

The Rock of Power and
the Hole of Control

We all need power people *and* control people in our lives. Without control people, life would be hopelessly chaotic. Without power people, it would be hellishly static and regimented.

Power and control are a classic rock and hole. Without control, power is unfocused and ineffective. Without power, there's nothing to control.

As you'll recall from chapter 12, power people make things *happen*. They act. They move. They mobilize. They break through. Often, they break rules.

Control people make things *work*. They manage. They organize. They coordinate. They strategize. They devise and enforce the rules.

No human being is *solely* a power person or a control person. Every sane person has both orientations inside them. It's a classic *both/and* arrangement.

But folks with the most serious internal power/control imbalances *aren't* healthy. People with obsessive compulsive disorder lean way too far toward control. People who lean way too far toward power tend to end up as violent criminals, prison inmates, or corpses.

Most of us have a distinct leaning in one direction or the other. That's usually sane and healthy. It's only the folks with the most extreme leanings who run into trouble—and often create it.

Many successful professional relationships involve a power person and a control person. Think of the celebrity and their agent or manager, the CEO and their COO and CFO, the chef and their prep cook, or the disc jockey and their engineer.

Unfortunately, many therapists largely misunderstand power and control. They use the terms interchangeably, as if they were equivalents rather than two sides of the same coin. It's a bit like thinking that *therapist* and *the rapist* mean the same thing.

Power and Control for Two

In most committed couples, one partner leans more toward power and the other more toward control.

If you're a power-oriented person, you're likely to get together with a control-oriented partner, and vice versa. Each of you brings to the relationship something the other lacks.

But when you exercise this complementary quality within your partnership, your partner may not like it one bit. When they exercise *their* complementary attribute, you probably won't like it, either. You'll recognize this as the inherent paradox of rocks and holes. And when it occurs, of course, nothing is going wrong.

When both members of a couple understand and acknowledge this, they can use it to create greater intimacy and a smoother day-to-day life. When they don't, they may drive each other crazy and create boatloads of dirty pain.

There's one other *both/and* aspect to this: it's not unusual for couples to shift their power/control balance based on the context.

Meet the Extremes

Someone with an extreme power orientation tends to be impatient and impulsive. They like to *act*, not study options, or plan strategies, or build consensus. Their main focus in life is trying to get everyone else to do what they want. They get extremely uncomfortable sitting around talking but doing nothing.

Power people tend to respond from their heads, not their hearts. When you ask for their opinion, they'll usually say, "I think it's a smart move" rather than "That seems right to me."

People with strong power leanings usually find partners who have strong control orientations—and for good reason, because they often have difficulty controlling or managing their impulses. But, of course, when their partner tries to control them, they get pissed as hell.

What people with extreme power orientations most need to develop is self-control.

In contrast, somebody with an extreme control orientation spends a lot of time pondering, considering, and worrying. But they don't often *act*—and when they do act, it rarely involves something new, different, or challenging.

Control people usually have strong emotions and opinions about everything—especially their partnership, their partner, and their partner's behavior. They may spend much of their time correcting or commenting on what their partner does.

People with very strong control leanings usually experience themselves as powerless, so they find partners with strong power orientations. The partner brings to the relationship a sense of purpose and effectiveness, and an ability to get things done. But, of course, the control-oriented person instinctively does everything they can to regulate these very qualities in their partner.

What people with extreme control orientations most need to develop is motivation: a willingness and ability to act.

As with all rocks and holes, power has a control underbelly, and control has a power underbelly. But when someone with an extreme control orientation finally accesses their power, they can easily misuse it at first. The same is true when someone with an extreme power orientation begins learning to use control. They're both like Frankenstein's monster learning to use his limbs for the first time.

When Leanings Turn Cruel

When there has been physical cruelty in a committed relationship, often it's because at least one partner has an extreme leaning toward either power or control.

A talented therapist can help the couple examine this issue, unhook it, and create a more evenly balanced relationship.

Unfortunately, when therapists work with someone who has been physically cruel to their partner, they often make this series of mistakes:

First, they reflexively designate the person who was physically cruel as the *perpetrator*, and the person they were cruel to as the *victim*. (Sometimes, in the case of hetero couples, they reflexively declare the man the perpetrator and the woman the victim, without knowing the couple's dynamics, or the details of their backstory.)

Second, they tell the so-called perp they have a power problem and then build a therapeutic intervention around that problem.

Sometimes this is exactly the right call. The person *does* have an overly strong power orientation, and their physical cruelty was an attempt to influence their partner through force.

But this isn't always the case. Often the person who was physically cruel doesn't have power issues at all. Instead, they're way too oriented toward control.

ELOISE AND AMAHD

Over the past year, Eloise has had three affairs, while lying to her husband, Amahd, about them. "Of course I'm faithful," she tells him time after time. "If I wanted to be with someone else, I'd leave."

Yet Amahd can sense that something isn't right. He doesn't confront her on her statements, but he does his best to monitor and track her.

One evening, an hour after she told him she needed to work late, he sees her enter a hotel lobby. He runs inside and confronts her as she waits for the elevator. Caught in the act, she is speechless at first. Then she says in a small, firm voice, "I'll do whatever I want. You can't stop me."

Amahd grabs her arms and pushes her up against the elevator door. "Why did you lie to me?" he demands.

Eloise glares at him. "Are you going to hit me now?" she says angrily. "You'd enjoy that, wouldn't you? Go ahead and try it. I'll put your ass in prison and walk away with everything we own."

Amahd lets go of Eloise and takes a step back. He opens his hand, pulls back his arm, and gets ready to slap his wife across the face. But when he sees her eyes widen, he stops himself. He takes a few deep breaths, then turns and walks away.

Obviously, Amahd and Eloise have some serious issues to work through. Those issues involve much more than just infidelity and violence. But saying that Amahd has a problem with power completely misses the mark. His problem is with *control*. His brief physical cruelty came from a completely different emotional place than the punch from the guy who told his therapist, "This is a dog-eat-dog world. You got to show your bitch who's boss, because if you don't, she'll make you *her* bitch."

For years I worked with groups of offenders who had been physically cruel to their partners. Everyone in every group was considered to have issues around power. But I quickly learned that many actually had issues around control. Because extreme-power folks have completely different mental templates from extreme-control people, I needed to develop two complementary approaches, one for each mental template, to help my clients heal. Whenever I began working with a new group of offenders, I had to first identify which people used which template to navigate the world.

When I work with people who have extreme power leanings, I usually sit very close to them, touch them frequently, and make comments such as, "Dude, I get it, man. It really hurts you deep inside." As they tell me their stories, I often ask them, "How did that affect you emotionally?"

All of this freaks the shit out of them. Eventually they say something like, "Dude! Why are you touching me and sitting so close?" I look surprised and ask, "Does that make you uncomfortable?" "Hell, yes!" "So, what do you sense about me?" "I'm really pissed and I wish you'd back the fuck off."

Now that they've moved out of acting—and into experiencing their own emotions and physical sensations—my foot is in the door. "Do you want to get up and punch me?" "Hell, yes!" "So tell me what you're noticing in your body right now. Do you experience it as a fire? Like the fire is growing? Is that the same thing you experience when you're pissed at your partner?" I say this because power-oriented people usually have a limitation around their hearts and their emotions. (In contrast, control-oriented people usually have a limitation around their heads and around action.)

When I work with people who have extreme control leanings, I sit far away with my arms crossed. I'll be attentive, but I'll display only a small amount of empathy and act a bit bored.

Usually they begin by telling me, often in great detail, their many emotions. As soon as they finish, I say, "Okay, so tell me what you're going to do about that." When they drop back into talking about their emotions, I ask again, "So what do you plan to do to handle that?" I repeat this question in various forms until the client finally answers it—or says something like, "This is bullshit. I'm leaving" or "I'm seriously thinking of punching you in the face right now." Either way, they've begun to move from emotions into action.

Growing up is never easy. But it's a hell of a lot easier when you've got a therapist who actually understands who you are and how you see the world.

Here are three more cases that illustrate the complex dynamics of power and control:

HENRI AND VALERIE

Henri and Valerie came to see me about some serious physical cruelty that had disrupted their marriage.

For years, Valerie complained that Henri didn't pay attention to her. He spent most of his free time on the Internet or watching cable TV. When the two went out together, Henri would reflexively answer his phone whenever it rang, even if they were in the middle of dinner or a conversation.

At home, when Henri wasn't watching television, or on the phone, or surfing the Internet, he was warm, chatty, and fully present. "But when he'd use an electronic device," Valerie told me, "he was *gone*—completely hypnotized. I could walk right up to him and say, 'Henri, I just screwed all three of your brothers on the kitchen table,' and he wouldn't notice. *Maybe* he'd nod or say 'okay.'"

For nearly three years, Henri and Valerie ground together on this issue—but not in a clean way. Valerie never stood up to Henri and said, "There's something important I need to talk with you about, right now. I need you to turn that thing off and focus on me." Instead, every time, she'd sit down next to Henri and start talking. When he ignored her, she'd get frustrated, curse him, and stomp out of the room.

She also never stood up to herself. She never asked herself, *Why do I get so upset when I want Henri's attention right away and don't get it?*

One Sunday afternoon, while Henri was lying on the couch watching football, Valerie got a phone call from her sister-in-law Patti. Through sobs, Patti told her that her brother Matt had died in an auto accident a few hours earlier.

Crying, Valerie hurried into the den. She knelt next to her husband and took his hand. "Henri," she said, "can we talk?"

Henri nodded but didn't take his eyes off the screen. "It's only four minutes to halftime," he said.

That's when Valerie lost her mind. She got up and yanked the television plug out of the wall. Then she tore out all the plugs next to it and picked up the nearby table lamp.

"What the *hell*?" Henri shouted.

Valerie turned and glared into her husband's eyes. "You bastard. *For once in your life, you're going to listen to me.*"

"But the Packers are—"

Valerie ran to the couch and stood over her husband, holding the base of the lamp a foot above his head. "Pack *this*," she said, and let go.

It was clear that Valerie and Henri had some serious issues. At first I thought I had a handle on what the main ones were—but I was wrong. I discovered this when I asked, "When did the lamp incident happen?"

"Fifteen years ago," Valerie said.

I turned to Henri. "Has there been any physical cruelty between you since then?"

He shook his head.

Valerie shook hers, too. "Neither one of us wants a repeat of that afternoon."

"Have there been any threats of violence?"

"No," Henri said. "Violence really isn't an issue in our marriage."

"Trust is," Valerie said. "Henri doesn't trust me."

"Of course I don't trust you," Henri said. "You beaned me with a goddamn table lamp."

Valerie spread her hands. "That was fifteen years ago!"

This was one case where I did *not* tell my clients, "There's nothing wrong. Everything is happening just the way it should."

The table lamp gave Henri a large, painful bruise on his forehead and a smaller bruise just above one ear. His injuries certainly didn't help the marriage. Still, that afternoon was a turning point for both spouses.

It took a couple of years of therapy, but Henri woke up to his inattentiveness. He apologized to his wife, took himself on about his fondness for devices, and partly grew up. Valerie mostly grew up around the issue, too.

The two of them made several deals. They would spend at least an hour together every day, with all devices except phones turned off. When they were out together, neither one would answer their phone, except by prior agreement. And when either mate was at the computer or watching TV, the other wouldn't interrupt except for something important—in which case they would start by saying, "This is important."

Those agreements had worked well for almost fifteen years. Their issue was something else entirely.

On that painful Sunday afternoon, Henri stopped trusting his wife. That trust needed to be rebuilt.

The couple spent the next several years making amends to each other. They mostly treated each other with respect and courtesy. But whatever Valerie did, Henri never allowed himself to fully trust her again. The sweetness of the relationship evaporated. *That* was why the two mates were in my office.

I began to work with Valerie and Henri separately.

"We've both changed for the better," Valerie told me in one of our sessions. "Our communication is good. We're rarely rude to each other and certainly never abusive. But something big is missing. I want to have a good relationship with my husband. But Henri keeps holding back. A big piece of him isn't there."

"That's always been the problem, hasn't it?" I asked.

"It's different now. Before, he'd let himself get sucked into his electronics. But when the devices were turned off, he was there. Now, he's *never* all there—at least not when he's with me. After the lamp incident, he put up a wall."

Henri confirmed this in one of our sessions. "Of course I put up a wall," he said. "Wouldn't you put up a wall if someone dropped a lamp on your head?"

"Of course," I said. "But once I stopped needing the wall, I'd dismantle it."

"She's the one who forced me to build it," Henri said. "She's the one who needs to take it down. I've told her that, over and over."

Valerie didn't argue with that. "He *does* tell me that over and over," she said in her next session. "But I don't know what he expects me to do. I'd love to knock that wall down. But no matter what I do, he tells me it's not good enough, that he still can't trust me. In his mind, I'm still standing there holding the lamp over his head." She brushed her hair out of her eyes. "Sometimes I think he's making plans to leave."

I shook my head. "Henri isn't going anywhere. If he was interested in leaving, he would have left a long time ago. But here's the thing, Valerie. He's the one who put up that wall. He's the only one who can take it down. It's not your job to take those bricks out, no matter how much he tells you it is. In fact, you *can't* take them out, because the only handles on those bricks are on his side of the wall.

"Yes, you went berserk when your brother died and your husband ignored you. But that was fifteen years ago. Henri's lack of trust now is *his* problem, not yours. He needs to take himself on about this—but so far he hasn't."

"So what do I do?" Valerie asked.

"Go home and tell him that *he* needs to yank those bricks out. Say that you're done with trying to do the impossible." I leaned forward. "Valerie, the only way you're going to have the relationship you want with Henri is if he confronts himself about his own bullshit. Until *he* starts taking the bricks out, and stops trying to blow his fear through you, nothing is going to improve."

From the beginning of their marriage, Henri had controlled most of the relationship. For years he determined the couple's level of interaction, simply by shifting his attention. But after almost three years, in the heat of her grief and frustration, Valerie responded to Henri's ongoing control with an act of sheer, violent power.

During the fifteen years afterward, their relationship improved in some ways. But Henri continued to control their level of interaction by constantly withholding his trust.

Valerie needed to act from her power—not violent power, but the power to straighten her spine and tell Henri what she wanted from him.

She went home to her husband and explained that she wanted more from their relationship. She told him it was time for him to choose: either start tearing down his wall, or tell her through his actions that it would never come down—in which case she would have to make a choice of her own.

Valerie understood that she was giving her husband a choice, not an ultimatum. Ultimatums tend to create double binds rather than solutions. She realized that Henri might continue doing exactly what he had been doing for the past fifteen years—and, if he did, there would be nothing she could do to stop or change him. If he did decide to keep his wall in place, then the next move would be up to her.

LARRY AND STAN

When Larry first came to see me, it was because he'd been badly beaten by his partner, Stan, three years earlier. The two had been together for almost five years. Larry did not fight back, or call the police, or leave the relationship.

Larry sat slumped in the chair across from me. "I saw you on *Oprah*," he told me in our first session, "and people told me that you can really help abuse victims. I'm here to get some support."

As you've figured out by now, that's not how I work. I don't hand out support like it's Halloween candy. I want to learn what the dynamics of the relationship are first. And in some cases, my "support" might involve suggesting to my client that they get up off their ass, straighten their spine, and call the police.

"Tell me why you're here," I said.

"I don't understand what's wrong with me. I'm thirty years old. This is my fourth serious relationship—and in every single one, my boyfriend abused me." Larry explained that the abuse wasn't always physical. One partner had stolen his credit cards; another had an emotionally sadistic streak.

"Were they all abusive from the beginning?" I asked.

"No. Never at first. Always after a year or so. It's like I'm an abuse magnet. I'm here to find out whether it's the people I pick or the things I do in the relationship."

That's a shitty set of choices, I thought. *Either way, you've made yourself responsible.*

"When your lovers treat you badly, do they blame you for it or say you deserve it?"

Larry brightened a bit, but stayed slumped. "Yes. That's it exactly."

"So what do you think you need to do about it?"

"I don't know."

I waited. We sat in silence for half a minute. Larry started to look uncomfortable. I waited more. Eventually he said, "Are you going to ask me more questions?"

"No," I said. "I'll ask you the same one again. What do you think you need to do about it?"

"That's what I'm here to find out, isn't it? I'm looking for your guidance."

"I can give you my best guidance if you tell me the things *you* think you can do. That will give me something to work with."

Our conversations went on like this for three sessions. But I was willing to wait and to continue to be a broken record. Sooner or later something else would show up.

When Larry came in for our fourth session, the slump in his shoulders had largely disappeared. He seemed tense and angry.

"How are you doing?" I asked.

"Fine," he said in a clipped, hollow voice. "But I don't think this therapy is working. People told me you were really good, but I haven't heard you say anything helpful yet."

Larry was confronting me. He'd *never* done this with any of his partners. Something inside him was beginning to shift.

I said, "It seems like something's going on for you. You might have a little anger toward me."

The moment I named the anger, he retreated. "I'm not angry."

I moved in. "Larry. Now's the time to decide whether you have enough power to be able to soothe yourself and actually tell me what's going on for you."

"I'm not angry."

I held my ground. "Larry, right now you get to decide what you want to do. What you've always done—which is shut up, suck it down, control it, and not move with it—or something different."

Then I went silent. I sat back and let it cook.

I saw in his face that he was going back and forth. *Say something; don't say something; say something; don't say something.*

Finally he said, "You're not going to say anything?"

"You can keep trying to blow it through me, or you can take it forward. It's all on you."

We sat in silence for another five seconds. Then he said angrily, "I thought you were going to be able to help me."

I said, "Are you disappointed that I can't help you?"

We sat silently for a while longer. Then he said, "You scare me."

"I know I do."

"I hate the way you're treating me. I wish you'd act like a normal therapist."

I leaned forward. "You're finally doing it, Larry. You're confronting someone and telling them what you want. That's exactly the skill you need to practice. Now you have a chance to learn to tell people what you want from them. That's what you're going to need in order to not pick another asshole—and to stand up straight whenever you don't like the way someone is treating you.

"You can't be cavalier about this, because you're still in a dangerous relationship. Notice what's happening in your body right now, and embrace it."

Larry looked at me sadly. Then he said, "I'm not in danger. Not anymore. Stan left me last week."

We sat in silence for some time.

After about a minute, I said, "You're going to have to give birth to a new Larry now. You've already started. I can just see the crown of the head poking out, but you're going to have to keep pushing."

Larry stared at me for a moment. Then we both burst out laughing.

"You know something?" Larry said. "You're a fucking nutbag."

"I know, I know. Listen, Larry—you're going to have to transform the way you think and who you believe you are."

"Now you're *really* scaring me." But he was smiling. He was getting it.

It took Larry years to heal and grow up. At times he went too far in the other direction, calling people on the mild bullshit that most of us let slide. But it was good practice for him as he learned to straighten his spine and live into his own power.

JUDI AND BRANDON

Judi was the assistant police chief of a major Midwestern city. From the time she first joined the force at age twenty-two, she learned not to take shit from anyone, especially men.

Her husband, Brandon, worked in a call center for a large retailer. His job largely involved taking shit from people all day. He didn't like his job at all; he wanted to be a writer. But whenever he talked to his wife about taking some college-level writing classes, she would push back—hard. "Get real," she'd say. "We have two kids to raise."

Occasionally Brandon would take the debate further. "I'm not looking to be a poet or novelist," he'd say. "I'm talking about training to become a publicist or a corporate communications specialist. They make three times the money I'm making at the call center."

Judi always responded by pushing back harder. "Yeah," she'd say, "and so do I. And you know why? Because I don't sit on my ass dreaming about what might be. I work in the real world. You need to take Jimmy to soccer practice now."

Every couple of months, Brandon and Judi would get into a loud, lengthy argument. The topics varied, but their tactics were always the same. Brandon would do his best to make a logical, sensible case. Judi would respond with an angry refusal, then call Brandon lazy or foolish or unrealistic. Brandon would say something like, "You're not being fair." Judi would respond, "You're not being very smart. Listen, I can do this all day if you really want to. You think I got to where I am by being weak and stupid?" Eventually Brandon would sigh and let the matter drop.

Sometimes Judi accused Brandon of lacking motivation. To his credit, he didn't buy it. "I've got plenty of motivation," he'd say. "But whenever I try to do something new or different, you stand in my way."

"No," Judi would reply. "When you try to do something *lame* I stand in your way."

After a few years of this, Brandon stopped trying to convince his wife that his professional hopes or dreams had any merit. Instead, he signed up for a two-day writers' conference and told her about it only after he'd registered. That led to another fight—but this one ended in a standoff, partly because he'd already paid the nonrefundable registration fee.

Two days before the conference was to begin, Judi told him, "I need to work this Saturday. The chief came down with the flu. He asked me to come in to handle part of the workload. I'll need you to watch the kids."

"I've got the writers' conference on Saturday and Sunday," Brandon reminded her. "I'll call your mom to see if she can take them."

"Jesus Christ. You can't even watch your own kids. You're useless, you know that?"

"You've known for weeks that I have plans for this weekend."

Judi glared at her husband. "I'm not sure I want to be married to you anymore. I'm not sure I even respect you anymore. I *know* the kids don't."

Brandon took a deep breath, thought about his options, and agreed to watch the kids on Saturday. "But on Sunday I'm going to the writers' conference," he insisted. "You can take care of them or send them to your mom's—whichever one you want."

On Saturday, Judi came home about 7 p.m. and ate a quick dinner with the family. As she and Brandon washed the dishes, Judi said, "Listen, I'm tired. *Really* tired. You're going to have to handle the kids tomorrow."

For a moment, Brandon froze. Then he dropped the dishtowel, picked up a plate, and smashed it to pieces against the edge of the counter. "Fuck you."

"*What* did you say?"

He turned to Judi. "I'm not taking any more shit from you. Do you hear me? I'M NOT TAKING ANY MORE SHIT FROM YOU."

She took a step toward him.

He hit her hard on the cheek. As she staggered backward, he threw himself on her.

She went down, and they struggled on the floor for over a minute. Finally she wiggled free, ran into the bedroom, and locked the door. As he kicked at it, she pulled her cell phone from her pocket and dialed 911.

Eventually Brandon kicked the door down. But by then his fury was spent. He sat down on the bedroom floor and put his head in his hands. Judi stepped around him and ran into the front yard.

When the squad cars pulled up a few minutes later, Brandon was waiting outside to be taken away.

When Judi and Brandon came to see me as a couple, eight years later, they had both done some of their own individual therapy. But they were still on the verge of divorce. "You're our last stop before we file divorce papers," Brandon told me. "If you can help us crawl out of this pit, great. Otherwise, we're both ready to call it quits."

I looked at Judi. "Is that how you view my role, too?"

She shrugged. "Sure." She turned to her husband. "But you're still going to pay for what you did to me."

I'm used to someone talking trash to their partner's face in their first therapy session, so I let that comment slide. I said to them, "Like it or not, the two of you are in this pit together. But let me be clear. It's not my job to get the two of you out of something that you spent years digging yourselves into."

Judi gave me a nasty look but didn't say anything.

I said, "The first thing the two of you have to do is stop being so cruel to each other—which I know is a tall order for you two. So let me spell out what that means. No physical cruelty. No emotional cruelty. No cruelty with words.

"How serious the two of you are about this will determine whether or not you file divorce papers. Either way, it's your call, not mine."

It took Brandon and Judi years to transform their relationship. But they were both tenacious and resilient people. Sometimes incrementally, sometimes in small leaps, they began to examine and unhook their hurtful dynamics.

Judi began to see how she had developed a reflexively aggressive response to anything that seemed at all threatening. Over time she learned to step back, soothe herself down, and consider her options. She also learned a variety of responses to use in place of her take-no-prisoners approach.

For his part, Brandon began to learn how to stand in his own power without trying to make a convincing argument—and without being cruel or violent. After about a year, the two actually began to joke about a line he learned to use regularly: "I don't take shit, and I don't dish it out."

What broke things open for the couple was when Judi's sister was busted for cooking and dealing meth. The headline of the local paper—*Assistant Police Chief's Sister Arrested on Drug Charge*—reduced her to tears. Then came the unavoidable questions from reporters—especially, "How could you not know your own sister was cooking meth?" For the first time in her adult life, everything seemed utterly out of her control—and she was powerless to stop it.

Terrible as the news was, it was exactly what she needed. It cracked her wide open. In my office, for the first time in many years, she admitted her fear and vulnerability.

I knew that she and Brandon had a chance when, choking back tears, she took her husband's hand and said to him softly, "Bran, I can't do this alone. Will you help me?"

COMPASS POINTS

- Power is the ability to influence. Control is the ability to regulate. We all need power people and control people in our lives.

- Power and control are a classic rock and hole. Without control, power is unfocused and ineffective. Without power, there's nothing to control.

- No human being is *solely* a power person or a control person. Every sane person has both orientations inside them. It's a classic *both/and* arrangement.

- Unfortunately, many therapists largely misunderstand power and control. They use the terms interchangeably, as if they were equivalents rather than opposites. This sometimes prevents clients from healing and growing up.

- In most committed couples, one partner leans more toward power and the other more toward control—though it's not unusual for couples to shift their power/control balance based on the context.

- People with very strong power leanings usually find partners who have strong control orientations—and vice versa.

- When there has been physical cruelty in a committed relationship, often it's because at least one partner has an extreme leaning toward either power or control.

- Growing up is never easy. But it's easier when you've got a therapist who understands who you are and how you see the world.

34

How Our Culture Needs
to Grow Up

As I write this chapter, three stories about celebrity athletes are in the news. The first involves a man who fatally shot his girlfriend. The second is about a woman who will soon go to trial for assaulting her nephew and half sister. The third involves a man who punched his fiancée in the face, knocking her unconscious.

Six months earlier, the media buzzed with stories about three famous singers. One story involved a woman who physically attacked her brother-in-law. Another was about a couple who, after twenty-two years of marriage, had become physically cruel to each other.

When most of us read these stories, a sense of righteous indignation wells up in us. An inner voice says, "That's wrong! Something needs to be done."

So we speak our mind on blogs and call-in shows. What we usually say is, "Put that monster in jail!" We pop the buttons off our shirts and pull them open, so everyone can see the "S" on our chest.

But that's all we do. Most of us don't give an extra dollar to a women's shelter or a violence prevention or treatment program. We don't volunteer our time, either. We just "stand behind" the victim, make a lot of noise, and preen in front of the world. We don't actually want to help anyone heal or grow up.

As part of our reflexive response, we typically make the person who was physically cruel into a villain, the person they were cruel to into a victim, and ourselves into a hero. This cartoonish, childish view of reality is also known as the *victim/perpetrator/rescuer* stance.[26]

In this view of the world, everyone plays a predetermined role. The victim is always helpless and powerless, the villain is always evil, and the hero always rescues the victim and then captures or annihilates the villain.

In modern times, we've added a fourth role to this cycle: the reporter. After Superman has delivered the villain to the authorities for punishment, Clark Kent writes about it for the *Daily Planet*, and the story goes viral.

Occasionally, a celebrity in one such story may refuse to play the role we assigned to them. They straighten their spine and say to the media, "Please respect our privacy as we work through this together," or "My partner is not a beast; we're committed to making this relationship work."

When they do this, we go ballistic. "What the *hell* is wrong with them? They don't even realize they're a victim! We didn't pop the buttons on our shirt so they could go crawling back to the villain. They must be human debris, too!" We make *sure* they realize they're a victim by victimizing them.

We confuse justice with healing, and comic books with real life.

How did this happen?

Strangely, it's the result of enormous progress.

How We Got Here

Commonplace physical cruelty is as old as our species. So is *uncommon* physical cruelty—rape, murder, torture, and enslavement.

Today, those four crimes continue to be routinely practiced in parts of the world. Over time the faces and places change, but the crimes continue. Overwhelmingly, the people who commit these crimes are men and their victims are women.

We think that in the United States we've crawled out of such a primitive, lawless, amoral, male-dominated approach to life. And we have—mostly.

---

26 My mentors, Dr. David Schnarch and Dr. James Maddock, and Dr. Noel Larson, Dr. Maddock's widow, have done some of the best work on the victim/perpetrator/rescuer triangle. Particularly valuable are the essay "Beyond Victimhood: Altering the Paradigm for Psychotherapy" by all three authors; Dr. Maddock's and Dr. Larson's book *Incestuous Families: An Ecological Approach to Understanding and Treatment* (Norton, 1995); and Dr. Maddock's essay, "An Ecological Approach to Abuse and Violence."

Today, 15 percent of women will get raped at least once. A third of all women murdered in the United States are killed by their male partners.

Still, grim as these statistics are, they represent an enormous improvement over how things used to be.

In the United States, through the late 1950s, women were routinely brutalized—and sometimes raped or murdered—while our culture looked the other way. When people beat their partners, often no one called the police. When the police did get called, they would take the batterer around the corner, give them a talking to, and leave. There was little accountability, little prosecution, and no therapeutic intervention. There were also few therapeutic practices available. There was no such thing as crisis intervention. There were no women's shelters. Beating your partner was not usually considered sufficient grounds for divorce.

Women were not protected by police, by courts, by psychologists, or by religion. Furthermore, if you and your partner were gay, or lesbian, or hetero and unmarried but living together, you could be arrested.

Psychology was especially idiotic. Homosexuality was considered a mental disorder. So was leaving your husband. (Leaving your wife was considered perfectly sane.) Psychoanalysts believed women derived sexual pleasure from being beaten by their partners; as late as 1964, an article in the *Archives of General Psychiatry* explained that wives whose husbands were physically cruel to them had a masochistic need for pain that their husbands' aggression fulfilled.[27]

By the 1950s, women had had enough of this crap. They began to take matters into their own hands. They created underground safe houses—places where women could be safe from their physically abusive partners. These were reminiscent of the safe houses of the Underground Railroad during the Civil War; they were also precursors of women's shelters, which would appear in the mid-1960s.

For the next two decades, things improved steadily—almost solely because of women's organizing, advocacy, activism, and hard work. Law, public safety, psychology, and government—all of

---

27 Such errors have not been limited to sexuality and aggression. I could write a large book on the subject (and perhaps someday will). One of the most outrageous and idiotic was the ostensible "mental illness" of *drapetomania*, the desire to flee enslavement. In 1851, physician Samuel Cartwright diagnosed this "condition" as a dysfunctional refusal by enslaved Black people to accept enslavement as the natural order of things.

which were heavily male-dominated—mostly sat on their hands, and occasionally got in the way.

Women activists wisely gave up trying to engage with these fields. Instead they said, "We don't trust you to do a goddamned useful thing, so we won't ask you to. But at least get the hell out of our way so we can make the world safer." That's exactly what happened. Women's organizations set up hotlines, crisis centers, counseling programs, shelters, and peer support groups. Men largely stood on the sidelines.

It took a long time for social workers, psychologists, courts, and police to get seriously involved. When psychologists and social workers did finally step up to the plate, often the first thing they did was spout total bullshit. This did not help to build trust.

In the mid-1970s, the issue of physical cruelty in couples began to get some serious traction. The National Organization for Women declared marital violence a major issue and established a national task force on it. In 1978, the National Coalition Against Domestic Violence was formed, and the Family Violence Prevention and Services Act was introduced in Congress. (It was not passed until 1984.)

In the late 1970s and early 1980s, men at last began to wake up. In 1980, Ellen Pence and Michael Paymar developed the Domestic Abuse Intervention Project in Duluth, Minnesota. This was a curriculum for treating domestic abuse offenders. It was based on the premise that, in our culture, men are encouraged and expected to control their partners.

This curriculum soon became known as the Duluth Model. It spread across the country, eventually becoming the most widely used approach for dealing with physical cruelty in committed relationships. Today it's considered the gold standard.

The Duluth Model was a huge step forward. For the first time, it created cooperation among police, courts, social service agencies, and other relevant players, so that everyone in the community worked together. It provided a structured, standardized course of treatment for people who had been physically cruel to their partners. It created clear and consistent policies for holding these people accountable.

The Duluth Model helped our country do many good things. We dramatically reduced the number of people being murdered and beaten. Police routinely arrested people who had been physically cruel to their partners, instead of talking to them and sending them back home. Communities were able to craft integrated and coordinated responses.

Before the Duluth Model, the American approach to physical cruelty in committed partnerships was childish, piecemeal, and often counterproductive. Ellen and Michael brought us out of childhood and into adolescence. I'm deeply grateful to them for these important changes. I knew Ellen professionally (she died in 2012) and I'm proud of that association.

But the Duluth Model was created in 1980. More than four decades later, that's the model we still use and look up to.

This would be fine if the model worked well for everyone. But it doesn't. Two studies—one in 2003, another in 2011—concluded that the Duluth Model's effectiveness in helping people heal and grow up was just above zero. As with anything that human beings create, it has limitations and gaps, many of which only became visible over time.

In fact, after using the model for years, Ellen herself came to doubt and criticize it:

> By determining that the need or desire for power was the motivating force behind battering, we created a conceptual framework that, in fact, did not fit the lived experience of many of the men and women we were working with. Like those we were criticizing, we reduced our analysis to a psychological universal truism....We all engaged in ideological practices and claimed them to be neutral observations. . . . It was the cases themselves that created the scratch in each of our theoretical suits of armor. Speaking for myself, I found that many of the men I interviewed did not seem to articulate a desire for power over their partner.[28]

The Duluth Model has other serious drawbacks as well. For starters, within each couple, it always designates one person as perp and the other as victim. Then it requires the perp to come in, submit to the mental health professionals, and admit to their awfulness. The person is told, "Admit you're a batterer. If you don't, you'll do more jail time—or another thirty-two weeks of treatment." Both threats scared the piss out of people.

There are certainly people for whom saying "I'm a batterer" is a necessary first step in healing—but as a required protocol, it's unnecessarily rigid. In any case, who *wouldn't* admit to perphood

---

28 The 2003 study was published by the U.S. National Institute of Justice, the 2011 study by the FISA Foundation. The quotation from Ellen Pence is from the book *Coordinating Community Responses to Domestic Violence: Lessons from Duluth and Beyond*, edited by Melanie F. Shepard and Ellen L. Pence (SAGE Publications, 1999), page 29.

when faced with the prospect of more jail or treatment time? If I were jailed—whether fairly or unfairly—and given this choice, *I'd* admit I was a batterer, or a Shetland pony, just to be done sooner. But I'd be thinking, *You shrinks are total dipshits. Fuck you.*

The Duluth Model is primarily legalistic and punitive. It focuses on reducing the incidence of physical cruelty, and on getting dangerous people off the streets and into jail and treatment. These are all good things. But the treatment itself is designed to educate and control people, not to help them heal.

Given the less-than-enlightened positions that psychology has taken on physical cruelty over the years, it's hardly surprising that this model has far more respect for law and safety than it does for therapy.

Still, merely reducing violence isn't enough. No successful marriage has ever been built on the withholding of physical cruelty.

Where We Need to Go

In our culture, we're so afraid of physical cruelty in committed relationships that our entire discussion of the subject focuses on law enforcement and legal issues.

As a society, our response to this cruelty is to try to turn down the heat around it and to tiptoe around the subject.

We need to grow out of this. We need to be less frightened of physical cruelty. We need to stand in our own integrity and address it in a way that helps people and couples actually grow up.

We train people to stop beating their partners. That's better than nothing. But we don't train them to actually heal, to be redeemed, to grow up into fully adult human beings. And we should. We know we should.

This chapter is a call for something better than what we've settled for over the past four decades.

One final thought: if everyone who called a radio station or wrote a comment on the Web would volunteer at a shelter or treatment program for just one hour, our society would quickly change for the better.

COMPASS POINTS

- When we hear about physical cruelty among celebrities, we typically respond by speaking our mind on blogs and call-in shows. We shout, "Put that monster in jail!" and declare ourselves heroes. But that's all we do. We don't actually help anyone heal or grow up.

- In the United States, through the late 1950s, women were routinely brutalized—and sometimes raped or murdered—while our culture looked the other way. Women were not protected by police, by courts, by psychologists, or by religion. And if you and your partner were gay, or lesbian, or hetero and unmarried but living together, you could be arrested.

- By the 1950s, women began to take matters into their own hands. During the decades that followed, things improved steadily—almost solely because of women's organizing, advocacy, activism, and hard work.

- In 1980, Ellen Pence and Michael Paymar developed the Domestic Abuse Intervention Project, a curriculum for treating domestic abuse offenders. It was based on the premise that, in our culture, men are encouraged and expected to control their partners.

- This model created cooperation among police, courts, social service agencies, and other relevant players, so that everyone in the community worked together. It helped our country dramatically reduce the number of people being murdered and beaten.

- But the model has not helped people heal. It's primarily legalistic and punitive. It focuses on reducing the incidence of physical cruelty and on getting dangerous people off the streets and into jail and treatment.

- As a culture, we need to take the next step forward.

- We need to be less frightened of physical cruelty. We need to stand in our own integrity and address it in a way that helps couples actually heal and grow up.

PART 3

Intimacy and Alchemy

35

The Integrity of
Confronting Yourself

Self-confrontation takes place mostly in the body, and it always involves metabolizing pain: fully experiencing, discerning, accepting, and moving through it.

For that pain to be clean instead of dirty, you need to learn how to hold on to yourself, *not* your partner, in the midst of conflict and uncertainty. Your partner needs to learn the same thing. Each of you also needs to learn to lick your own wounds rather than try to blow your pain through your lover.

In addition, each of you needs to learn to tolerate *the other's* emotional pain. Often when we see our partner hurting, we get anxious. Then, to ease our own anxiety, we try to soothe their pain, or tell them they shouldn't blame themselves for getting into trouble. We can't tolerate our own discomfort around their pain, so we make things worse by blowing our anxiety through them.

But dealing with your anxiety—even if it grows out of empathy with your partner—is *your* responsibility, not theirs. You need to soothe *yourself* down, not stick your nose deep into your partner's business.

Anchoring 101
At the heart of self-confrontation are the five anchors. These enable you to slow yourself down so you can see what's happening and make conscious choices, rather than follow the dictates of your lizard or bee brain.

As you know by now, the five anchors are:

1. **Soothe and resource yourself** to quiet your mind, calm your heart, and settle your body.

2. **Pause, and then notice the sensations, vibrations, and emotions in your body** instead of reacting to them.

3. **Accept the discomfort** instead of trying to flee from it.

4. **Stay present and in your body** as you move through the unfolding experience, with all its ambiguity and uncertainty, and respond from the best parts of yourself.

5. **Metabolize any energy that remains.**

When you first use the anchors in any new situation, you'll normally employ the first four anchors in sequence. You soothe yourself in order to calm down and notice what you're experiencing in your body. You become aware of your bodily sensations in order to accept them. You use this awareness as a baseline, so you can pull yourself back to the present when your brain starts to stray. This entire initial sequence may take only a few seconds.

However, once you're moving through the experience, you'll find yourself practicing all four anchors at once, or moving back and forth among them.

The five anchors are not tactical or technical. Their use is an art, not a science. They are not so much plans to carry out as ways to live into uncertainty in real time.

The more you practice these anchors, the more capable and comfortable you'll get with using them. Eventually they'll become your natural first response to conflict or difficulty.

Let's look at the anchors in detail, so you practice them whenever the heat under you gets turned way up.

Anchor 1: Soothe and resource yourself to quiet your mind, calm your heart, and settle your body.

In an ideal world, when a conflict starts to boil, you'd be able to leave the room, take ten deep breaths, meditate for five minutes, and walk around the block. But in the real world, you'll almost *never* have that kind of opportunity. In the heat of a conflict, you need to be able to soothe yourself down *quickly* in order to move into the second anchor. Here are some ways to practice Anchor 1:

- First and foremost, *shut up*. For a few seconds, don't say anything—no matter how much you might want to, or how much you have to say, or how loudly your partner is yelling. Just breathe.

- If you're holding something, let it go or put it down.
- Sit down. Put your hands in your lap or on your knees.
- Pause. Take a breath—or two or three.
- Mentally tell yourself, *Stay calm* or *Keep it together* or (my own favorite) *Calm the fuck down.*
- Go to the bathroom. Say, "I need to use the john. I'll be right back"; then go in and close the door. I know this sounds silly. But in many situations, it's the best way to get two minutes alone to catch your breath and move into Anchor 2. If you just walk away or say, "I need to be alone for a minute," your partner might come after you. But they probably won't follow you into the toilet. (Be sure to return and reengage after a few minutes, if possible.)
- Do something else to slow things down without dissing your partner or running away. Say, "Hang on, it's hot in here," and take off your sweater; take a long, slow drink from your mug; open or close a window; reach over and pet the cat.

Anchor 2: Notice the sensations, vibrations, and emotions in your body instead of reacting to them.

This is the key to staying in the here and now. Here are some ways to practice this anchor:

- Pay attention to what your body experiences in your clothes. Notice how and where your body touches your underwear, your shirt, your pants, your skirt, your socks or stockings, your hat.
- Notice any other body sensations: your back against the chair, your tongue against the roof of your mouth, the wind blowing against your face. Move into and name each sensation: heat, cold, tightness, relaxation, hollowness, looseness, weakness, trembling.
- As thoughts and emotions and possible reactions arise, don't run off with them. Bring yourself back to your body and its sensations.

Anchor 3: Accept the discomfort instead of trying to flee from it.

At first this will be difficult, but with practice it will get much easier. Here are some ways to practice this anchor:

- When you experience an urge to tamp down or push away the discomfort, don't. Keep your attention focused directly on it. Stay with it.

- When you get the impulse to analyze or think about the discomfort, bring yourself back to the discomfort itself.
- When your mind spits out strategies for what to do next, don't grab onto them. Just sit with the discomfort.
- When thoughts or images about the past or future pop up, let them float past you. Stay with your body.

Anchor 4: Stay present and in your body as you move through the unfolding experience, with all its ambiguity and uncertainty, and respond from the best parts of yourself.

Continue to use the first three anchors to hold on to yourself. At the same time, slowly move with your partner into the heat, peril, and possibility of the conflict. You and your lover will need to go forward into the unknown, moment by moment. Here are some helpful tips:

- When you find yourself focusing on the future or the past, use the first three anchors to bring yourself back to your body and the here and now.
- When your attention moves to what's wrong with your partner or what a jerk they're being, use those first three anchors to bring you back to the present.
- Find a place in your body where you experience warmth, love, or concern for your partner. Focus on that spot.
- Don't try to know what will happen next. It's impossible. If your partner asks you a question and your only honest response is *I don't know*, say, "I don't know."
- Don't try to wrest or finagle a particular response from your partner. This only creates dirty pain. What's happening isn't about what your partner does or doesn't do. It's about the evolution of your partnership.
- Act from the best parts of yourself—from your noble integrity. As events unfold, you'll sense what these parts are.

Anchor 4 always involves uncertainty. It can take many minutes, or sometimes even hours, to play out. There will be some situations—especially during your first few months of practicing the anchors—when your lizard or bee brain gets overwhelmed and you temporarily go bonkers. This happens occasionally to almost everyone—including us therapists.

If and when you do briefly lose your mind, this doesn't mean you've blown it, it's too late, and you might as well go berserk, smash a window, or file for divorce. In fact, *exactly the opposite is true*. Every new moment is a new opportunity to catch yourself.

Whenever you lose your way—or lose your mind—while using any of the five anchors, simply go back to Anchor 1, and use it to soothe yourself and slow yourself down. Then move forward again into Anchors 2, 3, and 4.

Anchor 5: Metabolize any energy that remains.

This anchor is underused and poorly understood, but it is no less important than the others. Use this anchor only *after* you and your partner have worked through the conflict—or agreed to stop grinding on it for now.

If you watch animals in the wild, you'll see that after a high-stress situation has passed, they'll instinctively discharge their built-up energy. A zebra that has just outrun a lion will vigorously shake itself or ripple the skin along its back. Other animals will roll on the ground, or run in a circle, or pick brief mock fights with each other. They're metabolizing their excess energy by discharging it autonomically.

After you and your partner have been in the heat of a conflict, this same kind of energy is bottled up in your bodies. But we humans need to metabolize it differently than animals do. We need to process it internally by pausing, reflecting on what we have just been through, and absorbing what it may have taught us.

This is sometimes done in the moment, but often it happens later. Sometimes it occurs suddenly, in a rush of bodily understanding. More likely, though, it gets metabolized slowly and gradually, in the same way that a meal digests or a wound heals.

After you come out of a high-stress situation with your partner, you may experience an urge to release some of the excess energy through physical activity. This is fine, but keep in mind that this will simply discharge the energy, not metabolize it. So if you want to walk, or exercise, or play a sport, or do some physical labor afterward, do that. But don't use it to bypass or avoid the all-important task of letting your body fully process the experience you and your partner have just been through.

One of the most common forms of bypassing is make-up sex. While this will blow off some of the excess physical energy—and it will create pleasant sensations—it can also encourage a cycle of dirty pain in which the two of you alternately become cruel to each other, then have sex to dull the pain. In such a cycle, the two of you never work through your conflicts or grow up.

After you and your partner have been in an emotional bottleneck, a second kind of energy also needs to be metabolized: an energy of love and caring. *This* form of energy needs to be processed through an exchange with your partner.

The exchange needs to honor the relationship, maintain a sense of connection, and send this message: *We're cool now. I love you.* You might take your partner by the hand and begin dancing with them. Or you might kiss them on the forehead, then the neck, then the mouth.

Often such exchanges take the form of a very simple gesture:

VINCE AND WENDY

After Vince and Wendy worked through an emotional bottleneck that had bothered them for months, they were both pleased and relieved—and uncomfortably buzzed by the built-up energy. Suddenly Vince said, "I'm going for a bike ride to chill out; see you in an hour," and headed out the door. To Wendy, it seemed like Vince was discounting her and running off, even if only for an hour. As the back door slammed shut, she opened her mouth to say, "Not so fast, Lance Armstrong." But she caught herself, kept her mouth closed, and began working with the first four anchors.

Fortunately, Vince caught himself, too. After a few steps, he turned around, went back into the house, took Wendy by the shoulders, and kissed her on the forehead. "I love you," he said. "Want to go for coffee when I get back? Or would you like me to pick some up for you on my way home?"

Do you see how this is an act of discernment and resource cultivation?

Life Reps and Invited Reps

No matter what we do, life is regularly going to put each of us in positions of conflict and uncertainty. Each situation forces us up against ourselves—and provides us with an opportunity to confront ourselves, hold onto ourselves, and grow up.

When you're in a committed relationship, life is going to regularly put you and your partner in these situations. Each of these is a chance for you and your partner to use the five anchors, and to choose clean pain and discomfort instead of dirty pain. Each of you can choose to hold onto yourself rather than each other, straighten your spine, lick your own wounds, experience your own pain, and metabolize and move through that pain. This will happen over and over, for as long as you are alive.

Each time you choose clean pain and discomfort, you will build greater discernment and resilience. Each time you and your partner both choose clean pain and discomfort, you will both grow up a bit more. This will temper and condition your relationship, and help the two of you—separately and together—to be more able to navigate life's turbulent waters.

Each time you choose clean pain and discomfort, you are repeating an elemental practice that can help you grow into your best self.

Repeating a practice, over and over, is the same process through which human bodies build muscle, endurance, and flexibility. It's also the same process by which we learn to sing, write, dance, paint, solve equations, create inventions, address problems, become great athletes, and become loving partners or parents. Through repetition after repetition, we learn and grow.

Each time you use the five anchors, that's a rep.

As you've seen, each time that life forces you into conflict and uncertainty—and you choose the anchors and clean pain—that's a life rep.

But there is a second type of rep, too: the invited rep. You practice an invited rep when you choose to step forward into clean pain and discomfort—and into peril and possibility—even when life isn't pushing you to do so at that moment. You practice an invited rep because you recognize that if you don't step forward now, sooner or later your circumstances will force you to. Because you love your partner—and because you care about yourself—you choose to accept conflict and pain, and deal with it in the present, rather than ignore or deny it, and wait for it to bite you on the ass later. Because eventually it will.

Here are some examples of invited reps:

- You tell your lover, "The next three weeks are going to be brutal for me at work. So, if I get grumpy or sullen, that's why. It won't be about you. If I say or do anything thoughtless, call me on it, okay? I love you."
- The last three times you and your partner had sex, they seemed distant and distracted—but each time you had a

huge, body-quaking orgasm. In the morning after the third time this happens, while you and your partner drink coffee, you say, "Hon? Can we talk for a little? Over the last couple of weeks, it seems like sex hasn't made you very happy. Can you tell me what's been going on for you?"

- You are a thirty-year-old man who was born in Bangladesh and whose family moved to South Carolina when you were three. You have been dating an African American woman for the past seven months. You have just gotten engaged but have not yet told anyone. Tonight she will meet your parents for the first time, at the country club to which they belong. You are nervous as hell and a little scared. You say to her that morning, "I'm anxious about tonight. My parents can be unpredictable and judgmental, so I have no idea how this evening will go. I want them to like you and accept you. I hope they do. But if they don't, that's their problem. If they say anything demeaning to you, I'll stick up for you. If we have to, we can leave. Whatever happens, I love you."

The Importance of Checkpoints

In Afghanistan, where I spent two years working with military contractors, many of the roads have frequent checkpoints. At each checkpoint, men with guns stop you, look at your ID, ask you questions, and decide whether to let you through or turn you back.

As you practice using the five anchors, you'll discover your own internal checkpoints—places where you have the opportunity to stop, look at yourself, ask yourself some important questions, and decide whether to plunge ahead or turn back.

Your internal checkpoints are specific physical sensations—a clench in your stomach, a tightness in your chest, a queasiness in your belly, a tingle at the back of your neck, an involuntary bracing, the sudden emerging of an impulse or urge.

Whenever one of your checkpoints is activated, investigate it. Pay attention to what you experience and where you experience it. Notice any accompanying images, thoughts, and emotions. Ask yourself these important questions: *What are these sensations telling me—or warning me about? What are they encouraging me to do? How can I respond from the best parts of myself?*

Internal checkpoints often get activated in a predictable sequence. For example, your partner says something nasty to you, so your stomach tightens. You know this means you're getting irritated. When your partner slams the bedroom door for no reason two minutes later, your heart speeds up. You know this means that your irritation is turning to anger. When they poke their head into the room and say, "Were you planning to make dinner any time today?" you can sense the blood rising up into your neck and jaw. Now you're aware that you're seriously pissed. You also know that if you don't quickly hold on to yourself, you'll curse out your partner the next time they do something annoying—which, you also know, will be soon.

Because you've paid attention to your checkpoints, you're careful to practice the first four anchors as you cook dinner. You're also prepared when, a few minutes into the meal, your partner says, "And who, exactly, told you it would be a good idea to put so much goddamned garlic in the stew?"

Your heart starts pounding furiously—just as you expected. The impulse to shout, "You know what? Go fuck yourself," also rises up inside you—but you expected this as well. Because you were ready for these physical and mental responses, you're able to you lean forward, look at your partner, and say softly, "I'm not sure what just happened, but I don't want to do it like this. I'm not trying to piss you off. I love you, and my plan was to have a pleasant dinner with you. But right now I don't know where to go next." You stay open and connected, even though your body is quaking with peril and possibility—and even though you have no idea what will happen next.

Or, maybe, your lizard brain is threatening to take over and push you into a fight, flee, or freeze response. You know that trying to tamp down or ignore these impulses will only strengthen them. You also know that either fighting or fleeing will create a hot mess of dirty pain. Most importantly, you recognize all of this as a yellow flag that your body is waving at you.

So, wisely, *you show your partner that flag.* You say, "Hon, I'm getting close to a place where one of my fuses might blow. I don't want that to happen. I need us to eat in silence for a little while. I care about you and I care about us. So, whatever we need to deal with, I'll go there with you—but later. Not now. Maybe later tonight, maybe tomorrow—whenever works for both of us."

Alternative Anchors

The five anchors are profoundly effective, but there's nothing magic or extraordinary about them. They are practices to be repeated regularly in your day-to-day life, not mere inspirational quotes to repeat to yourself when you need a pick-me-up. They're also a way of framing a process of self-discovery and mindful action that other therapists also recognize and teach.

Dr. David Schnarch created his own version of this process, which he calls the Crucible Four Points of Balance™. You can learn more about the late Dr. Schnarch and his work at crucible4points.com. (The five anchors stand on the shoulders of the Four Points of Balance and grew out of some of my work with Dr. Schnarch.)

Dr. Peter Levine, a key figure in body-centered therapy who has done groundbreaking work in dealing with trauma, has a somewhat similar process called SIBAM or SIMBA. The letters in SIMBA stand for Sensations, Images, Meaning, Behavior, and Affect. I use a modified version of SIMBA, called VIMBASI, in my work with clients.[29] VIMBASI stands for physical and energetic *vibrations*; *images* and thoughts; *meaning*; *behaviors* and urges; *affect* and emotions; *sensations*; and *imaginations* (or *imaginings*). These are forms of human intelligence that are often slighted or ignored in favor of cognitive thinking. We can all benefit from paying closer attention to each of these, because each has its own weight, charge, speed, and texture—and its own underlying wisdom.

I also often encourage my clients to *soul scribe*, which is the practice of writing down the VIMBASI they experience. I encourage you to do the same whenever the spirit moves you—or when (or soon after) you have a strong or unusual VIMBASI experience.

When possible, please soul scribe in longhand. I've discovered that the physical act of writing using a pen or pencil helps most people better process the energy involved.

Another useful framework is called Stop, Drop, and Roll. I invented this framework a few years ago, when I led therapy groups for men. Stop, Drop, and Roll compresses key elements from the five anchors into three steps:

Stop whatever you're doing and thinking. Don't keep rushing down whatever mental and emotional path you're on.

Drop back and notice what you're experiencing, what's happening to you, what's happening to your partner, how the situation is unfolding, and what your role in it is.

Roll with what's going on instead of trying to control it, or run from it, or blow it to smithereens.

---

29 You can learn more about Dr. Levine and his work at traumahealing.org.

Yet another helpful way to resource yourself is through what I call *resource icons*. These are images, symbols, and phrases that quickly soothe, support, or encourage you when the heat gets turned up under you.

Resource icons are memories, images, or reminders that you can quickly access whenever you need to. Below are a few examples—but I encourage you to create your own.

- The smile on your best friend's face when the two of you go running together and get into the zone.
- Your sister telling you that you're the best brother she could ever want.
- The taste of a ripe, fresh-picked strawberry from the patch in your backyard.
- The sensation of having your diploma placed in your hand at your graduation.
- The soft breathing of your sleeping cat between your feet as you lie in bed.

All of these frameworks are yours to use, however and whenever you like.

You now have a detailed process for growth at your fingertips. Whatever system of self-discovery and mindful action you use, and whatever conflicts you face, your choices will always be the same:

- Stay with the present or try to avoid it.
- Accept clean pain and discomfort, or create dirty pain.
- Confront yourself or flee yourself.
- Offer your partner the possibility of dealing with a grown-up— or fight with them.
- Grow up or don't.

As I asked you at the beginning of this book:

- Do you want your lover to rock your world? Good.
- Do you want to rock theirs? Even better.

Now you know what to do. Remember: It's always up to you.

COMPASS POINTS

- Self-confrontation takes place mostly in the body and always involves fully experiencing, accepting, and moving through pain. This process of tolerating emotional pain—both your own and your partner's—is one of the most important things anyone can bring to an intimate partnership.

- At the heart of self-confrontation are the five anchors.

- After you and your partner have been in the heat of a conflict, energy is bottled up in your bodies. This energy should be metabolized as soon as reasonably possible—through exercise, sports, dancing, physical labor, etc.

- A second kind of energy also needs to be processed: an energy of love and caring. This involves an exchange that honors the relationship, maintains a sense of connection, and sends a message of love and safety.

- No matter what we do, life regularly puts each of us in positions of conflict and uncertainty. Each situation forces us up against ourselves—and provides us with an opportunity to confront ourselves, hold onto ourselves, and grow up. When you're in a committed relationship, life is going to regularly put you and your partner in these situations. Each of these is a chance for you and your partner to use the five anchors, and to choose clean pain and discomfort instead of dirty pain.

- Each time you use the five anchors, that's a rep. When life forces you into conflict and uncertainty—and you choose the anchors and clean pain—that's a life rep. When you choose to step forward into clean pain and discomfort—and into peril and possibility—even when life isn't pushing you to do so at that moment, that's an invited rep.

- Each of us has our own internal checkpoints—places where we have the opportunity to stop, look at ourselves, ask ourselves some important questions, and decide whether to plunge ahead or turn back. These are specific physical sensations—for example, a clench in your stomach, a tightness in your chest—with specific meanings. Our checkpoints often get activated in a predictable and repeatable sequence.

- Whatever system of self-discovery and mindful action you use, and whatever conflicts you face, your choices will always be the same: stay with the present or try to avoid it; accept clean pain or create dirty pain; confront yourself or flee yourself; offer your partner the possibility of greater intimacy or fight with them; and grow up or don't.

36

The Brightened Self

If a couple reaches critical mass and chooses to accept the pain of growth, a profound shift can occur.

This shift is neurobiological—not just mental and not just emotional. The whole body's energy realigns. The person's eyes focus and brighten. Their spine straightens. Often they stand or sit straighter, or lean forward. They make direct eye contact. Their voice becomes clear and assured. Their energy is strong and vibrant, or calm and quiet but full of commitment. Their entire body undergoes a profound vibratory change.

This shift is sometimes called the brightening of self.

A brightening of self occurs when someone makes a leap. Suddenly they know, deep in their body, who they are, what they experience, what they stand for, and, often, what they need to do. The look in their eyes says, *I'm here. I'm fully present. And what's going to happen from now on isn't going to be what happened before.*

I see this brightening regularly in my therapy office. I see it when one lover takes the other's hand and says, "Honey, I love you to death, but I'm not going to let you emotionally hurt me or our children again. Ever." I see it when the man who has never stood up to his in-laws tells his partner, "I know how important your family is to you, but I'm done taking shit from them." I see it when a woman whose fiancé has been sexually unresponsive for two years says to him, "You know what? I'm not following you around like a dog anymore, begging for sex. If you don't want to fuck me, and you don't want to ever talk about *why* you don't want to fuck me, that's your decision. But that doesn't mean I'm going to stop wanting it, or letting you know that I want it. And I want the sex that we do have to be better. But now I have to make a decision about what *I'm* going to do, because I've given up on thinking that sex will improve for us if I beg for it—or just suck it up and shut up about it."

The key is not in the words, but in the vibes and the intent. A brightened self has an unmistakable vibratory signature.

When this brightening happens, the person is no longer the same human being they were a minute earlier. A transformation has occurred. You can see it in their eyes, their expression, and the way they hold their body. They're aware, unafraid, fully engaged, and not interested in being anywhere else. It's a beautiful and awe-inspiring thing to see, like watching a wise man or woman come down from the mountain.

Each brightening is unique, but it always includes this message: *I'm not going to do this anymore. There's got to be something else. With or without you, I'm going to figure out what that something is. In that process, I'm going to stand up straight. And I accept the pain of doing this.*

When a brightening occurs, everyone in the room sees it and intuitively knows it. If the person's partner is in the room, they immediately realize the game is up. They can't do their usual dance anymore. They've got no more room to move. They either need to grow up or flee.

The brightening of self is always an act of health, sanity, and courage. It's also nothing less than an embodied spiritual transformation.

Alice Walker's *The Color Purple* provides a wonderful example of the brightening of self. The narrator, Celie is married to a selfish, abusive, much older man who has beaten her for years. For much of the story, Celie observes and admires Sofia. She is also fascinated by a beautiful singer named Shug, who eventually becomes Celie's lover. Both Sofia and Shug do not allow themselves to be mistreated.

After years of acquiescing to her husband, Celie reaches critical mass with him. She decides to leave him and move out of town with Shug. When Shug announces this over dinner with Celie and her husband, he replies, "Over my dead body." That's when Celie's brightening begins. "You a lowdown dog," she says to him. "It's time to leave you and enter into the Creation. . . . [You] ain't dead horse's shit." Her husband reaches over to slap her, and—in the film version—she grabs a knife from the table. It's the first time she has ever fought back against his abuse. (In the book version, the brightening is just as full and strong, but there's no knife. And, just to be clear, I never recommend using a knife to make a point.)

A few days later, just before Celie and Shug leave, Celie's husband confronts her again. "Look at you," he says. "You black, you pore, you ugly, you a woman . . . you nothing at all."

Celie's reply is simple and certain: "Until you do right by me . . . everything you even dream about will fail. . . . I'm pore, I'm black, I may be ugly and can't cook, but I'm here."

Like most brightenings, Celie's experience has nothing to do with thinking or making a conscious, cognitive decision. In a letter to her sister Nettie, she writes, *I give it to him straight, just like it come to me. And it seem to come to me from the trees.*

Brightening is an unthwarting. It is creation itself being revealed.

We've all seen the brightening of self in lots of movies. It happens to many heroes and heroines. After many trials and lots of emotional bottlenecks, at a certain point their situation reaches critical mass. Suddenly there's something the character has to do. They have no other choice and no other place to turn. Either they step up and face the situation or they fold and shrink away.

That's when the person changes. They take on a hero's gaze. We can see in their face and body that they know just what to do, and they're committed to doing it.

This brightening of self occurs in almost every type of movie, from *Rocky* to *The Karate Kid* to *Kill Bill* to *Moonrise Kingdom* to *The Secret Life of Bees.*

TWANYA AND MARCUS

Twanya and Marcus came to see me because of a year-long affair Marcus had been having with his coworker Leslie.

For the first two months, whenever they came to therapy, Twanya spent much of the time crying or sighing or looking at the floor. When the pressure got too high, she'd sometimes get up and leave the room for a few minutes.

A few weeks ago, Twanya and Marcus hit critical mass. For several minutes, Twanya sobbed into her hands as Marcus explained why he couldn't just break off with Leslie. "We've been together a year," he said. "I can't just walk away like I'm hanging up the phone."

Suddenly Twanya stopped crying and put her hands down. She turned and looked straight into her husband's eyes. I saw the brightening.

Marcus saw it, too. He went silent and leaned back. He started fiddling with his wristwatch. He looked at me. "Dude, don't look at me," I said. "Look at your wife."

He did, and Twanya said softly, "Marcus, I'll tell you what. You do whatever the fuck you want to do. I'm done trying to tell you what I think you should do. Screw Leslie all you want. But from now on, whatever you do, it will tell me which of us you want to be with. You can have her or you can have me, but if you choose me, then this shit with Leslie stops. I'm not playing about this."

As I looked at Twanya, I could see the brightening in her eyes, in her face, and in her body. She had raised her game big-time.

Now, at last, instead of arguing continually about Leslie, they could begin to talk about the ways they had been grinding against each other for years. Marcus often attempted to evade responsibility. Twanya regularly tried to control Marcus and the relationship. Long before Leslie came along, each of them had lost respect and trust for the other because they both kept avoiding tough choices.

When they hit emotional stalemates, Marcus wouldn't confront himself and take a stand. Instead, he'd find some way out of his own personal dilemma. For years he'd go into the basement and pound his punching bag, or go into the backyard and chop firewood. He'd never reengage with Twanya.

After Marcus began his affair with Leslie, he did much less punching and chopping. He also showed up for dinner much less often and sometimes stayed out all night.

At the same time, instead of taking herself on, Twanya played the role of victim and assigned Marcus the role of perp. She complained about him to her friends and relatives, but she never took a stand—until now.

Each partner had stopped trusting that the other would grow up. As they grew older together, their respect for each other decayed. They both needed to rebuild that respect by acting in ways that earned it.

Their choice now is not about Leslie. It's about whether they're each going to choose to grow up. It's about whether they can move through the pressure and heat of their relationship—and become the best people they can.

Since then, in therapy sessions Twanya is usually present and engaged. Sometimes, though, she slips back. When she looks down or sighs, I say, "Twanya, look at me. Stay here. Don't go away. Stay here." A moment later the brightening returns, and she's present once again.

I don't know what Twanya and Marcus will ultimately decide. But now they are doing the real work of a committed relationship. Marcus has broken off with Leslie. For now, at least, he and Twanya have chosen to work on growing up.

We usually think that an affair is all about the person who has it, and that the other partner is a victim. But every affair is really about both partners—or, more accurately, about the ecology of their relationship. Together, the two people have created so much grinding and heat and pressure that they can't tolerate it without growing up—and both refuse to grow up. So the two timing partner disperses some of that heat and pressure by blowing it through someone else. Instead of confronting themselves, the person having the affair gets to split their energy between two different people. (This is why people who have affairs rarely leave their spouses on their own; they can't stand the heat of *any* committed two-person relationship.) Meanwhile, the person being cheated on also gets to avoid confronting themselves by focusing on the affair and their two-timing partner. The pressure and heat get divided up between three people instead of two.

Open marriage and swinging with other couples have the same function: under the guise of pleasure, freedom, liberation, experimentation, or even maturity, partners turn down the heat that creates growth and transformation.

It's no accident that the brightening of self always involves a literal (as well as a metaphorical) straightening of the spine.

The spine is like no other part of the human body. It's at once a physical, emotional, and spiritual organ. It keeps us erect, and it serves as the main conduit for the body's electrical and emotional energy.

Your spine needs to be both solid and flexible. If it's not solid enough, you won't be able to hold on to yourself in conflicts, difficulties, and danger. You'll wimp out and give in.

But if it's not flexible enough, you won't always be able to adapt or respectfully compromise. You'll dig in your heels just when you need to reach out or open up. (Former Congresswoman Michele Bachmann once boasted that she had a "titanium spine," but such a solid, stiff spine would actually be terribly brittle and dysfunctional.)

Many spiritual traditions speak of the spine as the main pathway for the body's spiritual energy, often known as *kundalini, chi*, or *prana*. The ancient icon for the practice of medicine, which depicts a snake coiled around a rod, also represents the energy pathway up and down the spine. The equally ancient Egyptian symbol known as the *djed*, which represents stability, is also a symbolic spine. And in the Kemetic faith, the spine is a symbol of transformation and grace.

No one can predict when a brightening of self will occur. It can't be willed or planned or created. We don't make it happen; it happens *to* and *in* us. It is part miracle, part mystery, part grace. But it only happens through intense pressure, heat, and friction. And it only happens after we make an internal commitment to growing up.

COMPASS POINTS

- When a couple reaches critical mass, and one member chooses to accept the pain of growth, a profound shift occurs. This shift is physical and neurobiological, not just mental and emotional. The body's energy realigns; the person's eyes focus and brighten; they make direct eye contact; their spine straightens.

- This shift occurs when someone makes a leap. Suddenly they know, deep in their body, who they are, what they experience, and what they stand for.

- Each brightening is unique, but it always includes this message: *I'm not going to do this anymore. I'm going to stand up straight. And I accept the pain of doing this.*

- The brightening of self is always an act of health, sanity, and courage. It's also nothing less than a spiritual transformation.

- No one can predict when a brightening of self will occur. It can't be willed or planned or created. We don't make it happen; it happens *to* us. But it only happens after we make an internal commitment to growing up.

37

Healthy Monsters and
Healing Relationships

In earlier chapters, I emphasized that emotional and spiritual development don't occur only—or even primarily—in the cortex. They take place in the body, and they are experienced throughout it.

That's why taking good care of your body is so important. The better your health, the more reliable an anchor your body can be—and the easier holding on to yourself becomes—whenever your boat begins to rock. (That said, if you're disabled, or have a chronic illness, or are in your tenth or eleventh decade of life, you can still learn to practice the five anchors effectively.)

This chapter offers some simple strategies and information for supporting your physical and spiritual health—and, in turn, your emotional well-being.

These are all general strategies, not specific prescriptions. Please adapt them for your own body, psyche, and situation. Talk to your doctor before beginning any exercise program. Talk with your spiritual leader or therapist about anything that intrigues or concerns you. And go ahead and further investigate any topic I discuss here.

I'm not a physician. Nothing in this book is intended as medical advice, and nothing in it is meant to replace the guidance of a qualified medical professional. Nor am I a spiritual leader or teacher. I'm simply an experienced psychotherapist and clinical social worker, giving the most helpful general guidance that I can.

One more note about health: lots of folks are quick to blame other human beings for their physical conditions, chronic illnesses, and/

or body shapes. Please don't do this. Each human body is affected by a very large welter of factors, including the person's environment, upbringing, choices, range of available choices, social location, genetics, epigenetics, and a great deal more.

It's unwise to jump to conclusions about why someone else's health—or body—is what it is. You might be thin as a chopstick at age sixteen, and forty pounds heavier at age sixty-six, all because of your genes—or partly because of your genes, a job that requires you to sit for at least seven hours a day, and the fact that, for the past thirty years, you've been married to a first-rate pastry chef.

I am no exception to this. I do all of the things I recommend in this chapter; I work out regularly; and people often tell me that I look great—yet my cholesterol is chronically high.

I'm also well aware of the current and historical reverberations among body shaming, anti-Blackness, and a variety of other *I'm-better-than-you* mindsets. Some of these are overt, some subtle, and some largely invisible. (Two excellent books on these reverberations are *Fearing the Black Body: The Racial Origins of Fat Phobia* by Sabrina Strings and *The Body Is Not an Apology: The Power of Radical Self-Love* by Sonya Renee Taylor.)

Lastly, I'm committed to regularly interrogating and challenging my own limitations (and my own perceived virtues) around health, body size and body image, and well-being.

Creating a Growth Routine

Growing up takes focus, energy, resilience, patience, and tolerance for uncertainty. All of these require good nutrition, mindfulness, enough sleep, some regular moments of simple enjoyment, and at least some physical fitness.

Your regular efforts to maintain these form your *growth routine*. Your growth routine serves as a mooring post in your life. It helps keep you stable when life with your partner becomes painful, difficult, or uncertain. Without such a routine, the winds of change, and the heat and pressure of intimacy, can tear you apart.

When everything else in your life is painful or confusing, you need at least one thing that *you* can hold on to. You need something that you *know* will help keep you sane and stable, no matter what happens. That "something" is your growth routine.

The essential elements of a fully effective growth routine are:

- Enough restful sleep (typically seven to eight hours a day)
- Regular exercise (based on your ability)
- Good nutrition, often including beneficial supplements
- Simple pleasures, enjoyed regularly
- Being present with yourself and the world

In the pages that follow, I'll discuss each of these elements and review a range of potential pieces of your own growth routine. You can't possibly adopt them all, any more than you can go shopping at the supermarket and come home with one of everything. The suggestions in this chapter are simply options to choose from and adapt.

You need to design your own growth routine so that it suits your life and your body. Don't just copy someone else's, even if they swear by it and say, "It saved my life and restored my health and sanity." The person is probably telling the truth—but you don't live in their body, and they don't live in yours. No matter how much my blond colleague Judy swears by a particular brand of tanning cream, I have no use for it. What *I* need is effective sunscreen.

Especially don't copy your partner's growth routine. You need to create your own—one that is ideal for you. If, after some experimentation, you discover that a growth routine that's much like your partner's works well for you, then go for it. But follow it because it works for *you.*

If your partner doesn't have a growth routine of their own, don't pressure them to create and follow one. Just continue to follow your own. It's up to your partner to decide what to do or not do in support of their own health.

Here's what I've noticed, though: when one lover regularly follows a growth routine for several months or more, their partner usually begins to acknowledge (at least to themselves) the value of such a routine. Over time, the positive results of your own growth routine may, slowly and subtly, encourage your lover to take better care of themselves.

It may also turn up the heat between you. Your partner may be threatened by your growth routine, and perhaps try to sabotage it. If so, then this will likely create an emotional bottleneck—one that the two of you will need to go through.

When you first begin to follow a new growth routine, it's usually best to *not* try to overhaul everything at once. Most people get the best results if they start out with modest changes, and then make additions and adjustments over time—gradually, gently, one by one.

Experiment. Play. If something doesn't suit you, replace or adjust or adapt it, until you find what works well for you.

When you or your lover are under stress of any kind—an emotional bottleneck, a sick child, long hours at work, or the death of a friend—you will have lots of good reasons to not follow your growth routine. *Yet this is precisely when following your growth routine is most important.* The harder your boat rocks, the more you need your routine.

In fact, during times of extreme stress, try to *strengthen* your routine. Get thirty to sixty more minutes of sleep each day. Avoid alcohol and other mood-altering drugs entirely. Exercise a few minutes longer, or a bit more often. Eat as healthily as you can. Reward yourself with a few extra small pleasures every week. And stay as grounded and as present as possible.

Get Enough Sleep

Doctors recommend at least seven to eight hours of sleep each day for most folks. Some people need even more for optimal health. If you do need more, you'll know it, because you'll routinely be tired and dragged out when you get up.

You don't have to get all your sleep at night. Many people find that they're more alert during the workday if they sleep less at night and take a regular nap, especially in the afternoon.

Getting enough sleep can improve your life in multiple ways:

Learning and memory: Sleep helps the brain concentrate and retain new information. In multiple studies, people who slept after learning a new task did better at it later.

Metabolism and weight: Chronic sleep deprivation may create weight gain by affecting the way our bodies process and store carbohydrates and by altering levels of hormones that affect our appetite.

Safety: Sleep deprivation contributes to more frequent falls, mistakes, and traffic accidents—and, of course, to falling asleep during the day.

Mood: Too little sleep can result in irritability, impatience, and other forms of moodiness. Too little sleep can also leave you too tired to do the things you like to do. A chronic lack of sleep has been linked to the symptoms of some mental and emotional disorders.

Healing: Sleep bolsters your immune system, so getting enough sleep is essential to recovery from illness or trauma. As a rule of thumb, the more healing you need—whether physical, emotional, or spiritual—the more sleep you need as well. Healing from clinical depression is an exception.

Cardiovascular health: Serious sleep disorders have been linked to hypertension, increased stress hormone levels, and irregular heartbeat.

Most people think that each of us has an internal sleep bank—that if we deprive ourselves of sleep during the work week, we can catch up with extra sleep on weekends. But that's not how sleep works. When you don't get enough sleep on Tuesday night, you'll be less healthy, happy, focused, and alert on Wednesday, no matter how much sleep you got the Sunday before (or plan to get the Sunday after).

It's also important to create a regular sleep pattern, including a daily routine of winding down at the end of your day. This makes it easier to fall asleep *and* easier to wake up, because your body adjusts to the regular rhythm over time. This doesn't mean you have to go to sleep and get up at exactly the same time every day. You just need to create enough regularity that your body knows when to naturally shift into sleep mode.

Exercise Regularly (But Not Painfully)

Most people need some regular exercise to be at their best, and to show up fully for themselves and their partners. Physical exercise also helps release the pent-up energy that we store in our bodies as emotion and stress.

Multiple studies have demonstrated the mental health benefits of regular exercise. It can increase our resiliency and improve our mood.

An ideal exercise program focuses on building cardiovascular strength. This means doing exercises that will raise your heart rate for thirty minutes or more at a time. Brisk walking, jogging, swimming, or biking all give your heart a decent workout. This type of exercise also releases depression-fighting endorphins.

If you don't like to exercise, then simply take a brisk walk of at least two miles, five days a week. This won't be physically taxing—at least after the first few weeks—and it can pay off by improving your mood and your physical health.

Your exercise routine doesn't have to be grueling or painful. But it does have to be real and consistent. Shoot for at least five days a week, thirty to sixty minutes a day.

It's fine to start out slow and work your way up. Once a routine gets easy, make it longer or more difficult—or vary it.

I repeat: before beginning any new exercise routine, check with your doctor.

Eat Well

You already know that the mind and body are inextricably linked. A good diet promotes the health of both. It also helps to improve your mood and stabilize your energy. (A not-very-good diet can lead to big swings in mood and energy.) Here are some useful tips, which I invite you to adopt (or adapt for your own body):

Drink eight to nine cups of water each day. Every day you lose water through your breath, perspiration, urine, and bowel movements. Most people don't drink nearly enough water—which means that most people go through life dehydrated. For your body to function properly, drink eight to nine cups—about half a gallon—of water or water-based beverages (tea, sparkling water, vitamin water, etc.) every day. Monitor your water consumption daily, and deliberately increase it if necessary.

Focus your diet on fresh vegetables and fruits, lean proteins, and whole grains. Limit your consumption of highly processed foods.

Eat reasonable amounts. If you tend to overeat, avoid eating while you're doing anything else, such as talking on the phone, working at the computer, driving, or sitting in front of the TV. Set a time in the evening after which you won't eat anything until morning.

If you find yourself *losing* your appetite, carry healthy snacks with you, or keep them easily available at home or work.

Try eating more often and smaller amounts. Eating five or six times a day is ideal. This may help stabilize your blood sugar level. It's also less taxing on your digestive system than two or three large meals a day. Set your phone to remind you to eat something every few hours.

Become aware of your tolerance for gluten. Gluten is a complex protein that is found in all types of wheat, as well as in some other grains, such as rye, barley, triticale, and spelt. Most people can handle gluten fairly well, but a significant percentage can't.

Gluten intolerance, which is usually genetically inherited, is an inability to absorb gluten. Symptoms of gluten intolerance include headaches; ulcers in the mouth; weight loss or gain; skin problems, such as eczema or dermatitis; depression; exhaustion; irritability; cramps; numbness or tingling; dental problems; and immunity issues. Women with gluten sensitivity might also experience infertility or miscarriage; affected infants and children may grow unusually slowly.

The most common symptoms of gluten intolerance are gastrointestinal and can include diarrhea, vomiting, abdominal pain, flatulence, bloating, or dyspepsia (an uncomfortable sensation or pain in the upper part of the stomach). Inflammation and joint pain are also common and can be especially troubling in older people.

I can't tell you how many of my clients have seen huge improvements in their health, digestion, and mood once they've stopped eating gluten. When I suspect that gluten sensitivity may be at work, I say to my client, "Don't eat gluten for the next week or two and see what happens." If nothing about their body or health or energy changes, then they and I know that gluten isn't a problem for them. But I've had lots of clients show up at their next appointments with smiles on their faces. "Resmaa," they tell me, "I thought all that talk about gluten was pure bullshit. But I can't tell you how much better my body seems and how much more energy I have."[30]

Physicians now have a simple blood test for determining gluten intolerance and other food sensitivities. If you think you may have a problem digesting gluten, get tested.

If you are gluten intolerant, avoid eating it whenever possible. This *doesn't* mean not eating bread or pasta. Grocery stores and bakeries now routinely offer a wide variety of gluten-free products, including pasta and bread, many of which are delicious.

Sidestep refined sugar. Naturally occurring sugars, such those found in fresh, whole fruit, are healthful. But refined sugar—including corn syrup—can upset your blood sugar levels and contribute to weight gain. Limit your refined sugar intake.

Raw, unfiltered honey, unsulfured blackstrap molasses, pure maple syrup, rice syrup, stevia, agave, and date sugar are better for you than refined sugar, and they are usually healthy when eaten in moderation.

Watch your alcohol consumption. The healthiest choice is to simply avoid alcoholic beverages, especially when you're under lots

---

30 In my clinical experience, when clients have high anxiety or serious depression, their physical and mental health problems sometimes resolve when they stop eating gluten and begin taking vitamins D3 and CoQ10 in appropriate doses.

of stress. If you do drink, though, having one or two drinks per day is *far* healthier than drinking more.

For socializing, try naturally sparkling spring water with a twist of lemon or lime. It's refreshing, hydrating, and far cheaper than alcohol—and you'll fit right in with the folks drinking gin and tonics.

Replace most of the fats in your diet with olive oil and butter. Not all fats are bad; in fact, healthy oils and fats supply your body with essential fatty acids that promote longevity, hormone balance, heart health, sharp vision, moist skin, and sufficient energy.

Avoid hydrogenated fats (also called trans fats), which are used in many processed foods, including many margarines, commercial mayonnaises, commercial cookies, and solid shortenings such as Crisco. Trans fats are also added to many commercial peanut butters. However, old-fashioned nut butters made of roasted nuts with nothing added (except perhaps salt) contain good fats; enjoy them.

Eat foods that support healthy serotonin levels. These include walnuts, bananas, pineapples, kiwis, plums, plantains, and tomatoes.

Eat foods that are rich in tryptophan. These include turkey, dairy products, bananas, eggs, meat, nuts, beans, and fish.

Be wary of "white foods." Limit your consumption of white flour products, including white bread, pasta, crackers, etc. These can make you sleepy, and they may upset the biochemical balance in your gut. The same is true for white rice. Instead, eat brown rice, sweet potatoes, and other carbs with more nutrients and more fiber.

Limit your intake of most commercially processed or cured meats such as bologna, salami, frankfurters, corned beef, and pastrami. Many varieties of these are full of chemicals.

Go easy on the caffeine. Caffeine can pick you up and give you a buzz, but it can sometimes contribute to irritability and anger. It can also interrupt your sleep pattern, especially if you drink it later than midafternoon.

Coffee, most colas, most sport and energy drinks, and many teas have caffeine. I generally advise people to have no more than one, or at most two, caffeinated drinks a day.

The healthiest caffeinated drink is green tea, which one health researcher called "the healthiest thing you can drink." It's full of antioxidants, improves blood flow, lowers cholesterol and blood pressure, helps prevent a wide range of heart-related problems, and may help prevent Alzheimer's disease. It also has only about a third of the caffeine of coffee. (If you want the benefit of highly concentrated antioxidants, try taking green tea extract as a supplement.)

Most black teas have roughly half the caffeine of coffee. Most herbal teas are caffeine-free, and many have health benefits as well.

Read nutrition labels. In any list of ingredients, the earlier in the list that an ingredient appears, the higher a percentage of it is in the food. In particular, look for sugar and corn syrup, which are added to a wide range of processed foods, including foods that don't taste particularly sweet, such as cereals and canned soups.

If you take a moment to read the packaging, you'll notice an amazing amount of chemicals added to many packaged foods. Some of these are harmless, but many are not. Avoid artificial preservatives (e.g., BHA, BHT, nitrites, nitrates, sodium benzoate, etc.), which are commonly found in many processed foods. Bypass foods and beverages with artificial coloring (which is especially common in sodas and candy) or artificial flavoring. Also avoid artificial sweeteners such as aspartame, saccharine, and sucralose (which are often added to diet sodas, diabetic foods, and other low-calorie processed foods).

Diet, income, and social class are inextricably linked. You don't have to be an economist to know that it's much harder to eat well if your food budget is tight (or nonexistent)—or if you live in a food desert. If you don't have the money to follow all of the above guidance, please don't throw up your hands in despair. Simply do the best you can.

Consider taking healthy, carefully chosen, affordable supplements. When people are unwell or under stress, taking the right supplements may help them return to full health faster. Although you can choose from thousands of different supplements, only some are beneficial— and some may even be harmful. Also, some are overpriced.

I should also note that, because supplements are rarely covered by health insurance, many people simply can't afford the additional out-of-pocket costs. This is only one of many systemic ways in which being poor—or having little or no discretionary income—can lead to poorer health.

In my work, I've watched some people's physical and mental health significantly improve when they created and followed a growth routine, took therapy seriously, and took some or all of the following supplements under the guidance of a qualified nutritionist:

A multivitamin derived from food (rather than chemicals). If you're eating a consistently healthy diet, you don't need a multivitamin.

But most of us don't eat as well as we should. Furthermore, a stressful lifestyle can deplete the body of key nutrients. As a result, many of us are deficient in calcium, magnesium, vitamin A, and vitamin C. A good multivitamin can fill in these gaps.

A food-derived B-complex vitamin. B vitamins are nutritional powerhouses that play a vital role in both physical and mental health. Make sure the variety you take includes folate (or folic acid, the synthetic form of folate), a particularly beneficial B vitamin.

Vitamin D3. This helps prevent and address a wide range of physical and mental health problems.

Magnesium. Magnesium is vital to maintaining metabolism and heart rate, preserving immunity, and strengthening bones and teeth. It may also decrease panic attacks, insomnia, and high blood pressure.

Flaxseed oil. Flaxseed contains omega-3 essential fatty acids, lignans, and fiber. It may help reduce the risk of heart disease, cancer, stroke, and diabetes.

CoQ10. This is a powerful antioxidant that supports basic cell functions, heart health, oxygen utilization, and energy production.

Observe your body. If your body or energy or mood seems off, ask yourself, *Is there something I'm doing—or not doing—that might be contributing to what I'm experiencing?* Then change that habit or behavior for a few days and see what happens. If you improve, consider making the change permanent.

Simple Pleasures

Make a list of small things you enjoy that you can easily do for yourself—taking a walk, watching the sunset, gardening, having a meal with a friend, etc. Do at least one each day, every day. *Build these simple pleasures into your schedule.* Only skip this regular self-care for genuine emergencies.

Being Present and Noticing

Part of any growth routine is learning to be fully present—in your body and in the here and now.

Here's a simple exercise in being present that I use with most of my clients. It takes only a minute or two—though when some people practice it on their own, they slow it down and take more time. I call it simply *coming into the room.*

- Find a chair and sit down on it comfortably. Take two or three breaths, then close your eyes.
- Imagine that you're in outer space, looking down at the Earth turning below you. Just watch it for a few seconds.
- Now zoom in slowly until you're looking just at the landmass of whatever country you're in. You're positioned directly over it like a GPS satellite, so it seems to be standing still.
- Slowly zoom in further, so that you're looking down on the state, or city, or valley, or other area you're in right now.
- Zoom in still further, until you're looking down at the top of the building around you. If you're outside, zoom in far enough that you can just make out your own body below, as if you're seeing it from an airplane.
- Continue zooming in slowly, until you can clearly see your body in detail, as if you're hovering a few feet above it. Notice your clothing, your posture, and any movement.
- Then, slowly, descend the rest of the way to your body and slip inside it.
- Take a few moments to simply breathe and be in your body.
- Now, starting with your hair or the top of your head, slowly scan your body from top to bottom. Pay attention to each part as you work your way down. What is tight or constricted? What is loose or expansive? Where is there pain? Where is there relaxation?
- When you reach the bottoms of your feet, take a moment to experience the sensation of them on the ground.
- Now experience the pressure of the chair against your legs and thighs.
- Now experience the chair against your back.
- For the next few seconds, just let the chair do its job. Relax and let it support you.
- Notice what it's like to be right here, in your body, in the chair.

I normally start each therapy session with this brief exercise. I encourage you to do it, too, at least once each day.

This isn't a trance or even a meditation. It's just noticing and being present with your whole body. You can do it almost anytime and anywhere.

Over time, with practice, you'll get better and better at being present in your body. You'll also get better at noticing when your mind is flittering off into the past or the future. When this occurs, you'll discover that you can bring it back just by noticing your body.

Eventually you'll bring this noticing to everything in your life.

Being present isn't some mystical or ethereal concept. It's what our bodies and minds are designed to do.

Most of us spend a lot of our time worrying about the future, which can create anxiety, or obsessing over the past, which can encourage depression. Learning to be present simply means learning to live *in* the present, where your life is actually taking place.

Being present isn't only for when the pressure is off you and you're calm and connected. In fact, if you're only fully present when you're on a yoga mat or at a meditation retreat, you're missing the point.

Growing up doesn't happen in some ashram or isolated woodland retreat, far from the pressures and grinding of life. It happens *in and through* those pressures and grinding.

As you'll discover, being present is *especially* useful when your boat is rocking like crazy, and when it seems like you're going to get hurled overboard.

When you and your partner are looking at each other and wondering how the hell you're going to make it through uncharted waters together, that's when being fully present can help the most.

Some foundational practices for being present are what I call *primal reps*: small, simple movements that make us more aware of our bodies and of the energies that move through them.

These are not new-age practices developed by a yoga or meditation master. They're exactly the opposite: age-old (i.e., older than the human species) practices built into our bodies. They're also built into the very fabric and flows of the universe.

In chapter 35 you read about life reps and invited reps— opportunities for using the five anchors to build discernment, resiliency, and connection. Primal reps are much briefer and much more basic. You practice them almost entirely bodily, with minimal cognitive direction.

Primal reps serve a deeply valuable purpose. Over time, they can temper and condition your body so you can be more present to it; so it can better hold the weight, charge, speed, and texture of conflict; so you are more able to accept, experience, and metabolize clean pain and discomfort; and so you can grow up.

Primal reps help your body become a container in which emergence can take place. When you and your mate both practice primal reps regularly, they also help your *relationship* become such a container.

Most of these primal practices are things your body does naturally. In fact, as you'll see, some of them are things that many living creatures do, from lower primates to fish to single-cell organisms. These practices tie us back to creation. Each time you do a primal rep, you express the universe and your full participation in it.

I'll list and describe seventeen of the most common such practices below. I suggest doing any practice you choose for three breaths at a time, while noticing what you experience in your body. Three breaths equals one rep.

A single rep should give you enough time to pause, focus, and notice what your body is experiencing. But if your body wants to do more than one rep—and if that creates positive sensations and energy—then by all means do more.

If a particular primal practice is painful for you, don't do it.

Otherwise, there are only two other general guidelines: do primal reps often, and do them for as long as you live.

Pausing and noticing. Simply stop what you're doing. For three breaths, sit or stand still. Notice what sensations arise in your body.

Orienting. Slowly turn your head, first in one direction, then the other, until you've scanned a 360-degree circle. This should include briefly looking behind you. Notice any colors or shapes that stand out. Note any sounds you hear, any aromas you smell, any warmth or coolness. Many people do this daily, when they first get out of bed and stand up.

Entering and leaving. When you walk from one room into another—or from indoors to outside, or vice versa—pause for three breaths. Orient yourself, then notice what changes you experience in your body. (You can also do this when getting in or out of a car, on or off a bicycle, into or out of an elevator, etc.)

Grounding. Notice the outline of your skin and the slight pressure of the air around it. Experience the firmer pressure or the chair, bed, sofa, floor, or ground beneath you. Then pause and notice what else you experience in your body—pressure, constriction, release, pleasure, pain, etc.—and where you experience it.

Scanning. Starting at the top of your head, slowly bring your attention down through your body. Notice each sensation as your attention passes through: coolness, warmth, relaxation, tightness, numbness, pressure, release.

Wiggling[31]. Wiggle your whole body gently using your whole spinal column, from your neck through your hips, the way a fish wiggles.

Pumping. Using your hips and knees, gently pump your body up and down.

Curling your spine. Push out your chest and belly, curling your spine forward. Then pull your spine back and your shoulders forward, so that your upper body curls in the opposite direction.

Swaying. Using your hips—and while staying balanced—sway from side to side, or forward and backward.

Touching. Place your hand gently on any part of your body that asks to be touched. Let your hand rest there for three breaths. Notice what you experience in that body part, in your hand, and in the rest of your body.

Squeezing. Gently squeeze any part of your body with your hand, or with two or more of your fingers; hold the squeeze for three breaths; then release. As a variation, gently curl your fingers into relaxed fists.

Pushing and pulling. While maintaining your balance, gently push against a wall or table; then gently pull yourself back toward it. Or, plant your feet shoulder-width apart, then make pushing and pulling movements into the space around you. As a variation, hold your palms open and upward, as if you are offering and receiving.

Stretching. Stretch out any body part(s) that want to be stretched, in any direction that your body wants to stretch; hold for three breaths; release.

Softening. Relax all the muscles in your face and head. Let your eyelids droop (but not close). Let your jaw hang. Let your tongue fall to the bottom of your mouth.

Curling up. Lie down on a comfortable, even surface—a bed, a trampoline, the ground, etc. Slowly pull your body into a fetal curl; hold the curl briefly; then uncurl.

Infant positioning. Lie down on a comfortable, even surface. Turn your head to one side. Put your hands in a "stick-em-up" position on both sides of your head, letting them rest comfortably. Using the muscles in your thighs and lower back, raise your knees partly toward your head, until your feet are off the ground. (This is

---

31 My thanks to Liz Koch, who recommends and describes wiggling, pumping, and curling up in her book *Stalking Wild Psoas*.

the position an infant will often take when you lay them on their back to change their diaper.) Hold your knees and legs in this position for a few breaths, while letting all your other muscles relax. Notice what vibrations, images, thoughts, meanings, urges, emotions, sensations, and imaginings arise—especially those related to submission or protection.

Working with your joints. Move your head in a few slow circles; repeat in the opposite direction. Do the same with any or all of these joints, one by one: shoulders, wrists, hips, knees, ankles. If you like, do this with your thumbs and then each finger, one by one.

When I talk about primal reps in classes and workshops, people usually flood me with questions: *How many different primal reps should I do each day? Which ones should I do? What times of day should I do them? In what order should I do them? How fast or slow should I go? Can I do more than one type of primal rep at once? Should I spend ten minutes a day doing them, or twenty, or thirty? Which ones are best for someone with scoliosis? How do I know whether I'm doing a primal rep correctly or incorrectly? Are two reps better than one? Are ten reps better than two, or are ten reps too many?*[32]

I don't answer these questions because I don't know the answer to any of them. But your body does. Do the practices your body wants to do, when it wants to do them, in whatever ways it wants.

Of course, don't do any primal rep in a situation where it might disturb or distract others. For example, don't curl up like a fetus or sway your hips back and forth during a job interview.

Approach these primal reps with openness and curiosity. Be like Frankenstein's monster after he leaves the lab, exploring and testing out his body, getting to know its abilities and limitations. Notice what arises, emerges, or gets released as you do each practice. You may discover that certain practices help excavate and release trauma that has gotten stuck somewhere in your body.

Primal reps are *not* physical or spiritual exercises; forms of self-improvement or self-actualization; things to do with your mate in designated primal-rep sessions; things to perform in front of others in order to demonstrate your coolness or wokeness or spiritual advancement; ways to show your partner that you're working on the relationship—or that you're working harder on it than they are; things

---

32 Some of these primal reps can also be done in groups. I describe some of these collective primal reps in *My Grandmother's Hands*. A therapist might also suggest to a couple that they do certain primal reps together—and provide then with more specific instructions.

to become a supposed expert in; things to lead special workshops on; and/or things to "teach" and charge money for.[33]

Over time, with enough reps, many of these practices will naturally become parts of your life.

Other Ways to Care for Yourself

Here are some other simple ways to support your health, happiness, and balance.

Avoid tobacco. No amount of cigarette, cigar, or pipe smoking is healthy. The same goes for snuff and chewable tobacco. If you want to smoke a cigar once a year on your birthday, that's not a big deal. But spend the next 364 days tobacco-free.

Also try to avoid inhaling other people's smoke. Secondhand smoke can damage your lungs and throat. If your partner smokes, get them to smoke outside.

Monitor and limit your drug use. Use prescription drugs mindfully. Take as much as has been prescribed, but no more. With over-the-counter medications, take as little as possible to obtain the desired effect. Taking too much of any drug—even Tylenol—can sometimes be harmful, or even deadly. The fourth leading cause of death in the United States is the improper use of medications.

Be especially aware of drug interactions—what can happen when you take two or more different drugs at once. If you're taking multiple drugs (including over-the-counter drugs), check with your doctor or pharmacist to make sure the combination is okay.

In general, avoid marijuana, cocaine, hallucinogens (such as LSD), and other recreational drugs. These can seriously impair your judgment. Most recreational drugs, especially heroin and meth, can cause serious harm—and can be addictive.

Notice if you begin to fall into a negative feedback loop. For example, suppose you stay up late worrying about your partner. Because you go to sleep too late, your brain doesn't shut down, but keeps running through the same thoughts and memories. That keeps you awake, and the next day you're dragged out and exhausted. So you drink coffee all day to keep going, which makes it harder to sleep the next night. Eventually the chronic lack of sleep also gets in the way of your immune system, so you catch the flu—and so on in a self-perpetuating circle.

---

33 If you do any of these things, you will be an asshole. Please don't do any of them.

The best way to break a vicious circle is to rely on—and, if possible, strengthen—your growth routine. This will help stabilize your body, mind, and spirit.

Remember that everything naturally changes—including your body, your psyche, your partner, and your relationship. As you and your partner age, each of you will naturally go through physical, mental, emotional, and spiritual changes. For example, once you reach middle age, you may become more forgetful. You may have less energy at certain times of the day. Sex will almost certainly change, and it will usually be less athletic, and possibly less frequent. Your body will hurt more—and those pains will take up a big chunk of your energy and attention.

You know what I'm going to say: when these things happen, *nothing is going wrong.* It's how aging works. If couples are not mindful about this, they can end up blaming each other for changes that are completely normal.

Part of growing up is learning how to grow older together. Some of the changes—especially those involving sex—will rock your boat big-time. But simply respond the way you've learned to respond to other conflicts in your relationship. Use the five anchors to hold on to yourself and stay present and engaged. Then reach out to your partner and invite them to move through the changes with you, if they can.

And if they can't, it's *your* job—not your partner's—to take care of your own emotional, physical, and spiritual needs. Following a regular growth routine will help you do this.

In fact, when you follow a growth routine and commit to growing up, everything gets better as you age. Sex gets better, even though it may be less vigorous or less frequent. Conversations get better, even though your hearing and memory aren't as strong as before. Your ability to appreciate and enjoy life gets better, even as you adjust to your body's new limitations. Love gets better, even as the wrinkles form.

Learning to love and care for yourself is essential, not optional.

Becoming a healthier, happier, more anchored human being doesn't just benefit you. Over time you will discover that it also helps you better love and care for your partner.

From Self-Help to Well-Being

Everything you've read in this chapter so far involves *self-help*: things you can do to support your and your partner's health and happiness.

Now let's look at something less personal and more emergent: *well-being*.

Well-being is built on collective energies, communal support, and an awareness that the health, happiness, and fates of all of us are closely bound together.

Well-being is ongoing and timeless. It is not personal, tactical, or transactional. It is about being connected with others, the Earth, and the energies of creation itself. Perhaps most of all, it is about *belonging*.

No amount of self-care—and no amount of strategy—can create well-being, or substitute for it. Instead, well-being *emerges* from a profound connection with your fellow human beings—and with all of life.

If well-being currently eludes you, don't try to buy it, design and build it, track it down and trap it, seduce and ravish it, or receive it from a guru or mentor. You'll fail every time.

But as you grow up, over and over, day by day, you may discover that eventually well-being finds you.

COMPASS POINTS

- The better your health, the more reliable an anchor your body can be, and the easier holding on to yourself becomes when your boat begins to rock.
- All of us need good nutrition, mindfulness, enough sleep, the enjoyment of simple pleasures, and at least some physical fitness. Your regular efforts to maintain these form your growth routine.
- You need to design your own growth routine. Don't simply copy someone else's—especially your partner's.
- If your partner doesn't have a growth routine of their own, don't pressure them to create and follow one.
- Eating well means drinking eight to nine cups of water each day; eating mostly fresh vegetables and fruits, lean proteins, and whole grains; eating reasonable amounts; becoming aware of your tolerance for gluten; sidestepping refined sugar; watching your alcohol consumption; replacing most of the fats in your diet with olive oil (and, if you like, a small amount of butter); eating foods that support healthy serotonin levels; eating foods that are rich in tryptophan; being wary of "white

foods"; going easy on the caffeine; reading nutrition labels; and paying attention to the what your body experiences.

- Take healthy, affordable supplements each day.
- Practice being fully present—noticing what's going on, both inside and outside you.
- Practice primal reps regularly.
- Avoid tobacco; monitor and limit your alcohol and other drug use.
- Notice if you begin to fall into a negative feedback loop.
- Remember that everything naturally changes, including your body, your psyche, your partner, and your relationship.
- Becoming a healthier, happier, more anchored human being doesn't benefit just you. Over time you will discover that it also helps you better love and care for your partner.
- Well-being is built on collective energies, communal support, and an awareness that the health, happiness, and fates of all of us are closely bound together. Perhaps most of all, it is about belonging.
- No amount of self-care—and no amount of strategy—can create well-being. Instead, well-being emerges from a profound connection with your fellow human beings—and with all of life.
- As you grow up, over and over, day by day, you may discover that well-being finds you.

38

Why Our Culture Sometimes Drives You Crazy—and What You Can Do About It

Like each of us as individuals, our culture is always being called to grow up. Like so many of us, it often refuses.

American culture, like all cultures, is shot through with unhealed trauma—much of it historical, intergenerational, and persistent and institutional.

American culture, like all cultures, is awash in dirty pain.

Each of us is routinely bombarded by cultural messages that encourage us to spread that dirty pain by blowing it through others—as well as cultural messages that encourage us to pause, hold onto ourselves, explore that pain, and metabolize the energies behind it.

Over and over, our culture presents us with emerging perils and possibilities.

As you may already intuit, much of what you have learned in this book about your relationship with your partner also applies to relationships with your neighbors, your fellow countrymen, and all other human beings.

Since 2016, my work has focused primarily on Somatic Abolitionism, the healing of racialized trauma, our collective growing up around race, and the building of a living, embodied antiracist culture. But race is not its own separate bubble. Both individually and collectively, the more we grow up in any aspect of our lives, the more room we create in our bodies for further growth—and the more growth we encourage in others.

You, your partner, I, and everyone else need to grow up as individuals. We also need to grow up collectively—as couples, families, communities, cultures, nations, and a species.

Please commit to being an ongoing part of that growth.

COMPASS POINTS

- Like each of us as individuals, our culture is always being called to grow up. Like so many of us, it often refuses.
- Over and over, our culture presents us with emerging perils and possibilities.
- Both individually and collectively, the more we grow up in any aspect of our lives, the more room we create in our bodies for further growth.
- We also need to grow up collectively—as couples, families, communities, cultures, nations, and a species.
- Please commit to being an ongoing part of that growth.

PART 4

How Therapy Really Works

39

People in Therapy
Are Heroes

In therapy, you make yourself vulnerable. You open yourself to a process that you can't control or predict—or even understand in a cognitive way. If you stick with it, you may move through something new and unknown, and you may become a different person.

Don't tell me that that's not heroic.

The changes people go through in therapy can be brutal. It takes great strength to sit in a therapy session and face the truth about yourself and your partner.

Often I tell clients, "I really hope you guys make it through this together. I'm going to do everything I can to help you, and I want both of you to be happy. But I don't know if you're going to be together when you come out the other end." When I tell this to partners and they say, "All right, Resmaa, let's do it; let's go through this," that's heroic.

In my office I see transformations that ministers and rabbis and imams tell me they wish they could witness. I see couples hit emotional stalemates, go through critical mass, and come out the other side as different people, with their relationships transformed.

Afterward, these couples thank me. But I always say, "Let me tell you something. Watching you two go through this process was inspiring. You did something deeply spiritual. You're heroes to me."

People usually come to therapy wanting to confront their partners. Then they discover that they have to confront themselves. They have to show up, face the truth about themselves and their lovers, and take themselves on.

When they finally do this, it's never pretty. No one ever thinks, *Oh, this is great; I'm really glad I'm doing this.* It's always, *Oh shit. I've been doing some nasty stuff for a long time. I need to stop.*

This is exactly the opposite of what people expect in therapy. They think they'll learn to lean on each other and prop up each other. After the second or third session, when it sinks in that something very different is happening, clients look at me and ask, "What the hell's going on? This isn't what I expected at all." I tell them, "That's exactly right. Nobody expects it." That's when most people curse and then laugh.

Even though the process of growing up can be brutal, there's a lot of laughter in my therapy sessions. Clients keep coming up against the absurdity of what we all have to deal with as human beings. Whether you're a client or a therapist, you can't do this work without laughing sometimes. Our lives are a combination of Mary Shelley's *Frankenstein* and Mel Brooks's *Young Frankenstein.*

At first most people try to hold on to their partner, because they've never been taught to hold on to themselves. Eventually each partner sees that they need to develop this ability to hold on to themselves when things get tough and painful.

Some people call this new ability personal strength or personal integrity; others see it as an aspect of creation unfolding. Either way, they learn to settle down and be soothed and cared for and grounded, without having to turn to their lover for it. They learn to be present with what is, no matter how much it hurts.

Nobody does this willingly. They do it when they've hit a wall, when they've got no other options and nowhere else to go, except out of the relationship.

When you can learn to confront yourself, hold on to yourself, let yourself be pulverized and shredded and transformed, and laugh about it at the same time, that's nothing short of heroic. And what's amazing is that people do it all the time.

COMPASS POINTS

- In therapy, you open yourself to a process that you can't control or predict. If you stick with it, you move through something new and unknown—and become a different person.
- Therapy is always about letting go of who you are and becoming the person you most want to be. This takes courage and a tolerance for uncertainty.
- When you confront yourself in therapy—and that's always what happens in any real therapeutic process—it's never pretty. You see things about yourself you never wanted to see. And then, instead of turning away, you straighten up and look more closely.
- Therapy is exactly the opposite of what most people think. They think it's a forum for confronting their partner and helping them wake up. It's not.
- Instead, *you* always end up looking in a mirror. That's about the most heroic thing a person can do.

40

Underground Therapy

When most people hear the name Harriet Tubman, they think of a little Black woman who helped refugees from plantations make their way north via the Underground Railroad.

That's true, but there was much more to her. For one thing, she was part of the Union Army, serving as (among other things) a spy. For another, she carried a shotgun.

The shotgun wasn't for fighting Confederate troops. It was for keeping plantation refugees focused.

Over time, Tubman gleaned that once people had gotten a certain distance from their old plantation, many would begin to have second thoughts. They knew that, going forward, they would face danger and the complete unknown. But if they returned to the plantation, they'd be back in a familiar setting—one they despised and feared, but understood. Sometimes people would change their minds and tell Tubman that they wanted to go back.

That's when she would raise her shotgun and say, "You are going forward. You can't go back. You can go all the way north, to a life of freedom. Or you can turn around and try to go back—but if you do, I'll shoot you dead. You choose."

This wasn't just a matter of motivation. She knew that if someone did go back or get captured, they would tell the plantation owners about the routes that were used to help people escape. This would put other refugees in danger.

Tubman didn't freak out when she heard dogs in the distance. Instead, she said to the person in her care, "Keep your ass moving. There is no going back. You are not going to jeopardize this operation because you don't think you can do it. I'm telling you, you can do it. *Now move."*

Tubman told the people she assisted, "I know who I am, and I'm good with it. And right now you might not know who you are. You might think you're a slave. But I'm telling you, *You are not a slave.* You have *been* enslaved. But you aren't a slave. There's a difference. Something *happened* to us Black folks.

"Now you are no longer enslaved. You can be who you are. But, right now, you need to get your ass up that road."

I don't know the exact words Tubman used, of course. But her essential messages were certainly along these lines.

I also don't know if Tubman would have been able to articulate the five anchors that I discuss in this book. But she certainly used them with herself, over and over—and she reinforced them in others with her shotgun.

When you're familiar with something, even if it's bad for you— even if it's a living hell—there's still an energy to it for you. You're afraid to leave it. When you're away from it, you sense its absence— and that it is pulling at you to return to it.

During the Civil War, as refugees went through the trials and tribulations of freedom, enslavement sometimes started to look better to them. Freedom meant they would be on their own in a world they didn't know or understand. They knew they would have to grow up very, very fast. The north meant some relative freedom, but it also meant an onslaught of clean pain.

Therapy is a similar process. It helps people escape from a world of old, familiar, dirty pain into safety and freedom. But it always means going to a new and unfamiliar place—a place they may not recognize or understand. It always means going through clean pain and discomfort. And—if the therapist is any good—it always means growing up.

When you go to a therapist, it's like leaving a mental and emotional plantation. Everything that's familiar will change. And once you've decided, you can't go back. You have to keep moving forward.

Here's what I tell every one of my clients when we begin our work together: *This is going to be tough. You're going toward freedom, toward growing up, toward a different type of relationship with your partner, and with yourself, and with the world. You're moving toward clean pain and discomfort instead of dirty pain. At times it will look like the hardest thing you can possibly do. But you have to keep going forward.* I don't carry a shotgun, but part of my job is to help each client keep moving in the right direction.

Sometimes, once people have done some real therapy, they change their minds and try to go back to how they were before. But it's too late. The very act of moving forward, even a small amount, has changed things irrevocably. They're not the same person they were before. What they try to go back to will be different as well.

There are times when I half-wish I did have a shotgun in my office. When a couple is losing their minds and screaming at each other (*You're a slut, just like your mama! Well, you're an asshole, just like your scumbag daddy!*), I'd like to be able to raise the gun and say, "You two are here because you've left the plantations of your families of origin. You're on the road to freedom. And I swear to you, you are *not* going back."

I'm never going to do any of this, of course. As much as I want growth and freedom for all my clients, I know that I can't force those things on anyone. It would also be a huge violation of professional ethics—and a generally lame-ass move—to even try.

As a therapist, I know to do just the opposite. When chaos erupts around me, I use the five anchors to hold on to myself. Then, from a centered and present place, I hold both people to the direction of growing up, and to the principle of freedom.

Instead of raising a gun, I raise my voice just a bit and say, "Freedom and growth are where you're going. I don't know how the two of you are going to get there, and there's going to be some twists and turns and clean pain and discomfort, but you'll find your way. You're not going back to the way things were. And I'll have your back—even when you don't want me to."

COMPASS POINTS

- When something is familiar, there's an energy to it, even if it's painful. You're afraid to leave it. When you're away from it, you sense its absence and seem pulled back to it.

- Therapy helps people escape from a world of old, familiar, dirty pain into safety and freedom. But it always means going to a new and unfamiliar place—a place they may not recognize or understand.

- When you go to a therapist, it's like leaving the mental and emotional plantation. Everything that's familiar will change. And once you've decided, you can't go back. You have to keep moving.
- Once you've done some real therapy, you can't go back to how things were before. The very act of moving forward has changed things irrevocably. You're not the same person you were before—and what you try to go back to will have changed as well.

41

How Therapy
Mirrors Marriage

What people do in therapists' offices—in displaying their strengths and weaknesses, in avoiding and confronting themselves, and in getting stuck and breaking through—often mirrors what occurs in committed partnerships.

I've discovered that when I start working with a client, I learn a lot about how they relate to their partner simply by observing how they relate to me. Usually there are a great many parallels. Here are the biggest and most common ones:

Most people want to solve the problems in their relationships by getting their partners to change in exactly the way they'd like. When individuals and couples first come to therapy, they do the same thing, hoping that if they spend $200 or more per hour, the therapist will solve their problems for them. But that's not how the therapist-client relationship works.

Most people go to a marriage or family therapist because they sense that they're burning up. They can't handle the heat and pressure of their relationship. They want to lower the heat, take the pressure off, and find a way around their difficulties.

This mirrors what most of us try to do with our partners: we want them to make us happy, solve our problems for us, be exactly what we want them to be, or handle our pressure or responsibility or pain for us.

If you see a therapist, their job is to do exactly the opposite: to insist that you (or you and your partner) confront yourselves and go *through* your issues instead of around them.

Here are some other common ways in which the therapist-client relationship mirrors committed partnerships:

- Many of the things that seem like painful stumbling blocks will in fact be invitations to hold on to yourself and straighten your spine. (In many of these situations, this invitation also applies to the therapist.)

- The client and therapist will go through uncertainty and ambiguity together. There will be times when one or both will need to say, "I don't know what the hell to do right now, but let's stick with it and work through it together."

- All kinds of apparent dualities will appear, but most of these will be *both/and* rather than *either/or*.

- There will occasionally be periods of stasis, during which not much seems to happen, as well as periods of important, painful growth. There will also be a natural cycle of fluidity and rigidness. At times everything will seem to flow naturally and effortlessly, as if you and the therapist are in perfect alignment. At other times, the two of you will seem out of alignment with them—as if your relationship is rigid or awkward. Both states are normal. There's no need to scramble to recover a lost sense of alignment. If each of you is doing your job in therapy, that alignment will eventually return on its own (and then disappear again later, as part of the cycle). It's okay to let the therapeutic relationship be temporarily out of alignment. Meanwhile, hold on to yourself, keep your spine straight, and stay present.

- Everything that happens will be an opportunity to choose: grow up or don't.

COMPASS POINTS

- What people do in therapists' offices—in displaying their strengths and weaknesses, in avoiding and confronting themselves, and in getting stuck and breaking through—often mirrors what occurs in committed partnerships.

- Most people want to improve their relationships by getting their partners to change in exactly the way they'd like. This doesn't work. Similarly, many individuals and couples come to therapy hoping the therapist will solve their problems for them. This also doesn't work.

- A therapist's job is to do the opposite: to insist that you (or you and your partner) confront yourselves—not pass off the job to anyone else—and go *through* your issues instead of around them.

42

When Therapists
Cop Out

This chapter will seriously piss off many of my colleagues—and delight some others. But I'm not trying to anger or please anyone. And I'm very aware that I, and my insights, are not for everybody. Still, I'm simply saying what urgently needs to be said—which is this:

If a therapist reflexively helps you and your partner turn down the heat in your relationship, they're being negligent—and leading the two of you astray.

The things that create conflict for you and your lover are the very things the two of you need to lean into, because they're tied to your integrity. Your conflict needs to cook—and you can't cook without heat.

A good therapist won't reflexively try to turn down that heat. Instead, they'll help you and your partner learn to modulate it and navigate through it. They can't do this unless they know how to navigate that heat themselves. In their therapy office, they may sometimes modulate that heat, like a good chef, for the benefit of their clients—but they won't *reflexively* turn it down and then pretend that they're doing it for their clients' safety.

When clients get stuck in an emotional bottleneck in a therapist's office, the therapist needs to be able to hold on to themselves, stay present and connected, and help their clients get through the bottleneck together, if possible. This is especially true when people are screaming and cursing at each other, or squaring off like wrestlers.

Good therapists have fortitude, and they aren't afraid to use it in service of their clients' growth.

A therapist's job is to push their clients to grow up. But some therapists are wimps. They're not willing to confront themselves and do their own painful internal work, so they don't demand hard work from their clients.

Instead, they teach clients techniques for lowering the heat in their relationships. That may make the relationships less rocky, but it also keeps both partners from growing up.

Most therapists demand from their clients exactly what they demand from themselves. As a result, a therapist's limitations often line up perfectly with those of their clients. The therapist then takes the client only as far as the therapist is willing to go. It's a version of rocks and holes. Because they can't see beyond their own beliefs, fears, and limitations, the therapist doesn't push their clients far enough,[34] and the job remains incomplete.

When someone is losing their mind in a therapist's office, rocking the therapeutic boat like crazy, the therapist needs to straighten their own spine and stay present.

I'm not saying therapists need to be fearless. Sometimes we get scared, especially when people act like they may pull a knife or throw a punch. There have been times in my office when I've slowly reached into my pocket and clutched my phone, ready to dial 911. (So far, dialing that number hasn't been necessary.)

But in the heat of these moments, my fear is none of my business. My business is to use the five anchors to hold on to myself, so I remain connected with the human beings in my office as events unfold, and as we move into the unknown together.

When therapists do cop out, they typically use their professional authority to cool down everyone in the room—all in an effort to create a sense of safety *for themselves*. Here are their most common strategies:

- They refocus the client on some concept, theory, name, or term. "Halle, your husband is a sex addict." "Bonnie, some of what you've just described is consistent with borderline personality disorder." "Jung had some very important things to say about this." This enables the therapist to claim a superior position, while taking the focus off the very real—and deeply important—conflict in the room.

---

34 My mentor Dr. David Schnarch often noted this dynamic. He also observed that some clients will deliberately seek out a therapist whose limitations line up with their own.

- Instead of saying, "This must hurt like hell; I don't know what you're going to do, but let's stay with it," they use little tricks to buy time, and to mentally and emotionally catch their breath. They say, "Tell me more" or "How does that make you feel?" or "Well, what do you think about that?" or "That's interesting."

- They give clients tactical, technical advice: *Speak in "I" statements. Learn listening skills. Repeat what you just heard your partner say. Have you considered seeing a sex therapist?*

- They look at the client and say, "That's inappropriate" or "That's disrespectful." This sounds like expertise or maturity, but the actual message is: *What you just did or said or thought—you're fucked up for doing or saying or thinking it. You're even more fucked up for not realizing that it's wrong. And I get to speak for what's right and wrong because I have a graduate degree in psychology or social work.* The point is to control the interaction and establish authority over the client. This encourages the client to think, *What's wrong with me? Why didn't I know this already?* instead of *Either educate me or shut up; don't tell me I've crossed the line without telling me where the line is, or when and how I crossed it.*

- They play surrogate mommy or daddy by saying in a very controlled—and controlling—voice, "Let's all just calm down here for a minute." What they're really saying, though, is, *What you're doing scares the shit out of me. Take care of me by being nice and quiet and by deferring to me as an authority figure and expert.*

Therapists use these cheesy tricks all the time. They may look therapeutically sound, but they actually deprive couples of the opportunity to move through emotional bottlenecks and transform.

I'm not saying that concepts and theories and terms aren't useful or real. Also, certain actions—such as beating up your partner—clearly *are* inappropriate and disrespectful. But when an issue comes to a boil in a therapist's office, the therapist isn't supposed to run for cover. If their spine sags in the heat of an emotional stalemate, their clients are going to follow their lead and let their own spines sag as well.

Every therapist needs to develop the same straight, stable, flexible spine that they encourage (or should encourage) their clients to develop. They have to be able to tolerate their clients' problems and strong emotions, without being reactive to them. They need to hold on to themselves by using the five anchors, just like their clients.

Knowledge, experience, and cognitive insight can all be helpful. But when people come to therapy, it's usually because they or someone close to them has a dysregulated nervous system. What's most important in therapy is that the therapist be able to tolerate the rocking of the therapeutic boat and model a response that's present, centered, and connected.

Knowledge and experience and cognitive insight aren't what matter when the people in your office are screaming at each other. When people go to therapy, what they actually pay for is a therapist who won't break apart when shit is flying, or when people are going crazy in the office because of their own dysregulation. Because the therapist doesn't get caught up in the drama, they're able to respond from a place where they can actually help their clients grow up.

One of the most important things a therapist can bring to the table is a well-regulated nervous system.

COMPASS POINTS

- If a therapist reflexively helps you and your partner turn down the heat in your relationship, they're being negligent—and leading the two of you astray.
- Instead of trying to turn down the heat, a good therapist will help you and your partner learn to navigate through it.
- They can't do this unless they know how to navigate that heat themselves.
- Because some therapists aren't willing to confront themselves and do their own painful internal work, they don't demand hard work from their clients. Instead, they teach clients techniques for lowering the heat in their relationships. That may make the relationships less rocky, but it also keeps both partners from growing up.
- When therapists do cop out, they typically use their professional authority to cool down everyone in the room—all in an effort to create a greater sense of safety for *themselves*.
- If a therapist's spine sags in the heat of an emotional stalemate, their clients are going to follow their lead and let their own spines sag as well.

- What's most important in therapy is that the therapist be able to tolerate the rocking of the therapeutic boat and model a response that's present, centered, and connected.
- The most important thing a therapist can bring to the table is a well-regulated nervous system.

43

Why Therapy Often Doesn't Work

Therapy never succeeds when people run for cover rather than learn to tolerate heat, friction, and discomfort.

But that's not the only reason why couples therapy can fail. There are six other common causes:

1. Therapists who believe—against all evidence—that the key to healing and growth is cognitive insight. Most therapists and self-help writers have a high regard for meaning, which they see as the holy grail of emotional healing. The goal of these professionals is to help their clients have *aha!* moments, usually by delving deeply into their pasts. They believe that if they can help a client sort out meaning in their life, healing will naturally follow.

Clients of these therapists may have epiphanies galore. But they don't often transform, for two reasons: First, there's no processing of images, emotions, or bodily sensations, because cognitive insight tends to speed up mental processes rather than slow down bodily ones. Second, cognitive insight alone typically does little to help people access the best parts of themselves, build strength, and grow up.

We human beings naturally try to make meaning out of what happens to us. Often this is helpful, but in most high-stress situations, meaning-making tends to get hijacked by our lizard brain, which focuses entirely on survival. Our body shifts into a constricted, self-protected position. We close up just when we need to open.

Unfortunately, many therapists are addicted to meaning-making. When a client makes a connection in their office—when they slap their head or say, "Aha!" or "Oh shit"—it makes the therapist happy.

Sometimes it makes the client happy, too. But those cognitive insights are rarely enough to get people to actually transform. They may cognitively understand what they need to do, but they don't yet experience enough heat under them to do it.

Sometimes the therapist needs to ask a client or couple to put meaning aside for a time, in order to focus on their bodies and emotions. *These* are the places where heat gets generated, where issues and conflicts can cook, and where alchemical transformations occur. The process of cooking helps partners build their capacity for both autonomy and togetherness. This capacity is far more important than generating an insight.

When therapists focus solely on making meaning, the insights that arise—although usually genuine—tend to be small, constricted, or myopic, because they're the result of purely cognitive processes. But if the therapist first leads the client or couple through a process that involves presence, sensations, images, emotions, and their entire bodies, the result can be meaning that is not merely insightful, but transformational. It's the difference between knowing you're approaching orgasm and actually having that orgasm. The first pleases your brain; the second rocks your whole being.

2. Therapists who encourage clients to focus on the weakest parts of themselves. Many people who come to therapy think that the process involves reaching into themselves, pulling out their weakest parts, and saying, "Here—help me fix these." Some therapists agree with that approach, so they work with their clients to make those weaknesses less weak.

But that isn't the therapist's primary job. Their main job is to say, "I'm not here to help you repair your weakest parts. I'm here to help you access your best and strongest parts. Those are what you're going to need to get through what you and your partner are facing."

3. Therapists who force their ideas or beliefs onto their clients. For these professionals, therapy is less about human connection and presence than it is about advancing a philosophy or worldview. This may involve a particular flavor of psychology, or a set of beliefs the therapist was taught in graduate school, or simply an idea the therapist cherishes. Whatever it is, the therapist is ideologically beholden to it, and they insist to the client that it is the only correct way to see the world. What begins as therapy morphs into indoctrination.

4. Clients who make preemptive strikes. When a client breaks down in a therapy session, it usually looks like it's because they can't tolerate what's happening or the strong emotions they're experiencing. In fact, that's almost never the case. Much more often it's because they don't want to deal with what they sense is coming. By falling apart, they're making a preemptive strike. They're trying to distract their partner, or their therapist, or both, so they don't get pushed into a place they don't want to go.

The wise therapist or partner doesn't allow themselves to be distracted by a preemptive strike. They stay focused on the very place the other person doesn't want to go, while offering their presence, support, and care.

5. *Clients who therapist-hop.* When some clients are forced to choose between clean pain and dirty pain—or when they intuit that such a choice is just over the horizon—they weasel out by leaving the therapist. They tell others that the therapist wasn't right for them, or wasn't any good, or wasn't helping. Then they start over with a new therapist. Folks who are serious about not growing up can continue this game for years. (This is, of course, very different from finding a new therapist because the one you're seeing now genuinely isn't very helpful or talented or insightful or brave.)

6. *Therapists who suck—or mistreat their clients.* Like members of all professions, therapists range from wonderful to terrible. We have professional associations and review boards whose job is to monitor us, and ban or prosecute the worst of us. These boards generally take their job quite seriously. But they aren't perfect, so there are still a fair number of incompetents among us, as well as a much smaller number of predators and sociopaths.

When working with (or considering working with) any therapist, don't just trust the credential on the wall. Listen to what your body tells you about them. As with doctors, mechanics, and insurance agents, don't be afraid to comparison shop.

A wise therapist will help you heal and grow up. Don't settle for someone who demands less than this from you.

COMPASS POINTS

- Therapy never succeeds when people run for cover rather than learn to tolerate heat, clean pain, and discomfort. But there are six other common causes of couples therapy that fails:

  1. Therapists who believe—against all evidence—that the key to healing and growth is cognitive insight.
  2. Therapists who encourage clients to focus on the weakest parts of themselves.
  3. Therapists who force their ideas or beliefs onto their clients.
  4. Clients who make preemptive strikes.
  5. Clients who therapist-hop.
  6. Therapists who suck—or mistreat their clients.

- When working with (or considering working with) any therapist, don't just trust the credential on the wall. Listen to what your body tells you about them. If you like, comparison shop.

- A wise therapist will help you heal and grow up. Don't settle for someone who is less than wise.

44

Integrity, Presence, and Not Knowing

Good therapists know how to pay attention to bodily cues—what they see in their clients' bodies *and* what they see and experience in their own. The better we get at noticing and experiencing these signals, the more helpful we can be.

A wise therapist also knows how to look at each client—and each couple—through a variety of windows. Typically these include intimacy, parenting, money, sex, work, families of origin, age, personal habits, and many others. Over time, a wise therapist is able to get a 360-degree view of the entire ecosystem of the partnership—for example, how Zoe's drinking leads to Marlon's withdrawal, which feeds Zoe's resentment, which encourages Marlon's mother's disdain, which leads to fights between her and her son, which Zoe avoids by going out drinking with her friends.

We therapists also need to show and tell our clients, over and over, that we're exactly like them. We're not special. We're wired exactly the same as other normal human beings. We have the same kinds of challenges and problems, some of which involve our partners. And, like them, we have to keep growing up, day after day.

This doesn't mean we'll always know what to do. Sometimes we won't have a goddamned clue. But when we don't know what to do, we're honest and brave enough to say to our client, "I don't know what to do or suggest right now. But let's keep talking."

We can stay engaged, keep listening, and move through the unknown with our client, in the same way couples often have to.

This can be an act of deep support and integrity, because we're not bullshitting our client with feigned expertise.

Most of all, every therapist needs humility and a commitment to serve our fellow human beings.

COMPASS POINTS

- Good therapists know how to pay attention to cues in their clients' bodies *and* in their own.
- A wise therapist knows how to look at each couple and see the entire ecosystem of the partnership.
- We therapists need to show and tell clients that we face the same kinds of problems they do, and that we, too, have to keep growing up.
- When a therapist has no idea what to do, they should say so, stay engaged, and move through the unknown with their client.
- Most of all, every therapist needs humility and a commitment to serve.

CONCLUSION
Unfolding Purpose

In authentic therapy, the trajectory of people's lives is altered for the better. People learn to act from their strengths, not their weaknesses, and become who they most want to be—and who their partner most wants them to be.

People rarely understand this when they first show up in a therapist's office. They want to change their partner to their liking. Or they want the therapist to give them a magic solution. Or they want a script for turning their romantic fantasy into reality.

Yet the fact that they've walked into a therapist's office usually means they're willing to do more than just acquire easy answers. They've made a decision to go beyond blaming their partner, or themselves, or God. They don't want things to stay the way they are. They're ready for transformation.

When couples do the painful work of growing up, they willingly drop their fantasies. They get better at being aware of the sensations in their bodies, at staying present, at holding on to themselves—rather than each other—when their boats are buffeted by waves, at slowing down their thoughts instead of reacting from their lizard and bee brains, at loving each other, and at loving themselves. They begin to see their partners—and themselves—as they are, instead of as who they wish, fear, or imagine them to be.

Each person also starts to see the *relationship* for what it is: an opportunity to build both autonomy and togetherness, and to forge a loving, collaborative alliance.

Real psychotherapy is a deeply spiritual process—not usually religious, but reflective and alchemical. This process always involves someone standing in their integrity and saying, "This is who I am and this is what I want."

In couples, it means at least one lover choosing to stand up and straighten their spine. It means saying to their partner in the heat of an emotional stalemate, "I love you to death, but I'm not going to do this anymore. We're going to deal. I'm not going to hate you or leave you or blame you in order to get through this. And I'm not going to hate or blame myself, either. There's got to be something else. And I accept whatever pain I'm going to have to experience in order to go through this." Often it means coming out the other side a different person.

This is the unfolding purpose of the relationship—and of creation itself. It's nothing less than spiritual transformation, and it's experienced in the body.

This is the point and purpose of authentic psychotherapy.

This alchemical process can be equally spiritual for the therapist. It certainly is for me.

Over and over in my office, I watch people and relationships transform. I see clients willingly live into the unknown, knowing that it is rife with possibility and peril. I bear witness as someone's unique purpose unfolds.

When this happens, I know that I'm beholding the birth of Creation.

About the Author

Resmaa Menakem is a healer, a longtime therapist, and a licensed clinical social worker who specializes in couples, conflict in relationships, the healing of trauma, and domestic violence prevention. He is also a cultural trauma navigator and a communal provocateur and coach.

Resmaaa is best known as the author of the *New York Times* bestseller *My Grandmother's Hands: Racialized Trauma and the Pathway to Mending Our Hearts and Bodies*, and as the originator and key advocate of Somatic Abolitionism, an embodied anti-racist practice of living and culture building. He is also the author of *The Quaking of America: An Embodied Guide to Navigating Our Nation's Upheaval and Racial Reckoning*.

For ten years, Resmaa cohosted a radio show with former US Congressman (and later Minnesota Attorney General) Keith Ellison on KMOJ-FM in Minneapolis. He also hosted his own show, "Resmaa in the Morning," on KMOJ. Resmaa has appeared on both *The Oprah Winfrey Show* and *Dr. Phil* as an expert on family dynamics, couples in conflict, and domestic violence.

Resmaa has served as the director of counseling services for Tubman Family Alliance, a domestic violence treatment center in Minneapolis; the behavioral health director for African American Family Services in Minneapolis; a domestic violence counselor for Wilder Foundation; a divorce and family mediator; a social worker for Minneapolis Public Schools; a youth counselor; a community organizer; and a marketing strategist.

From 2011 to 2013, Resmaa was a community care counselor for civilian contractors in Afghanistan, managing the wellness and counseling services on fifty-three US military bases. As a certified military family life consultant, he also worked with members of the military and their families on issues related to family living, deployment, and returning home.

Resmaa helps people rise through suffering's edge. His work focuses on making the invisible visible. You can learn more about him at www.resmaa.com.

Deepening Your Experience of This Book

I invite you to use the Wyser app to get more out of this book. Wyser provides a chapter-by-chapter set of links that will take you to videos, websites, articles, essays, podcasts, and other relevant information and perspectives.

To download and use Wyser on your smartphone, scan the QR code below.